*Soap Fans*

# Soap Fans

Pursuing Pleasure and

Making Meaning in Everyday Life

C. LEE HARRINGTON AND DENISE D. BIELBY

 Temple University Press / PHILADELPHIA

Temple University Press, Philadelphia 19122

Copyright © 1995 by Temple University. All rights reserved

Published 1995

Printed in the United States of America

⊛ The paper used in this book meets the requirements
of the American National Standard for Information
Sciences — Permanence of Paper for Printed Library Materials,
ANSI Z39.48-1984

Library of Congress Cataloging-in-Publication Data
Harrington, C. Lee, 1964–
    Soap fans : pursuing pleasure and making meaning in everyday
life / C. Lee Harrington and Denise D. Bielby.
        p.   cm.
    Includes bibliographical references (p.   ) and index.
    ISBN 1-56639-329-9 (alk. paper). — ISBN 1-56639-330-2 (alk.
paper : pbk.)
    1. Soap operas — United States — History and criticism.   2. Fans
(Persons) — United States — Psychology.   3. Television viewers —
United States — Psychology.   I. Bielby, Denise D.   II. Title.
PN1992.8.S4H37   1995
302.23'45'0973 — dc20                          94-40796

# Contents

# List of Tables and Illustrations

# Acknowledgments

We were aided in many ways, by many people, during the course of writing this book. The project could not have been conducted without the participation of soap opera fans, actors, writers, directors, producers, fan club staff members, and the daytime press. We would like to thank the many participants who wish to remain anonymous. We also thank Sue Corbett, director of Fans of *General Hospital;* Polly Hazen, president of the National *Days* Fan Club; Olin Jenkins; the staff at *Loving,* who generously shared some of their fan mail with us; the staff at *Soap Opera Weekly,* who advertised our study in one of their issues; the production staff at *The Bold and the Beautiful* and *The Young and the Restless;* Blanche Trinajstick of the National Organization of Fan Clubs; and Diane Warren, who truly went out of her way to help us. We express our deep appreciation to those who provided invaluable assistance in our entrée into the industry, especially Michael Logan of *TV Guide* and the staff at *Pure Soap,* and Jean Rouverol of the Writers' Guild of America, west. All of the participants in this study shared their time and experience very generously; this book is dedicated, ultimately, to them.

We thank Miami University, Oxford, and the University of California, Santa Barbara, for financial support for this project. A Miami University College of Arts and Sciences Small Research Grant funded the initial contact with fans at a *General Hospital* fan club luncheon in Los Angeles. Miami University's College of Arts and Sciences Small Teaching Grant, Liberal Education Enrichment Grant, Affirmative Action Grant, and Committee on the Improvement of Instruction Small Grant enabled us to attend a Summer Professional Program at the Massachusetts Institute of Technology entitled "Ninja Turtles, the Macho King, and Madonna's Navel: Taking Popular Culture Seriously." The seminar was a wonderful source of knowledge and inspiration, and we extend our appreciation to the participants and particularly to Professor Henry Jenkins, who ran the seminar. We also thank the Department of Sociology and Anthropology at Miami University for various forms of support (financial and other) and the Scripps Gerontology Center for providing excellent research assistants: Donna Dudzinski, Heather Horn, Laura Songer, and Yumiko Nishizawa. Faculty Research Grants from the Academic Senate and the Interdisciplinary Humanities Center of the University of California, Santa Barbara, also supported this research. Portions of this project were presented at the American Sociological Association; the Popular Culture Association; and the Conference on Social Theory, Politics, and the Arts, with travel funding provided by Miami University and the Academic Senate of the University of California, Santa Barbara.

Others who deserve thanks are Elizabeth E. Berlese, Ph.D., for insights into clinical psychology; Professor David R. Dow for legal advice; Melissa Atchley for her wisdom and direction; Erindira, Chounaird, Willie, Lou, Ralph, Bean, Zeke, and Gus for their expert diversionary tactics; Professor Thomas Scheff for inspiring an interest in the study of emotions; Professor John Sutton, Professor Harvey Molotch, and Professor Rebecca Adams, whose comments and suggestions on earlier drafts of the manuscript were immeasurably helpful. Michael Ames, editor-in-chief at Temple University Press, facilitated every stage of the manuscript. Professor William Bielby provided unceasing encouragement, support, advice, wit, companionship, and the willingness to point out when we were losing our minds. Patience is indeed a virtue! Fan friends Norma Marquez, Connie McNeely, and Wendy Wagner provided many pleasurable hours of insight, inspiration, analysis, and play. Our students, past and present, at Miami University, Oxford, and the University of California, Santa Barbara, reminded us, in innumerable ways, of the importance of soaps in everyday life. And our families gave us their unflagging support and enthusiasm.

Mostly, this is for all the fans of daytime soap operas.

*Soap Fans*

# Introduction

> I guess I've written over a hundred fan letters over the years, most of which have been answered, some of which have been answered in a way that lets me know the letter was read, understood, and appreciated by the actor. I've received full resumés, complex descriptions from the actor's point of view of where his character is headed, exchanges based on genetic background of the actor, ethnic background of the character vs. the actor, etc. Many soap actors seem interested in how viewers see their characters, how viewers see the actors themselves, and are quite willing to take advice.

> It is impossible to offer a profile of a typical stalker, but . . . they're media addicts. Many are loners seeking greatness by destroying greatness. . . . Somehow the public figure becomes the object of a grand delusion and the obsessed fan feels there is some kind of meaningful relationship.

Consider these two quotes, one from a thirty-eight-year-old man who is a devoted soap opera watcher, the second from security expert Gavin De Becker, interviewed for a recent magazine article whose title begins, "When Fans Turn into Fanatics" (*People Weekly* 1990:105). Are these quotes reconcilable? Does the soap fan's belief that his letters are "understood and appreciated" by actors constitute the "grand delusion" that the security expert warns of? What distinguishes a casual media consumer from a media fan, or a normal fan from a delusional fanatic?

The contemporary image of media fans is not a pretty picture. By reputation, fans cannot tell the difference between fiction and reality and are consumed with the minute details of make-believe worlds. Fans are portrayed as either losers — love-struck teenagers or lonely housewives — or lunatics who pose serious threats to celebrities' physical safety. These images are so widely held and so rarely questioned that virtually all fan behavior — from the harmless to the violent — draws public ridicule and suspicion.

Criticism of fan behavior from both the popular and the academic presses has grown harsher in recent years. Early media coverage of fanship (individual fan behavior) was fairly benign. Articles appearing in teen magazines throughout the 1970s, for example, offered advice about starting or joining fan clubs and about participating in fandom, the realm of organized fan activity (Davidson 1973). The enthusiasm of sports fans was occasionally featured in coverage of a winning team; it was treated as both harmless and understandable. Beginning in the mid-1970s, trade magazines promoted personal computers as labor-saving devices for celebrities who wanted to send mass mailings to their fans (Swan 1987).

Over the last fifteen years, however, popular media coverage has shifted, focusing on fans' extreme or violent behavior. This shift is marked by the 1981 publication of an article in *People Weekly* magazine titled "Desperate to Fill an Emotional Void, Some Fans Become Dangerous to Their Idols" (Freedman 1981). Since the mid-1980s *People* has increased its coverage of extreme fan behavior, and other popular publications have followed suit. For example, an article about stalker fans bore the title "Vanna White and Teri Garr Ask the Courts to Protect Them from Fans Who Have Gone Too Far" (Schindehette 1990), and the January 17, 1994, *Newsweek* cover featured the attack on figure skater Nancy Kerrigan with the cover line " 'Why Me?' The New Fear of Stalking." By the late 1980s, infotainment television programming and television and radio talk shows had joined in with features on lunatic fans and celebrities' need for security protection. Increasingly, even the network news reports cases of celebrities threatened or assailed, such as the stalkings of David Letterman, Rebecca Schaeffer, and tennis star Monica Seles. Efforts of fans' victims to gain legal rights and protection also receive widespread coverage, most notably that of model/actress Theresa Saldana, whose face was disfigured in 1981 by a fan's knife attack. Current popular accounts suggest the existence of a dangerous, widespread, and psychologically unstable fan community.

This shift in the popular perspective on fans coincided with a growing market for news and gossip about celebrities — particularly entertainment celebrities — that was easily accessible to the general public. In many ways, the current fascination with celebrity is the consequence of a narrowing gap between the famous and the unfamous caused by changing definitions of fame (Schickel 1985). At the turn of the century, celebrities were members of wealthy elites: politicians, inventors, and entrepreneurs. Admiration from the public was expected and tolerated, but one group did not rub elbows with the other. Today, in contrast, the media reduce the perceived social distance between ordinary people and the famous by creating and maintaining an illusion of intimacy. The tabloids in particular encourage the unfamous to engage the famous. While their reliability is debatable (Kelm 1989), tabloids facilitate pseudointimacy by providing luridly detailed reports about celebrities' private lives gleaned from police bulletins, nosy neighbors, or unnamed informants. Readers have been so successfully lured into the role of Peeping Tom that they now feel entitled to information about stars' personal lives. This results, for instance, in the hoopla surrounding Julia Roberts's surprise wedding to Lyle Lovett, where both the public and the press complained they were shortchanged: not only were they not invited to the wedding, but they did not even know that Lovett and Roberts were romantically linked.

Tabloids along with other popular publications flaunt the invasion of privacy of media stars by embedding readers in an enormous network of publicly available gossip. Public gossip influences the image of *both* celebrities and fans. Just as journalists conduct a feeding frenzy on the juicy details of stars' lives, they promote an image of the obsessive fan by circulating gossip that focuses only on fans' extreme behavior. When private behaviors are brought under public scrutiny, they are usually sensationalized rather than examined or explained. Rarely does popular coverage of fans encourage an understanding of *why* fans act the way they do. It is far simpler (and more newsworthy) to attribute mysterious or incomprehensible behavior to lunacy.

Until recently the academic community cooperated with the popular press and the general public in dismissing and ridiculing media fans.[1] While scholars have documented changing meanings of celebrity and fame, they have devoted little serious attention to understanding fan behavior. Current psychiatric doctrine, for example, supports the lunatic image by linking fan behavior to erotomania, a disorder stemming from an idealized erotic delusion that one is loved by a person of higher status (*Diagnostic and Statistical Manual of Mental Disorders-III-Revised* 1987:199). As an explanation, erotomania ties fanship exclusively to the world of sexually based "craziness." Even entertainment field insiders readily accept this link. Critic Richard Schickel (1985), for example, says that an integral feature of the culture of celebrity is fans' "near murderous moments."

Research on television and film audiences further darkens this negative image. When one of the earliest studies on film audiences recognized the importance of fan mail to sustaining celebrity (Thorp 1939), other researchers dismissed the study's reliability because it focused on nonrepresentative subgroups of movie goers, namely teenagers and young girls. They further discounted the importance of fan mail with the observation that the vocabulary of fan-letter writers was severely limited (Handel 1950:10). Today's press supports the loser image by depicting letter-writing fans as "lonely people, latchkey children, and teen-age illitera[tes]" (Ciotti 1992:F25A). An article about *Twin Peaks* fans distinguished them from the stereotype by pointing out that "these people are educated, these people are upscale—these are not letters from the masses. Everything's punctuated correctly, the grammar and spelling are right" (Griggs 1991:2).

Why do we consider fans by definition abnormal? According to social theorists (Bourdieu 1984), fans are stigmatized and marginalized because they cross culturally defined boundaries of taste and rationality. Media fans particularly are subject to marginalization because their pleasure derives from fictional narratives rather than from something "real," like a basketball game. Sports fans who celebrate a World Series or SuperBowl victory are largely accepted by the same nonfan public (see Babad 1987) that ridicules comparable activities by media fans.[2] We especially stigmatize fans of television, because we define television not just as fiction but as bad fiction (see Brunsdon 1989). It is so bad, in fact, that people are embarrassed by their own viewing habits (McIlwraith et al. 1991; Whetmore and Kielwasser 1983) and routinely lie about how much television they watch or which programs they prefer. If simply *watching* leads to social degradation and personal embarrassment, then to say one is a *fan* of television is unthinkable. Television fanship is acceptable only among adolescents, who are presumed immature, and the mentally unstable, who are presumed out of control.

The negative stereotypes of media fans, like most stereotypes, are based largely on ignorance. Few of us understand what fans actually do and why they do it. Why do grown-ups buy soap opera magazines or dress up like *Star Trek* characters or flood the producers of *Beauty and the Beast* with complaining letters when the heroine is killed off? we ask. Don't they have anything better to do with their time? Academics have recently called for scholarship that seriously examines fan subcultures — more specifically, for works that move beyond the loser/lunatic image and examine fans "as a normal, everyday cultural or social phenomenon" (Jensen 1992:13). Several scholars have addressed the challenge with ethnographic studies of fan communities, most notably Henry Jenkins's *Textual Poachers* (1992b) and Camille Bacon-Smith's *Enterprising Women* (1992). Both authors focus on prime-time and feature-film fan cultures, especially fans of *Star Trek,* the most widely studied subculture of media fans. Their work offers a significant contribution to knowledge about fan activities and the internal organization of fan communities, particularly the nature and meaning of fans' relationships with one another.

We take a different approach in this book, focusing less on fan-to-fan relationships than on how fanship and fandom are shaped by the cult of celebrity and by fans' relationships with the entertainment industry.[3] We move outside the context of the fan world itself to explore how that world interacts with media production in general. Not that we ignore the private world of the fan; in fact, we pay particular attention to how one integrates being a fan into one's day-to-day leisure activities, experience of pleasure, and personal identity. In part, we aim to normalize fan behavior by expanding what is known about its range and diversity.

We decided to study fans of daytime soap operas. Both of us are long-time soap viewers, and our dabblings in the soap fan world convinced us that a study of the subculture would yield an important perspective on media fans. Soaps are at the absolute bottom of the television hierarchy, lumped with game shows and professional wrestling in terms of their perceived moral worth (see Alasuutari 1992). Being a soap viewer, let alone a soap fan, is about as low as one can sink on cultural taste hierarchies. For this reason, what we would discover about this community, we believed, should extend what is known about media fandom as a whole by revealing its borders. For better or worse, soap fans are considered the outer limit of fan cultures.

More important, we chose soap operas as a vehicle for exploring how narrative structure and aspects of production shape fan cultures, features overlooked in existing research. Fans of different narrative forms are not interchangeable, and the activities through which they engage texts are not the same. Because the soap opera genre relies on particular subjects, themes, and narratives, it attracts a viewing audience with similar interests. Its structure is unique within the world of television, and scholars have convincingly demonstrated how that structure resonates with and is interpreted by viewers (see Allen 1983, 1985; Brown 1987; Modleski 1983). This made soaps an easy type of programming for us to draw on in examining how generic elements like content, structure, and production significantly influence the activities, organization, interests, and pleasures of fans. In other words, it matters that *Star Trek* fans choose that particular program to be a fan of, or that soap fans choose to be fans of soaps and not, say, of *Jeopardy.* Fan behavior is not haphazard, accidental, or spontaneous. It reflects the cultural object or text it addresses.

A final reason we wanted to study soap opera fans is to expand what is known about the private meaning of fanship. The most recent studies of fans (Bacon-Smith 1992; Jenkins 1992a, b; Penley 1991) suggest that at the core of media fandom lie the alternative texts created and produced by the fans themselves based on the primary narrative, such as fanzines, song tapes, or original artwork. In this perspective, fan worlds are constituted by the public and semipublic activities of fans. Although we agree that fan texts provide intriguing evidence of fan culture, our initial experiences with the soap fan world convinced us that concentrating on activities obscures an important element of fan worlds: the process by which people identify themselves as fans. As we show, fans engage in negotiations over the meaning and relevance that being a fan has in their lives, and these struggles influence their degree of involvement with organized fandom. We propose that fanship is about both engaging in activity and managing identity, which allows us to rethink sociological understandings of subculture. We want to question not just what fans *do* but who they *are*.

Readers might be surprised that we do not take an especially gendered approach in our study of soap opera fans, for soaps were created for a female viewing audience (Allen 1985), and despite demographic changes the audience remains largely female (Rouverol 1992). In addition, feminist scholarship has convincingly analyzed soaps' particular appeal for women, in terms of both story content and narrative structure, and we draw on that literature in order to introduce the reader to the genre and to inform specific analytic points we make in the book. But while soaps' viewing *audience* is most appropriately analyzed in terms of gender, that variable is less salient to an understanding of the soap *fan community.* Once we begin investigating the semipublic and public world of fans, variables other than gender explain more.[4]

We drew upon a wide range of source materials for our study of soap fans, including fans' responses to a questionnaire we designed, in-depth interviews with many fans, letters and other materials in fan magazines, viewers' postings on electronic bulletin boards, and observations from our own participation in the world of soap fans. We also interviewed soap actors — from day players to divas — soap writers, producers, fan club staff members, and journalists who write for the daytime magazines as well as photographers who contribute to them. We quote liberally from these materials throughout the text but identify individuals by name only when they have given us permission to do so or when they have been interviewed by others for public attribution (for example, magazine and television features on soap celebrities and other industry participants). We report details about how our study was conducted in the Appendix.

The book is organized into six chapters. In the first we describe the soap opera genre and offer initial thoughts on the impact of the narrative form on the construction and activities of its fan community. In the second we explore how the celebrity-fan relationship is created collaboratively by the production industry, the press, and relevant others, and how in turn that relationship cultivates and sustains fanship. In Chapter Three we look at the dual processes of becoming and being a fan: fan as activity and fan as identity. Here we also discuss the stalker stereotype as it applies to the soap world. In Chapter Four we explore the issue of pleasure, focusing on a newly visible form of fan pleasure that plays with the boundaries between the real and the fictional. In the fifth chapter we examine the impact of fans on the media production process specifically and on the production of cultural meaning more generally, focusing on the possibilities for viewer and fan agency. In the concluding chapter we suggest how our findings contribute to the concepts of viewing pleasure, power, and agency and to the phenomenon of subculture in everyday life.

# Chapter One

## The Soap Opera Fan World

Jennifer and her mother pull into the parking lot of the lavish Los Angeles hotel at 11:30 on a Sunday morning. Jennifer is a fifteen-year-old high school sophomore, and her mother, Elizabeth, is an administrative assistant at a computer software company. They flew in from Chicago the night before. Neatly dressed, each clutches her camera and purse. Inside, they ask the concierge to direct them to the soap opera fan club luncheon. Once they have checked in, they join the cluster of fans and professional photographers outside the ballroom door. The fans gossip excitedly about which stars might show up, while the photographers share backstage dirt about the actors. Camera bulbs flash. The arriving actors smile and pose graciously, then disappear into a private room.

As the two fans make their way to their table, Elizabeth stops at the cash bar for a glass of white wine. Their table is well positioned near the stage and beside the red-carpeted aisle where the actors will make their grand appearance. They are seated with six other fans: a retired couple in their midseventies, a housewife from Des Moines, two sisters (an attorney and a graphics designer), and a middle-aged corporate executive who is attending her ninth daytime luncheon.

The fan club president approaches the microphone, greets the audience, and begins to introduce the actors one by one. Smiling and waving to the crowd, they make their way down the aisle to the roped-off section at the front of the ballroom reserved for them and their dates and families. A cacophony of sound carries them along: thundering applause, loud laughter and conversation, good-humored ribbing, and the simultaneous click of two hundred cameras. Tuxedo-clad waiters serve a meal so unappetizing that some fans and actors visit the cash bar instead. At the request of the fan club president, fans refrain from taking photos during the meal, but they are delighted when an occasional actor abandons the chicken Florentine to wander among the tables talking and posing for pictures. After lunch, during the entertainment portion of the afternoon some actors sing and others perform skits. A long, humorous, and often ribald question-and-answer session gets out of hand when several actors begin yelling to each other, in character, across the crowded ballroom, again to the delight of the fans.

The highlight of the event is the autographing session. The fan club president shepherds the actors to a long banquet table lined with pens and publicity photos and instructs the fans to line up by table number. To Jennifer and Elizabeth's disappointment, they are scheduled almost last. The autograph line creeps forward, as fans chat with each actor before getting an autograph and having a picture taken. As the afternoon lengthens, fans at the remaining tables become impatient and abandon the instructions for lining up. The club president pleads with them to remain orderly but everyone ignores her, and several squabbles break out when fans try to cut to the front of the line. Some actors also become impatient with the line's slow crawl and leave their stations to descend into the crowd.

By five o'clock the actors have left, and the remaining dozen fans appear exhausted but happy. Jennifer and Elizabeth exchange addresses with their table mates and emerge from the ballroom looking shell-shocked. On the way back to the airport they examine their goods. Between them they have snapped more than four rolls of photos and collected twenty-five autographs. Was it worth the sixty-five dollars per ticket? You bet. Will they be back again next year? You bet.

Joshua Gamson (1994) suggests that an appropriate metaphor for most casual celebrity watching is the hunt, where fans collect autographs or pictures or sightings of celebrities and compare their collections with each other. Whoever scores the most (or the best) wins the hunt. By contrast, the soap opera fan club event is akin to an extended family reunion. The participants have a symbolically intimate but geographically distant relationship to each other; they come together on a Sunday afternoon to share a meal, exchange gossip, catch up on old times, and take pictures; and

The fan club luncheon tableau. The actors on the dais hold the rapt attention of the fans. Used by permission of an anonymous fan.

finally they part, exhausted, knowing that the same thing will happen next year. What transforms a hunt into a reunion? What explains the greater intimacy between celebrities and fans in the world of daytime television compared to other celebrity-fan relationships? Is this intimacy an illusion? What does it mean to be a fan of soap operas?

While considerable research exists on daytime *viewers*, little is known about daytime *fans*. Most research on media fans focuses on only one type: individuals who create derivative products that reflect personal interest in a cultural text. Some examples include the group of female fans who write homoerotic fiction starring Kirk and Spock from *Star Trek* (Bacon-Smith 1992; Penley 1991), and the "filking" community, which creates and performs original songs extending the narratives of media texts (Jenkins 1992a). Most scholarship defines fans by the types of activities they engage in. A person "becomes a fan not by being a regular viewer of a particular program but by translating that viewing into some type of cultural activity. . . . For fans, consumption sparks production, reading generates writing, until the terms seem logically inseparable" (Jenkins 1988:88).

The popular perception of the fan is shaped almost exclusively by this subset of fans who engage in well-organized and public expressions of fanship. They create fanzines or original artwork, attend fan club conventions or luncheons, write letters to the stars, or, in rare cases but with much publicity, stalk a celebrity. But what is the private meaning of being a fan? What are the personal and interpersonal pleasures and meanings derived from the role? What does it mean to call oneself a fan of something?

We chose to study soap opera fans because they represent a unique type of fan world. The genre's distinctive textual construction lends itself to the creation of a community with little formal structure and fairly low public visibility whose participants are nonetheless more socially stigmatized than any other type of media fan. Little is known about soap fans, and the popular perception is that there is nothing of import *to* know.

Before we introduce the world of the soap opera fan, we must describe the structure of the serial narrative, because the nature of the genre shapes the daytime fan community and its activities, just as the nature of any text shapes its fans. To understand soap fans, one must first understand the soap narrative.

## Fans Clued in to Soaps' Nuance, Structure

Despite increased research on the soaps in the past decade or so, critics continue to characterize them as "curiously distorted reflections of empirical social reality" (Allen 1983:97) and soap viewers as people desperately seeking mindless fantasy. The stereotype of the soap watcher remains a bathrobe-clad housewife who has abandoned her domestic duties to sit weeping in front of the television set clutching a half-consumed box of bonbons. This vision, firmly entrenched in the minds of the non-soap-watching public, is negotiated consciously by serial watchers themselves. However, it is not the simplicity of soaps but their narrative complexity that has left them inaccessible to non–soap watchers (Allen 1983, 1985).

Several elements distinguish the soap opera from other narrative forms; most notable is its resistance to closure (Allen 1983:98). Daytime serials are open texts. Unlike most novels, feature films, or prime-time television series, where each story has a distinct beginning, middle, and end, soaps are characterized by an "endless middle"; story lines are never finally resolved. While subplots regularly reach resolution, the story itself goes on forever. "The soap opera trades an investment in an ultimate narrative telos — the most characteristic feature of traditional narratives — for a series of over-lapping mini-closures, which resolve a particular narrative question but are in no way read as moving the overall story toward its potential end" (Allen 1985:75).

Open-ended narratives engage viewers through the development of story telling within the text and foster the perception of soap characters as real, with human strengths and limitations. Daytime serials are also open-ended in the sense that a new episode is shown every weekday, fifty-two weeks a year, often for years on end. In 1995, ABC's *All My Children* celebrated its twenty-fifth anniversary. CBS's *Guiding Light* is in its fifty-eighth year of production, including its early years on radio. That television seasons are less clearly defined for daytime shows also makes the boundaries of the text more difficult to determine.

Open texts encourage multiple readings. Unlike a closed text with a "straightforward linear pathway of stimulus and anticipated response" (Allen 1983:99), an open text allows for endless interpretations (Seiter et al. 1989:223–224). Not that anything goes with narrative interpretation. Rather, a competent viewer knows the specific codes at work in the genre, including camera conventions, intertextuality, ideological codes, and so on (Allen 1983:100–103). This knowledge guides viewers' textual readings. While sharing certain codes with all television genres, soap operas have distinct codes of their own, such as character development, distortion of time, emphasis on domestic concerns, multiple narratives, commercials as a structuring device, and background music (Allen 1983). How each code is manipulated sends distinct messages to the viewing audience; none are accidental, and all are sources of meaning for viewers.

The textual code of each soap opera is important to the construction of the genre. While each serial shares the genre characteristics mentioned above, it also has its own narrative history, and experienced viewers make sense of the action on the show by drawing on their knowledge of this history, or "backstory" (Timberg 1981). The codes unique to each show are generally inaccessible to nonwatchers, who tend to view all soaps as interchangeable. But avid viewers come to know a fictional community and its characters so well that they recognize appropriate and inappropriate behavior by characters, just as in real life we know when our intimates are behaving falsely. The following extended quote illustrates the importance of backstory and the narrative structure to a viewer's interpretation of the action:

> Let us presume in scene one of a soap episode we learn from a conversation between Lucy and her friend Debbie that Lucy is pregnant with Rick's child. In scene three, Debbie tells her husband Chris of Lucy's pregnancy. In scene five, Chris warns his friend Billy against becoming too involved with Lucy. . . . In terms of the syntagmatic . . . dimension of the soap, such exchanges [are] redundant . . . [but the] experienced reader is able to read these exchanges as invokings of the paradigmatic network. It makes a difference that Lucy chose to confide in Debbie about her plight because Debbie was once married to Rick. Debbie's telling Chris of Lucy's revelation is read against the background of Debbie's inability to have a child and Chris' recurrent infidelity, and so forth. . . . To the experienced reader . . . soap operas' distinctive networks of character relationships open up major sources of signifying potential that are simply unreadable to the naive reader. (Allen 1985:70–71)

Textual codes thus generate meaning by drawing on the expert viewer's knowledge of the narrative history of a particular show, especially the history of its relationships.

Soap opera's structure could hardly differ more from linear, progressive narratives motivated through action, whose characters cease to exist at their conclusions. Serial textuality draws upon an aesthetic of repetition and redundancy that offers "an indulgent invitation to repose, a chance of relaxing" (Eco 1985:165). This description suggests why nonwatchers have difficulty recognizing and understanding the pleasures offered by soap narratives. Viewers learn soap opera conventions through repeated viewings, and ignorance of these conventions leaves novice viewers and critics uneducated about the meanings viewers derive from soaps. Meaning is thus partly generated by the viewer's understanding of the nuances of the genre.

## The "Femaleness" of Soap Opera

Soap operas have long been considered part of "women's fiction," which includes romance novels and melodramatic films, even though 20 to 30 percent of the soap audience is male (Rouvcrol 1992; Whetmore 1993) and has been for at least a decade (A. C. Nielsen Company 1981). This gendered typecasting is due partly to soaps' predominantly female audience, but primarily to their narrative structure. Certain conventions of daytime television can be characterized as feminine and especially resonate with the experiences of female viewers: the focus on networks of relationships and verbal interaction, the consistent use of close-up camera techniques, the fragmentation of story telling, the concept of the endless middle, and the emphasis on domestic concerns (Allen 1985; Archer 1992; Brown 1987; Modleski 1983).

What happens on daytime serials, the action, is less important than *reaction* and *interaction* (Modleski 1982). It is not the events that reoccur with alarming frequency in the world of daytime television that appeal to viewers — the kidnappings, murders, and reappearances of characters believed to be dead — but rather their "concentric ripples" (Archer 1992:92) of impact on the community of interrelated characters. "In soap operas, the important thing is that there always be time for a person to consider a remark's ramifications, time for people to speak and to listen lavishly. Actions and climaxes are only of secondary importance" (Modleski 1982:106). Why is this a feminine element? Research on women's psychological and moral development (Chodorow 1978; Gilligan 1982) suggests that by adulthood, women are more likely than men to define themselves in terms of attachments and connections to others. Women tend to perceive themselves not as having sharp ego boundaries, as men are presumed to have, but as embedded in a network of relationships. "Intimacy goes along with identity, as the female comes to know herself as she is known, through her relationships with others" (Gilligan 1982:12). The mature female is thus defined through attachment, the mature male through separation. Daytime serials celebrate relationships and affiliations, the "realistic terms of many women's lives" (Archer 1992:93).

A second convention that contributes to the genderedness of soaps is their emphasis on verbal interaction. The action or events on serials "are not important in themselves; they merely serve as occasions for characters to get together and have prolonged, involved, intensely emotional discussions with each other" (Modleski 1983:68). Such scenarios appeal particularly to female viewers because women, unlike men, tend to emphasize verbal self-disclosure in their own interpersonal relationships (Rubin 1984; Tannen 1990). Women define love and intimacy as residing in the sharing of personal and emotional information, the telling of secrets, whereas men have traditionally defined intimacy in terms of sexual contact or instrumental help (Cancian 1987:7). Comments one scholar: "Nowhere else in American popular culture do people spend as much time discussing and analyzing personal problems of other people. This is, in short, a female world" (Rosen 1986:50). Women place a high value on talk in their own lives and thus identify with the centrality of talk on daytime serials. "The genre's very existence is bound to [the] possibility, and necessity, of saying everything" (Peter Brooks, quoted in Modleski 1982:106).

Another gendered aspect of soaps is the preference for close-up camera shots. Unlike most media forms that either fragment the female body or make a fetish of it, serials rely on close-up facial shots of characters (Byars 1988; Modleski 1983; Timberg 1981). This technique instructs the viewer to pay attention to, indeed to worry about, the welfare of the characters. "Close-ups provide the spectator with training in 'reading' other people, in being sensitive to their (unspoken) feelings at any given moment"

(Modleski 1983:70). Concern over the needs and wants of others has long been a prescribed concern of women in the domestic sphere (Bernard 1981; Modleski 1983). Women have traditionally been socialized into roles that entail caring for others, often at the expense of self (Gilligan 1982). Unlike men, women are presumed to be natural caregivers with an intuitive ability to read people emotionally. Extended close-ups affirm these assumptions by allowing viewers not only to experience emotions along with characters but also to imagine and speculate on the source of those emotions. Close-ups "are the means of exercising the feminine ability to understand the gap between what is meant and what is said" (Fiske 1987:183).

The fragmentation of story telling, which has been explicitly linked to women's domestic labor (Brown 1987; Modleski 1983; Oakley 1974), also contributes to the classification of soap operas as female narratives. Consider, for instance, the frequent repetition of facts or information within a single episode of a serial (Allen 1985). In an hour-long program, a certain bit of news might get told four or five different times by as many different characters. A viewer who is simultaneously working and watching television does not need to worry about missing information if he or she is distracted by children, a timer, or a phone call because the information is sure to be repeated (Modleski 1982). Commercials serve a similar function. Soaps air for only five to ten minutes between commercials and often backtrack after each, for example, by reiterating the end of the previous scene. The formal structure of the soap opera is thus closely linked to the rhythms of women's work in the home (Modleski 1983:73).

A fifth gendered feature of serials is the focus on the private or "interior world" (Allen 1985) rather than the public or exterior one. While most daytime characters, both male and female, now have glamorous and respected careers as physicians, lawyers, or corporate executives, they are rarely seen actually working. Rather, the work setting is transformed into a private arena in which to confront and explore personal issues. "Because of the importance of interpersonal relationships in soaps, the work places depicted in them must allow for frequent contact with other characters and opportunities to discuss matters not directly related to work" (Allen 1985:74). Hospitals, for example, frequently serve as settings for soap

CHAPTER ONE / 18

narratives because "friends and family members [of a hospitalized character], imprisoned in waiting rooms . . . can discuss their feelings about the latest tragedy, and . . . go on to analyze the predicaments of their mutual friends, as well as the state of their own relationships" (Modleski 1982: 106–107). Every setting, then, becomes a private arena or a "home" where personal dilemmas are brought to the forefront (Brunsdon 1981:34).

This division between public and private spheres accompanied American industrialization, as women were relegated to domestic life when men took control of the public or exterior world (Bernard 1981). Despite women's increasing participation in the paid labor force since the 1960s, they are still held responsible for the private sphere (Hochschild 1989). The focus on the domestic arena in daytime serials and the transformation of public settings into private ones thus corresponds to women's lived historical experience and resonates strongly with female viewers.

A final soap opera convention geared to female viewers is the endless middle, the consequence of stories with no real beginnings or endings but instead a continuous interweaving of past, present, and future. The emphasis is on the "process rather than the product, on pleasure as ongoing and cyclical rather than climactic and final" (Fiske 1987:183). This structure especially holds for romance and courtship, a main focus of daytime story telling. As any knowledgeable viewer knows, a happy couple rarely remains so for long. Instead, characters move in and out of relationships and marriages, with destruction a constant threat to romance. (When the Super Couple phenomenon of the 1980s violated this convention, it led to story-line dead ends and frustrated viewers [Reep 1992]). Soap operas, like all romance texts aimed at women, emphasize not the end goal of heterosexual courtship (marriage and a family) but the courtship itself (see Haskell 1987; Radway 1984). This emphasis appeals to women whose own experience of married life or romance falls short of the ideal. Daytime serials thus invest pleasure in the central condition of women's lives: waiting (Modleski 1982:88). The focus on courtship is explicitly contrasted with the "masculine pleasure of the final success" (Fiske 1987:183).

These conventions contribute to the female-gendered categorization of daytime serials, and their low status and marginalization as a cultural product.

> If television is to be considered by some to be a vast wasteland, soap operas are thought to be the least nourishing spot in the desert. . . . In the same way that men are often concerned to show that what they are, above all, is not women, not "feminine," so television programs and movies will, surprisingly often, tell us that they are not soap operas. (Modleski 1982:86)

When a cultural text is denigrated and marginalized, so are those who consume it. Like other forms of fandom, the daytime fan world is decidedly female gendered. By studying fans through the framework of gender (along with other aspects of interpersonal identity) we can explore how fans' activities are an extension of issues central to their lives, not (as many assume) the consequence of a marginalized status.

## Soaps' Structure Shapes Fan Community

The genre's structure, including its genderedness, helps shape the soap fan community into a form of fanship (individual fan activity) and fandom (organized fan activity) oriented toward private uses and pleasures. In contrast, activities focus on creating, producing, and exchanging derivative texts in the fan communities based on prime time series and feature films — most notably *Star Trek* but including *Beauty and the Beast, Blake's 7, Starsky and Hutch,* and others (see Bacon-Smith 1992; Jenkins 1992b; Penley 1991). Consider, for example, K/S fandom, a female community that combines interests in romance, utopias, technology, and pornography to create homoerotic products based on the Kirk and Spock characters from *Star Trek*. K/S fans "are producing . . . real products (albeit ones taking off from already-existing heterogeneous elements) — zines, novels, artworks, videos — that (admiringly) mimic and mock those of the industry they are 'borrowing' from while offering pleasures found lacking in the original products" (Penley 1991:139).

Female *Star Trek* fans (among the most fully explored groups of media fans) create derivative narratives partly as a way of claiming space in male-centered texts (Jenkins 1988). Because female characters are absent from or marginalized in the narrative, fans struggle to identify with and find pleasure in the story. To access the text, some begin to create their own stories, either in fantasies or through dialogues with other fans. Creating an actual product is the predictable next step, "the transformation of oral countertexts into a more tangible form, the translation of verbal speculations into . . . works that can be shared" (Jenkins 1988:91). The form and content of male-centered texts lead to activities that provide a way for female fans to access masculine narratives.

Consider, too, the fictional texts produced by women engaged in K/S fandom (Penley 1991), which speak directly to women's marginalized position in a technological world and their ambivalent relationship with technological means of production. Participation in this community provides female fans with opportunities for self-revelation and self-development (Bacon-Smith 1992). Through fiction writing, fans carve out space for themselves in male-gendered roles and activities and are able to "construct a safe discourse with which to explore the dangerous subjects of their own lives" (Bacon-Smith 1992:203).

Why do daytime fans rarely engage in derivative activities?[1] Perhaps viewers and fans interact differently with narratives whose content and form place women closer to the center. Soaps, like other women's texts, do not marginalize women but rather "speak to very real problems and tensions in women's lives" (Modleski 1982:14; see also Ang 1985; Gledhill 1987; Radway 1984). While telling fairly traditional stories about personal relationships, a woman-centered text "allays *real* anxieties, satisfies *real* needs and desires, even while it may distort them" (Modleski 1982:108).

Some scholars argue that the repeated consumption of feminine texts has subversive potential for women readers because it allows them to redefine gender expectations, particularly the expectation to care for and orient toward others at the expense of the self. In this sense, women's consumption of such texts constitutes a form of "everyday resistance" to patriarchal dominance (Scott 1985). For example, Janice Radway argues in her study of romance readers that, in picking up a book, women "refuse temporarily their family's otherwise constant demand that they attend to the wants of others even as they act deliberately to do something for their own private pleasure" (1984:211). In these cases, women's pleasure lies less in carving out space in a male-centered narrative than in claiming that same space in a male-centered world. It is *because* female consumers of women's texts — including soaps — find it easier to identify with and find pleasure in the primary narrative that they rarely produce derivative texts. Instead, they struggle with the disparaged status of the primary text *as* a female text, and with the difficulty of articulating the pleasure they receive from such purportedly unrealistic stories of love and romance.

A second explanation for the difference in the activities of soap fans compared to those of other media fans concerns the structure of the soap narrative. Most media fans engage a closed text that makes limited install-ments of the official story available: a finite number of episodes, the occa-sional feature film, or reruns in syndication. Not only is the text limited in scope, but the gap between installments may stretch from a week in prime time and syndication to several months between seasons or even several years, in the case of feature films. Most media fans thus create derivative narratives partly to fill the gaps of production delays. Their fan commu-nities are fundamentally structured by the nature of the closed narrative and the production schedule of the entertainment industry.

Because serials' structure differs from that of other narrative forms, the fanship and fandom that surround serials also differ. The open-ended nature of the genre allows for an endless story. Fans receive a new install-ment of the story five days a week, potentially for decades. Why create alternative stories if the official one unfolds for you daily? Much like romance readers who are gratified by the repetitive consumption of famil-iar stories (Radway 1984), daytime fans find pleasure in the daily engage-ment with fictional characters that they come to know through long-term viewing.

The stance of the production industry also helps shape and define its relationship with viewers and fans. For example, the people in charge of *Star Trek* tend to treat fan-produced materials with "benign neglect" (Jenkins 1988:89) as long as they are handled on a nonprofit basis. Lu-casfilm, in charge of *Star Wars*, has come down harder on fan-produced material, viewing it as competition for the company's officially sponsored fan organization. Lucasfilm has been especially aggressive in its attempts to control fanzines; however, fans widely use an underground market to

produce and distribute fanzines (Jenkins 1988:90). The relationship between the industry and many fan subcultures is tense at best.

A different relationship exists between soap fans and the daytime industry, which supports, endorses, and legitimates fans' existence — mainly for
commercial reasons, as the industry equates happy fan with long-term
viewer. The industry treats fans as integral to the success of the genre, and
soap producers attempt simultaneously to cultivate new fans and retain
long-term viewers. While viewers and fans regularly contact the production offices to complain and offer advice about story lines and character
development, they essentially support the story that is offered to them and
feel little need to create alternative versions of the daytime world. Soap
producers therefore do not feel threatened or infringed upon by fans in the
way that prime-time or movie producers can be.[2]

## Who Views?

Most scholarship treats the television audience as a unified mass or as
comprising social categories such as gender, race, class, or age that modify
reception (see Ang 1991; Press 1991). We know little about differentiation
among viewers in terms of their viewing habits or the activities they engage in around viewership. Scholars conceptualize viewing as a process
that takes place in the private, domestic sphere (Lull 1982, 1988) and
fanship as the participation in public activities surrounding interest in a
cultural object. They make a sharp distinction between the private activity
of viewers and the public activity of fans, which we believe to be false.

Because being a serial fan presumes that one is a serial viewer, however,
the viewing habits of our survey respondents deserve some attention; these
are summarized in Table 1 (see the Appendix for a description of the data
collection and for demographics of respondents). Nearly every respondent has a favorite soap opera, but more than half watch three or more
serials on a regular basis. Most watch their favorite soap five times a week,
and almost half view a second soap every day as well. Nearly a third view
an additional serial just as often. The industry considers regular soap
viewers to be those who watch at least 2.5 times per week (Hornik 1994),
so our sample is composed of dedicated watchers. In addition, many of

## TABLE I
## Selected Traits of Soap Opera Fans ($N = 706$)

| Viewers who | Percent |
|---|---|
| Watch just one serial | 25 |
| Watch two serials | 23 |
| Watch three or more | 51 |
| Keep up with other serials, but do not watch regularly | 49 |
| *Viewers who* | |
| Watch by videotape | 45 |
| Watch when aired | 24 |
| Watch by videotape or when aired | 31 |
| Prefer to watch alone | 76 |
| *Viewers who* | |
| Talk with others on a regular basis | 96 |
|    Face to face | 54 |
|    Telephone | 32 |
|    Electronic bulletin boards | 3 |
| Talk regularly with four or more fans | 37 |
| *Viewers who* | |
| Subscribe to publications | 82 |
|    *Soap Opera Digest* | 65 |
|    *Soap Opera Weekly* | 62 |
|    All others | 46 |
| *Respondents' viewing preferences* | |
| *All My Children* | 31 |
| *General Hospital* | 32 |
| *Days of Our Lives* | 41 |
| *Viewers who* | |
| Watch celebrity-oriented programs | 60 |
| Are members of one or more fan clubs | 28 |
| Have attended fan events | 38 |
| Would like to meet a daytime celebrity | 45 |

these respondents keep up with soaps by talking with other viewers or reading plot summaries in fan magazines. Nearly half videotape soaps to watch at their convenience, while about a fourth watch them as they air during the day.

As noted, scholars typically conceptualize viewing as a process located in the private, domestic sphere, and our findings support this claim. However, we find that daytime viewers modify their practices in a particular way: they usually seek *privacy* for their viewing. Most respondents (76 percent) would rather watch soaps alone than with other people, and their choice is closely related to the pleasures of viewing. Solitary viewing allows freedom to respond emotionally to the program without being distracted or ridiculed by other viewers:

> It makes for a better cry when a cry is called for.

> I can react any way I like and not be considered weird or too involved with the characters.

> [I prefer watching alone] so when I want to react to it I won't feel as stupid.

Those who prefer watching in group settings also do so for the sake of personal pleasure; they like to be able to discuss and react with others to the events unfolding on the screen.

Our findings suggest that soap viewers are not a unified subgroup of the mass audience; rather, they can be differentiated from one another in a number of ways. For instance, viewers tend to orient to and find pleasure in very specific things when watching a show, whether it be the character, actor, story line or writing, and those who are focused on, say, quality of acting, find it difficult to relate to those who are focused on lighting or set design. Viewers can also be differentiated in terms of what serials they watch. Both industry professionals and viewers themselves can distinguish, for example, between a *Days of Our Lives* viewer and a *Guiding Light* viewer based on their likes and dislikes, the letters they write, their behavior at fan events, and so on. Viewers categorize themselves and others on the basis of what they like and dislike about soaps, aspects of viewership almost always overlooked by critics and nonviewers.

We have been describing what most would agree is a private activity: watching television. What distinguishes viewing as we have discussed it from public activity? In other words, what constitutes the difference between viewership and fanship? Is it true that "one becomes a fan not by being a regular viewer of a particular program but by translating that viewing into some kind of cultural activity" (Jenkins 1988:88)? While we agree that activities pursued around viewing habits are an important part of "doing fan," one of our major goals in writing this book is to redefine what it means to be a fan. Being a fan is more than engaging in publicly visible activities. It includes a wonderfully rich private realm of meaning and experience that has yet to be fully examined.

## Activities of the Soap Opera Fan

Fanship can entail both public and private acts. One of the most private is viewers' creation of oral culture (Fiske 1987), their ongoing dialogues and gossip about soap opera actors, story lines, and production news. In the female-dominated science-fiction subculture studied by Camille Bacon-Smith, gossiping is the most frequent and important fan activity. When a fan comes up with an idea to extend the narrative through the creation of an alternative text, she calls on other members of her community to help develop story ideas: fans are literally "talking story" (1992:159).

In the daytime community too, gossiping is a priority for fans, though the dialogue has a different orientation and serves a different purpose. Nearly all of our respondents (96 percent) talk with others on a regular basis about what is happening on their shows, and many (37 percent) have four or more people with whom they regularly discuss story lines, characters, and plot developments. Gossip usually occurs either face-to-face (54 percent) or on the telephone (32 percent); as one fan states, "I have enormous phone bills to prove it!" In addition, newly emerging modes of interaction such as electronic bulletin boards provide an open forum for entertainment gossip.

Gossip in the soap fan community is grounded in the primary narrative, the show's own story lines, and tends to be speculative (Bielby and Harrington 1994). Rather than brainstorming about a derivative text, daytime gossip involves playful guesswork about events on the show. The following comment from a *Loving* viewer, is typical:

> Seems to me that *Loving* changed when Agnes Nixon returned and the new producer took over. Ava could have a meatier story than she does now. It's getting old really quickly. Buck and Tess used to be majorly involved in stories, now they just wait around talking to other characters in their stories. Where's Tess's villainous streak? She could have been a match for Gwen if Gwen got in her way. Gwen wasn't nice to Dinah Lee when Trucker and Gwen were talking about Trisha, so much for being friends. And I would like to see something happen with Buck and Tess, remember they did have that night of drunken passion. She could be pregnant, Stacey could find out that Tess was the one Buck slept with, etc. Interesting possibilities.

Gossip is a central component of women's cultural production and consumption and a unique aspect of the pleasure women derive from feminine texts (Fiske 1987; Press 1991). In the daytime community, soap gossip holds a status similar to that of "talking story" in the *Star Trek* community, yet the processes differ in an important way: the former is grounded in an existing narrative while the latter is focused on the creation of an alternative narrative.

Another way that fanship is enacted privately is through the uses of videotape. Of the almost 50 percent of our respondents who regularly tape their shows, about half sometimes save the tapes. In most cases, fans want to preserve a special event such as a wedding, funeral, or romantic love scene. Some viewers save all the tapes in which a favorite character or couple appears, and others save every episode aired. Some fans construct specially edited tapes, one form of derivative activity that is common among soap fans. For example, we know fans who own more than twenty hours of videotape containing edited scenes of the characters Frisco and Felicia from *General Hospital* and more than twenty-five hours of the romantic couple Harley and Mallet from *Guiding Light*. Both tapes were produced by fans who wanted to preserve the couple's history and chronicle their relationship. Saving tapes allows fans the pleasure of rewatching favorite scenes or actors ("keeping the story alive") and of recapturing a story that has evolved and changed, as two respondents report:

> I have saved *every scene* with Matthew Ashford and Melissa Brennan [actors on *Days of Our Lives*] that has aired since April 1990!! I became so captivated by these actors and their storyline that I didn't want to tape over their scenes. . . . Some of their episodes have become "classics" to me and my friends. . . . Our tapes are like one long, continuous movie.

> I have a Frisco and Felicia [characters from *General Hospital*] video library. . . . I just want to look at them over and over, catch mistakes by actors or just enjoy the chemistry again.

If gossiping and uses of videotape are private ways to enact serial fanship, several activities seem to us quasi-public (or public/private), in the sense that they allow fans to engage with the daytime world yet remain shielded from public scrutiny and condemnation. These activities include reading fan magazines and newsletters, writing to those in the production industry, exchanging photos and videotapes with other fans, and communicating on electronic bulletin boards.

Most respondents (82 percent) subscribe to or regularly purchase soap opera newsletters or magazines. The most popular publications among those surveyed are *Soap Opera Digest* and *Soap Opera Weekly*.[3] Nearly one half of our respondents also regularly read general celebrity-oriented publications, especially *People Weekly* and the *National Enquirer*. These commercial publications, whether soap oriented or not, act as forums for public gossip and are in the business of circulating information about the entertainment industry. However, fans understand well that industry-sanctioned gossip is altered or manufactured for public consumption. So while they avidly read commercial magazines, fans' skepticism helps create and sustain the market for face-to-face gossip.

Not surprisingly, most fans in our survey say they read fan publications to find out about their favorite show, actor, or character:

> [I subscribe in order to] read about my soaps and the actors. . . . [They] are also good for upcoming cast changes and story plots, etc.

[I subscribe in order to] get pictures of actors I like, reviews of plotlines on soaps I'm not currently very involved in to see if they've [improved] at all, and information on other acting jobs (movies, prime time) my favorites have gotten.

Additionally, some fans read commercial magazines as a way to connect with each other:

[I like] to hear other fans' opinions.

[I subscribe to] *The Soap Opera Viewers' Voice* [because it] is the only publication dedicated to "viewers' voices."

Commercial publications offer fans access to others with similar interests and provide a way for fans to create interpersonal bonds and an organized fan community.

Letter writing lets fans connect with the industry yet avoid public scrutiny. About half our respondents (49 percent) have written at least once to a producer, writer, or director of a soap, and almost as many (43 percent) have written at least once to an actor. Fans write for many reasons: to show support, to complain about something, to ask for autographs or pictures, or to find out about joining a fan club. Some fans are able to engage in ongoing correspondence with actors or producers.

David Forsyth [an actor on *Another World*] is a very nice person and I enjoy writing to him and getting his replies. He seems to really care about what viewers have to say about the show and his character.

The exchanges are often just "thanks for the letter," but they are also often involved discussions of interpretations of actions, modes of action, language nuances, grammar, career goals, diet and exercise problems, religion, politics.

Fans' abilities to correspond directly with daytime insiders contributes immeasurably to the pleasure they receive from viewing.

Some respondents (27 percent) have also written to or telephoned a television station to complain about a show's preemption. One well-worn stereotype of the soap viewer is the hysterical housewife who floods the local television station during national emergencies with complaints about her story's being interrupted. Our respondents report contacting stations only when a show is preempted for what seems an insignificant reason:

> I do get irritated when a show is interrupted by news regarding something that could have waited until I watched the evening news or they take up a great portion of a show with what might be going to happen . . . or guessing and going on about all [the] possibilities about something. Let us know when the facts are in.

> I dropped a postcard about the failure of CBS to continue a program . . . when they broke in to cover Bush's atrial fibrillations. Didn't seem important.

Others note that the structure of the soap narrative itself explains viewers' frustration with preemptions: "Soaps tend to lead up to resolution — build, build, build and then *one* day — resolve. Resent that. Feel more flashbacks — especially when they know they've been pre-empted — would be great." Viewers know how these complaints fuel the negative stereotypes aimed at them: "[I have contacted local stations] but NOT for preemptions due to national emergencies or news more important than the soap. I HATE to hear of soap fans doing this — hurts the image of fans." Others suspect that viewer complaints actually lead to more preemptions. One viewer suggested that "networks feel daytime viewers are 'secondary citizens' who are not watching anything important."

A third quasi-public fan activity is exchanging photos and videotapes with other fans. Through informal connections, fans learn where to get high-quality photographs of celebrities and fan events, videotapes of classic episodes, and specially edited tapes of actors or story lines. These tapes are often of very poor quality because of the extent to which they have been recopied — a tape of a tape of a tape, and so on. These exchange networks are usually created through word of mouth, but they can become more structured when tapes and photos are advertised in the classified section of fan magazines or fan club newsletters, or appear for exchange on electronic bulletin boards. Like all expressions of fanship, the exchange of tapes and photos occurs for a variety of reasons connected to

*Classified*

FOR SALE: VHS TAPE LIBRARY OF "DAYS OF OUR LIVES" ORIGINAL EPISODES: JUNE 13, 1985 - OCTOBER 14, 1993. RELIVE THE FIRST DAYS AND EARLY STORYLINES OF THE MANY DIVERSIFIED CHARACTERS! GUARANTEED COMPLETE STORYLINES OF STEVE JOHNSON AND JACK DEVERAUX FOR THEIR ENTIRE RUN ON THE SHOW. STEPHEN NICHOLS [STEVE JOHNSON]: JUNE 13, 1985 TO OCTOBER 24, 1990 - MATTHEW ASHFORD [JACK DEVERAUX]: OCTOBER 30, 1987 TO OCTOBER 12, 1993 - MARY BETH EVANS [KAYLA JOHNSON]: MAY 23, 1986 TO OCTOBER 25, 1991 [SPORADIC THEREAFTER UNTIL HER EXIT MAY 1992] - MELISSA REEVES [JENNIFER DEVERAUX]: OCTOBER 7, 1985 TO OCTOBER 14, 1993 - CALIFORNIA AND CANADIAN ASSISTANCE FOR ALL PRE-EMPTIONS AND INTERRUPTIONS. SEND SELF ADDRESSED STAMPED ENVELOPE FOR REPLY WHEN WRITING, PLEASE SPECIFY: A] CHARACTER, B] DATES DESIRED, C] DETAILED DESCRIPTION OF STORYLINE [IF EXACT DATES KNOWN] MUST DEAL ON A FIRST COME, FIRST SERVED BASIS

CONTACT:

WANTED: ANY DAYS OF OUR LIVES FROM 1984 TO 1987. PLEASE CALL ANYTIME -

OR WRITE TO

WANTED: SPECIFIC 1992 AND 1993 "GH" EPISODES IN THEIR ENTIRETY INVOLVING MAC AND FELICIA STORYLINE. 1992: JUNE 16, NOVEMBER 4, NOVEMBER 12, DECEMBER 10. 1993: FEBRUARY 11, FEBRUARY 12, APRIL 19. WILL SUPPLY ALL BLANK TAPES AND POSTAGE REQUIRED.

Soap fans' advertisements. From *Soap World*, no. 7 (April–May 1994). Used by permission.

fan pleasure: to view for the first time a much-discussed episode, to recon-struct the history of a favorite couple, or to complete a scrapbook on an actor or character. And, like other forms of fanship, these exchanges allow avid viewers to join a subculture of people with similar interests.

A final form of semipublic fanship is participation on electronic bulletin boards (BBSs). In our sample, 13 percent of the respondents use BBSs regularly. Among respondents not solicited through a BBS, 3 percent use them regularly. Through on-line charges or subscription fees members can correspond with each other night and day, seven days a week, about a variety of topics including the entertainment industry, celebrities, and daytime serials. While BBSs can serve as a forum for photos and videotape exchanges, their most important function is to provide an arena for fan gossip (Bielby and Harrington 1994). Fans log on to offer commentary and opinions about serial events, speculate about upcoming plot or char-acter developments, and request and diffuse specific information, such as a missed plot twist or the backstory of a character or romantic couple. BBSs provide a ready-made network of fans who engage in gossip sessions that can be passionate, intimate, and confrontational. Participation on BBSs can also feed into organized soap fandom. For example, members of one bulletin board institutionalized themselves as a fan group by planning a trip to a CBS production studio. Others coordinate attendance at per-sonal appearances of favorite actors and organize regional get-togethers where they meet each other face-to-face. Still other groups hold regional reunions in the form of barbecues or slumber parties and produce annual yearbooks chronicling members' fan activities. Through these planned events, fans get to know each other in ways that are impossible to accom-plish through electronically based interaction, even on a daily basis. They share family photos, collectively view albums of soap memorabilia, and meet each other's families. Such occasions provide opportunities for those who know each other electronically to expand the basis for their friend-ships beyond their mutual specialized interest in soaps.

The fans who gossip on BBSs are less likely than nonusers to engage in traditional fan activities. They are less likely to regularly buy or subscribe to fan magazines (62 percent versus 85 percent), to write to a daytime celebrity (28 percent versus 45 percent), or to complain to a television station or network about preemptions (15 percent versus 29 percent). These differences suggest that using BBSs partially replaces the benefits and pleasures fans derive from engaging in other fan activities.

Buying and subscribing to fan publications, writing letters, exchanging photos or videotapes, and joining BBSs, all quasi-public activities, allow people the chance to interact with others with similar interests but exist largely outside the public arena. But it is the overtly public fan activities such as fan club membership that are mistakenly presumed by outsiders to represent the entire scope of daytime fanship. What constitutes this realm of organized public fan activity so often ridiculed by non-fans?

## The Soap Fan World

Fewer people participate in public fan activities than in private or quasi-public ones, yet these public acts seem to represent the ultimate expression of fanship. Why the contradiction? We think that the negative stereotype of soap viewers and fans strongly influences whether and how much people participate in activities that publicly announce them as fans. Because such participation is usually presumed to indicate an immature (adolescent), unstable fan-as-lunatic, or loser personality, fans are unwilling to go public with their interests. "Public attacks on media fans keep other viewers in line, making it uncomfortable for [them] to adopt such inappropriate strategies" (Jenkins 1988:86). Some respondents agree wholeheartedly with the negative images of fan club members. One wrote that people who join fan clubs "really don't have lives. . . . They are a whole group of desperate people. . . . These are the kind of people who end up as snipers on the top of a tower." Most fans do not condemn fan behavior outright but are reluctant to display their pleasure in daytime television openly. One woman told us she just went to her first fan event but had to reassure herself that it was okay by reminding herself that the proceeds went to a charity. Others hide their attendance at fan events from friends and family. One woman told us that several members of her church community had seen an advertisement in a fan magazine about our study, but even though they wanted to participate they did not send in their names because they feared being "exposed" as soap watchers.

Those who do choose to express publicly their identities as fans have a wide range of pleasures available to them. While the science-fiction fan community is structured around a series of conventions (Bacon-Smith 1992:9), the most formal and public aspect of the daytime fan world is the fan club. One-fourth of our respondents are members of one or more fan clubs, and over one-third have attended fan-related events such as luncheons or mall appearances.

Most fan clubs form voluntarily through collective and publicly expressed interest on the part of fans, who then staff and manage the club under the sponsorship of an actor, as is the case with the John Reilly Fan Club, or of a serial, as in the National *Days of Our Lives* Fan Club. Usually a club is started when a viewer contacts a favorite actor, offering to run his or her fan club, though occasionally a relative takes on the responsibility. Dennis Wagner, for instance, ran the fan club for his brother Jack, who appeared on both *General Hospital* and *Santa Barbara.* Some actors' clubs are initiated at the suggestion of the show's executive producer. An actor might ask a colleague to recommend a fan club manager or invite a frequent letter writer to run the club. One of our respondents was asked to start a club by an actor who was impressed with the sophistication and intelligence of her fan letters. Based on our interviews with presidents of several fan clubs, most fans' motives for initiating fan clubs are sincere. (One exception was an actor's fan club formed to give the club officers access to his studio and contact with *another* actor on the show.) Fans are especially interested in gaining access to the actor for themselves and others, which gives them status and privilege within the fan community. For some fans, this is the most gratifying aspect of directing a club. Not just anyone can be an effective organizer, however; operating a fan club demands financial and administrative skill and experience at motivating actors to attend to the interests of the group (London 1991).

Fans interested in running a club must receive formal approval from the actor or production staff of the show. As stated in *The Fan Club Guide,* a publication of the National Association of Fan Clubs: "Before making any plans at all to start a fan club you must first contact the celebrity you wish to honor and get his or her permission, preferably in writing, to form a fan club in his name. . . . Written permission from your honorary will make your club an 'official' one" (Trinajstick 1989:4–5). Most actors and se-rials have only one sanctioned fan club, if any, and occasionally disputes or misunderstandings arise when multiple clubs are advertised. Usually the dispute is caused by a club started by a fan without permission from the actor. Some clubs, while created in response to fan interest, are run not by fans but by the show's production staff. For example, the producers of CBS's *The Bold and the Beautiful* and *The Young and the Restless* are responsible for the shows' clubs, which are managed by paid staff mem-bers who take an active part in running the club and cultivating new fans.

Whether a club is organized by a volunteer fan or a paid staffer, clear norms operate in clubbing. Fans and fan club officials alike emphasize that clubs should be initiated by fans and run by them on a volunteer basis for noncommercial purposes. Clubs are usually financed by membership fees of ten to twenty dollars per year. Occasionally a show or an actor subsi-dizes a club, since "it is a well known fact that the fan club dues do not always cover all the fan club expenses" (Trinajstick 1989:29). According to Blanche Trinajstick, the president of the National Organization of Fan Clubs, clubs should be run like businesses (1992:45).[4] Those few clubs run for profit come under criticism within the fan community for being strictly commercial operations, expensive to join, and inattentive to fans' inter-ests. One respondent, who has managed two fan clubs and been a member of many, believes that for-profit clubs have "turned fan clubbing into a business from which [they] make money. This is wrong. Clubbing was not ever meant to be like this. A fan club should be run by a fan who cares about the actor. There should be dues, but no profit!" Many fans also disapprove of another departure from the no-profit norm, clubs formed by actors themselves (and their publicists) too eager to capitalize on the benefits of a fan club.

Fan club norms also apply to actions taken to encourage new members. Fans usually dislike being solicited into club membership or being targeted for writing campaigns on behalf of an actor. Said one respondent: "I wrote to her at the studio, and you know what I got in return? An application kit for her fan club! Weird. Who does she think she is? Somebody important? I didn't ask for this." This fan resents the presumption that she is inter-ested in an actor's career when all she really cares about is the character that actor is playing. Fans emphasize that decisions about how to channel their interest in soap operas are best left to them. Making such decisions is central to the process of identifying oneself as a fan.

The structure of individual fan clubs, as well as the fan club world, tends to be informal. Clubs are loosely organized, amorphous, and staffed by volunteers, and their division of labor is often unclear. The only known reliable listing for fan clubs from all fields of entertainment is *The Fan Club Directory,* published by the National Association of Fan Clubs. If they lack access to that publication, potential club members can find information about clubs through contacting the actor or serial production offices, by word of mouth, or through regular listings in fan magazines.

Fan club membership offers numerous benefits, including a membership card, an eight-by-ten-inch photo of the star or stars, and a regular publication, usually a newsletter (Trinajstick 1989:8). Produced by the fan club staff with input from the star, the newsletter typically includes interviews with actors, recipes, members' addresses, a letter from the club president, and something personal from the celebrity, such as a letter to fans or responses to fans' questions. Clubs may also provide members with inside information about the celebrity or serial, glossy professional pictures of the stars, information about pen pals, and video and photo exchange opportunities.

In addition, belonging to a club embeds the fan in a network of people with similar interests. Through exchanging videotapes and becoming pen pals, club members develop lifelong friendships with people they may never meet. One respondent who corresponds with an international network of fans says that it is "interesting and intriguing . . . that soap viewers want to reach out to each other through the mail." In addition, belonging to a club can offer what seems like a more intimate relationship with a celebrity: "I enjoy hearing the actor's thoughts and opinions on their story line, as well as getting to know them a little more, apart from their characters on the show. . . . The club also allows the actor to communicate with all his fans personally."

These perks are especially available to fan club staff, who interact regularly with the actors about club business and have the opportunity to become their acquaintances or friends. One respondent, the secretary of a fan club for a popular actor on an ABC serial, lists the benefits of her job as bringing with it a personal relationship with the actor; access to inside gossip about actors, networks, and other fans; and status among friends as a minicelebrity. She says that holding a staff position is a "power trip" for many, who love being able to visit studio sets whenever they want to and monitor other fans' access to actors.

But the fan club staff position has drawbacks as well, among them dealing with members' demands for special attention and managing competition among members for the recognition that comes with publication of their letters and other features written for the club's newsletter. Other staffers describe infighting among members for selection as club officers, positions that grant access to the celebrity or show. And on a more tangible level, the labor involved in running a club can be staggering, given that membership can run into the thousands. Actor Jack Wagner's club, for example, reached more than 7,500 members at one point.

The pièces de résistance of fan clubs in terms of providing access to celebrities are the club's annual or semiannual gatherings, usually nonprofit luncheons held in hotel ballrooms or large restaurants. These gatherings, which were introduced in the late 1970s, are a relatively recent development in daytime serial fandom. (Traditionally celebrity-fan interaction was limited to newsletters and correspondence between the celebrity and a club member, according to a letter to us from Diane Warren, president of the Christine Jones and Friends fan club.) For fifty to sixty dollars, fan club members and interested nonmembers enjoy a lunch, entertainment by the actors, and a chance to meet and mingle with the actors and other fans. Actors often ask other actors to join in the festivities of their individual clubs. Actors' attendance at a show's fan events is generally voluntary, although some producer's invitations are widely understood to be orders. Some serials arrange fan activities over extended weekends. *Days of Our Lives,* for example, annually holds a series of events around a long weekend, including cocktail parties, luncheons, and barbecues hosted by different actors. Information about all kinds of fan events are distributed through both club newsletters and commercial magazines.

The metaphor of a family reunion that we suggested earlier is apt. The atmosphere at these events is one of excitement and familiarity, at least from the fan's point of view. Fans feel an immediate bond with each other because they share an important interest, and they make time at gatherings to get acquainted. Over the luncheon tables they banter good-naturedly about their favorite actors and story lines, swap viewing histories, and share details of their lives. Many fans recognize one another from other events and offer warm greetings, stopping by each other's tables to catch up. Fan club luncheons, like family reunions, are settings for both creating and maintaining long-term friendships. This intimacy is apparent not only among fans but between fans and actors as well. Fans greet actors like long-lost friends or confidantes, and the physical and emotional intimacy they demonstrate can be a bit startling. These events evoke the feeling so common at family reunions: coming home.

Everyone involved in fan events—fans, producers, and actors—views them as a way to give something back to loyal supporters of an actor or serial. Ironically, while most fans enjoy going to club luncheons and meeting daytime celebrities, many of the actors they come to honor and celebrate find these events overwhelming and emotionally draining. While actors like meeting fans one at a time and are grateful for their support, in the great numbers that attend formal events—all wanting to personally connect with them—the fans are exhausting. As one actor lamented, luncheons are just "thousands of screaming people."

Nevertheless, fan clubs benefit producers and actors as well as fans. Executive producers vary considerably in how involved they become with clubs for their show and in how strongly they advocate fan clubs for their actors. Some actively encourage actors' relationships with fans, making certain that a club is organized for an actor if one does not already exist (particularly if warranted by lots of fan mail) and monitoring its management, or making recommendations for improving an existing club. These producers also become involved with managing the reputation of their show's fan club, the organization and content of its annual events, and the publicity staff at the production studio. They believe in getting to know fans personally and reading viewer mail, and sometimes they even respond to it themselves. In contrast, producers of other shows have little interest or involvement in fan clubs and (as several actors told us) simply endure their fans for the sake of the Nielsen ratings.

For actors, fan clubs can provide career publicity and support. Clubs encourage members to send mail to the actors at the studio, which then gets counted by producers and sometimes influences which characters are emphasized in upcoming story lines. Fan clubs also encourage members to write letters to fan magazines; if these are published, they may introduce actors to a new audience of potential fans. Clubs can also serve as markets for actors' products, such as T-shirts, coffee mugs, or audiotapes of songs. As personal profit-making enterprises, however, such practices violate the norms of clubbing and are often frowned upon by fans.

Most important, perhaps, fan clubs allow actors to connect with fans in ways less intimate (and less threatening) than individual contact. For example, one actor we spoke with tried to answer all of her mail personally early in her career, but because of the increasing volume (and the occasional disturbing letter) she now sends out newsletters through her fan club. The newsletter keeps her in touch with her fans, but at a safe distance. Since it is not directed toward a specific individual, it helps maintain the boundaries of the celebrity-fan relationship. The need to respect this distance is further articulated by Scott Thompson Baker, who has portrayed popular characters on *General Hospital* and *All My Children* and is currently with the cast of *The Bold and the Beautiful*: "I was warned about responding [to letters] personally because you set up expectations in people's minds. For me, the quarterly newsletter is the answer. I'm able to write a letter from my heart and make an impact without getting bogged down in the complications" (Bialkowski 1992:101). The well-publicized cases of celebrity stalkers have made actors more leery about casual, unmediated contact with fans. Communicating through the newsletter protects them from potentially disturbed people, while still allowing them contact with fans.

A well-managed fan club thus benefits actors in many ways. But when club management appears too self-serving or when clubs fail to provide fans with adequate information about the celebrity's upcoming career events or developments, fans feel exploited or ignored, with consequences that may damage an actor's career. For example, one respondent complained that her favorite actor's club "is scheduled to disband, but even if it doesn't, it's no longer much of a club. . . . If [the actor] were going to take a break from the business I could understand the lapse, but with [his feature film] coming out, he cannot afford the loss." Even the daytime press has concerns over actors' treatment of fans. A recent opinion/ editorial column in *Soap Opera Now!* debated whether it was appropriate for actors to use their fans to help get their story lines changed. Says daytime critic Gretchen Keene: "The idea of a soap actor rallying his or her fans to pressure writers into changing said storyline is WRONG! . . . To let [fan involvement] actually interfere with the writers' plan reduces soaps from entertaining storytelling to backstage politics played out on screen" (*Soap Opera Now!* 1993d:5).

Aside from fan clubs, the most publicized aspect of soap opera fandom is celebrity appearances at shopping malls, sporting events, and community fairs. Actors often spend their days off traveling around the country to appear at functions and meet fans. These events vary widely in terms of how much (if at all) the celebrity is paid, who organizes them, if they are profit oriented or charity related, whether or not they are sponsored by the show, and so on. Executive producers or personal agents often encourage actors to appear for publicity reasons, but attendance is ultimately the actor's decision. Again, fans can learn about celebrity appearances through club newsletters and fan magazines.

Aspects of the formal fan community that receive less publicity are serial or actor support groups and fan-produced publications. A fairly new development in the fan club industry, most support groups are geared toward providing career support for actors. Some are affiliated with sanctioned fan clubs, but many exist independently. Support groups engage in letter-writing and telephone campaigns; during a specific time period members inundate production companies with letters and calls about an actor's story line or character development. The June 1991 issue of one fan club newsletter, *Jack's Fan Connection,* suggested: "The producer [is who] you should be referring your letters to. Can you imagine if every member sent 5 letters to this address in the first month [of an actor's appearance on the show], that would be well over 10,000 letters. That would impress them." Support groups are met with varying levels of tolerance by producers, who sometimes discount the campaigns because of their overtly staged quality. As Al Rabin, the former producer of *Days of*

*Our Lives* notes: "When we get 500 letters from Pittsburgh, all in similar handwriting, but not from the same person, we know" (quoted in Welkos 1991:F10). To circumvent such skepticism, support groups often urge members to wage secret campaigns: "Let's all support the show we all love. Please write to the following people and give them your ideas and suggestions . . . but PLEASE do not tell them that this is part of a writing campaign" (*Fans of General Hospital Newsletter* 1991). The most well-known and well-respected support group for prime-time programs, Viewers for Quality Television, faces similar barriers from production executives, forcing the head of VQT to "advise members against identifying themselves with VQT in their letters" (Brower 1992:182). Actors tend to think more highly of support groups than do producers, for obvious reasons, and actively cultivate them.

Most support groups make legitimate efforts to nurture an actor's career, but sometimes their efforts can go awry. Two respondents, former members of a support group for a romantic couple on *Days of Our Lives,* report that members desperately wanted the actors to become romantically involved offscreen. To encourage this development, fans fed false rumors to the national press that the actors were involved. Both women describe the group's activities as "vicious" and regret having been members. As one lamented, "I could've been saving whales."

The few publications produced by and for fans are not well known among nonfans, partly because "fan culture makes no attempt to circulate its texts outside its own community. They are 'narrowcast,' not broadcast, texts" (Fiske 1992:39). Soap fan publications have a different orientation than the fanzines produced in other communities, which deal mostly with fantasy art and literature and are both irregularly produced and privately distributed (Wertham 1973:33; see also Bainbridge 1986). The science fiction community, for example, has a long history of producing fanzines that feature alternative fictional narratives written by and for fans (Bacon-Smith 1992; Jenkins 1992b; Penley 1991).[5] Soap fan publications, on the other hand, have regular publishing and distribution schedules, and their pages are filled not with fan fiction but with fans' responses to the primary text. (An exception is *Soap Opera Digest*'s "Pearl Street," begun in November 1993 as a serialized narrative about a fictional community. Although it qualifies as an alternative text, however, it neither references the narratives of actual soaps nor is it fan produced.) *Soap World* (formerly *Viewer's Voice*), a typical fan publication, is primarily devoted to printing fans' letters about serials and providing a forum for videotape exchanges, photo purchases, and pen pals. The former editor regularly mailed the newsletter to each soap producer and called each studio annually to determine whether or not the newsletter was "being thrown in the trash." He believes that most producers pay attention to and respect both the newsletter and the fan opinions it contains.

Clearly, fans engage in a wide range of activities, some visible and accessible to the nonfan public and others more private. Does engaging in fan activities, whether public or private, distinguish the fan from the ordinary viewer? Instead of the widely held distinctions between viewer and fan and between private and public, we believe continuums of viewership/fanship and private/public exist and that these are integrated in complex ways. (The terms *viewer* and *fan,* as we use them, do not necessarily refer to individuals at either extreme of the viewer/fan continuum.) Distinguishing a fan from a nonfan involves more than looking at an individual's activities, because becoming and being a fan involves parallel processes of activity engagement and identity management. Furthermore, the stereotypes surrounding all forms of media fandom make it difficult for viewers to identify themselves as fans. This difficulty is magnified for daytime viewers because soap opera remains one of the most disparaged televisual genres.

Nevertheless, despite the soaps' low status, their fans are not a marginalized social group. Some suggest that those subordinated by the dominant culture find in the organization and structure of media fandom the acceptance and means of obtaining status missing in their real lives. While the soap community *is* composed largely of females — a structurally disadvantaged group — they are not looking for social acceptance or a therapeutic release (Bacon-Smith 1992). Women watch soaps precisely because soaps *do* speak to issues in their everyday lives. Soap opera fans do not fight for space in the narrative but rather celebrate and identify with it. Involvement in the daytime fan world, whether public or private, is thus a logical extension of women's identities, not an isolated component or a specialized identity looking for an outlet. Soap viewers and fans do not live on the margins of society but are fully integrated into it: they are men and women from all social backgrounds, retired couples and young children, professional workers and blue-collar laborers, Ph.D.'s and high school dropouts. In short, soap fans are as diverse as the culture in which they live.

# Chapter Two

## Soap Fans' Subculture

I can't believe I just spent $750 for a dinner with Antonio Sabato Jr.!

—Soap fan at a charity event

I would come off a shift on the oil rig and not even shower. I'd be stinking up the TV room just so I could catch Asa on *One Life to Live*. Eventually the other guys understood.

—Soap fan reflecting on his priorities

Few of us would call ourselves fans of television. But many of us watch television for several hours every day, and our daily routines, activities, and social relationships are well integrated with it (Comstock 1989; Grossberg 1987; Livingstone 1990; Morley 1986). More than just an easy way to spend leisure time, television is a pervasive and taken-for-granted part of our daily routine and a fact of social life (Cavell 1982). This fact is especially true for soap opera viewers, because soaps' structure and content mesh with the familiar rhythm of the domestic realm where most television viewing occurs (Brunsdon 1989; Lull 1982, 1988). Because soaps draw upon and "spill over into the experiential world of the viewer" (Allen 1983), they are easily integrated into viewers' everyday lives. Indeed, because soaps are so accessible and familiar, many viewers invest substantial time and energy in following them, often without realizing the medium's centrality to their lives.

The soap opera audience is known for its dedicated and even contagious following of the genre. Viewers watch soaps for years on end and pass viewing preferences on to family members, neighbors, roommates, significant others, and co-workers. They continue watching through ups and downs of story lines and recasting of roles, and they will often tolerate major inconsistencies in narrative and character. They return to the genre after interruptions that may last for years and go to great lengths to follow story developments interrupted by vacations, family obligations, or career or educational demands. Daytime viewers' loyalty far surpasses the casual spectatorship typically associated with television viewing (see Fowles 1992; Kubey and Csikszentmihalyi 1990).

Soaps' appeal can be explained in part by their virtual reproduction of the substance, form, and rhythm of everyday life. Equally important are the affect, the attachment to characters and story lines, and the cathartic moments that viewers experience through prolonged engagement with soaps. "The soap opera genre moves its viewers so completely and draws them in so fully that from an audience's perspective, it is one of the most intriguing and important programs in all of television" (Whetmore 1992:159).

Much of the scholarly work on the appeal of soap operas emphasizes psychological gratifications derived by individual viewers (e.g., Compesi 1980). According to this perspective, the appeal of soaps lies in the emotional payoff viewers receive from continuous viewing: the longer the viewer-serial relationship, the greater and more complex the gratifications (Kielwasser and Wolf 1989). While we agree that gratifications are central to establishing and sustaining viewer interest and loyalty, they are only one of several factors that sustain an individual's interest in daytime serials.

We believe that focusing on individual gratifications overlooks the rewards of both the social interaction connected to viewing and the social organization of soap fanship.[1] Fans receive pleasure and tolerate displeasures from viewing. But what interaction occurs around viewing? What institutional and commercial arrangements cultivate and sustain soap fandom? For example, what roles do the actors, writers, and others in the industry who construct the texts play in soap fandom? How do fan magazines and the publicity departments of the serials and the broadcast networks contribute to the organization of soap fanship? In this chapter we focus on how fans engage the soap opera medium through formal aspects of fandom—the celebrity of daytime actors, fan club activities, and soap fan magazines. These aspects foster fans' affective ties, encourage particular activities, and facilitate gratifications.

## The Who, Where, How, and Why of Soap Fanship

The affective ties fans establish with characters and narratives are central to the subculture of soap fanship. Equally important are the feelings fans experience as they seek those ties. The soap fan subculture is organized through the connections fans make with industry participants, and it encompasses the relationships fans form with each other. While experiencing affect or mood is important to all types of fanship (Grossberg 1992a:56), soap fans are unique because they engage a cultural text that specializes in portraying feelings. "Personal life is the core problematic of the narrative" (Ang 1990:79); fans watch soaps in order to participate in a "subjective experience of the world, a 'structure of feeling' " (Ang 1985). In short, soap fanship is unique in that the emotions viewers experience mirror those embedded within the cultural text itself.

Subculture can be defined as "a set of understandings, behaviors, and artifacts used by particular groups and diffused through interlocking group networks" (Fine and Kleinman 1979:18). Like other media-based subcultures, soap fandom is an amorphous, geographically dispersed collectivity that organizes through its interaction over narrative texts, celebrities, public events, publicity, fan magazines, and gossip.[2] Soap fandom cuts across all categories of age, gender, race, ethnicity, income, education, and ideology, leading us to conclude that this subculture is not organized on the basis of location in the social structure. Instead, it comes together around common experiences and feelings in the pursuit of affective ties to soap narratives. Indeed, one can be a member of the soap subculture without having regular interaction with other fans. To the extent that a group of fans does interact regularly, it develops its own localized idioculture consisting of "the knowledge, beliefs, behaviors, and customs shared by members . . . to which [they] can refer and employ as the basis of further interaction" (Fine 1979:733–734).

As we noted earlier, people are able to participate in soap subculture through private activities that may only minimally engage its more public and institutional forms. Fans' pleasures become more visible as fans organize around them and interact with the soap industry itself. This points to the central role of participants, events, sites, and practices that tie together the hidden aspects of the subculture to its more visible ones. To understand how soap fanship is constructed, we have to consider the institutional arrangements of the soap industry and how they connect with fans' private concerns. We focus upon *sites* where soap fanship occurs, *participants* who contribute to it, and subjective *processes* that are specific to it.

Soap fanship originates with the viewing process itself. Viewers' subjectivity guides their interpretation of the soap narrative (see Ang 1985; Grossberg 1987). Subjectivity is the socially located position that the text "invites the viewer to occupy in order to understand it easily and unproblematically" (Fiske 1987:25).[3] How viewers relate their interpretations of the primary narrative to news, gossip, and information generated by the soap industry (the secondary text), and to viewers' own gossip (the tertiary text) (Fiske 1987) also affects the viewing process. Although a viewer's interests are the outcome of his or her subjective engagements with textual layers, soap fanship is also sustained by viewers' many sites of contact with each other and the forms that contact takes; by their access to actors, producers, journalists, and others involved with the production of the medium; by their own notions about soap audiences; and by the actions through which their interests are expressed.

The secondary text, which consists of news, publicity, criticism, and gossip, legitimates and sustains fans' interests in soaps by facilitating their involvement with the primary narrative and by representing soap fandom to fans and nonfans alike. Commercial fan magazines are a particularly important mediating link between the private interests and activities of fans and the public dimensions of the subculture. Within the last few years they have devoted increasingly more space to critical commentary from fans and industry participants. Through the expanding contribution of soap journalists, free-lance photographers, and critics in both print and electronic media, fans' access to soap news, gossip, and criticism has increased considerably, and their interaction with this secondary text has never been more visible.

Soap actors also participate in the secondary text, and a key process is their cultivation of perceived intimacy with fans. The celebrity that stems from the popularity of a soap character, a couple, or a favorite story line is a vehicle through which fanship is solicited and cultivated by the industry, in particular by the soap press through magazine popularity awards, and the broadcast networks through televised promotionals for characters and story lines. Most scholars ignore this aspect of celebrity, rarely moving beyond documenting the awe or adulation accorded celebrities (for an exception, see Stacey 1991). Soap actors pursue popularity through personal appearances at charity events, festivals, and shopping mall events, and through participation in fan club gatherings.

The institutionally generated secondary text would have a negligible effect in cultivating daytime fanship (and in further defining its boundaries for us to observe) were it not for the sites, participants, and processes in the tertiary text of fan gossip.[4] The discourse created by daytime fans as they talk on the telephone, interact on computer bulletin boards, and write fan magazines forms a web of interaction that surrounds the viewing process and is read back into it. Connecting with other fans and sharing viewing experiences is vital to both the social construction of shared meanings and to the persistence of long-term viewing patterns.

Fans display agency by taking initiative in many ways. They organize when deciding who to vote for (or who to block) in popularity polls, which gatherings to attend, what fan magazines to buy and share, or whom to collaborate with in writing fan letters. They make active attempts to shape popular interpretation and to influence the production process, and fans' claims of ownership of the narrative can create conflict within the daytime industry. The increase in sites for fan discourse, along with the changing role of fan magazines and the adoption of electronic bulletin boards as vehicles for collective fan discourse, have transformed the tertiary text by enabling fans who are otherwise isolated from one another to interact in new ways.

In Table 2 we present our schematic representation of soap fandom. The most relevant participants in the subculture of soap opera fans are the viewers themselves. While the fans engage primary, secondary, and tertiary texts in their search for the affective experiences they value, the fandom also exists because of the actions and interpretations of other participants, who help create these affective experiences. The subculture of soap fanship thus draws upon both institutionally based and experientially based elements. While the term *subculture* implies a coherent whole,

TABLE 2

## Elements of Soap Fandom: Participants, Sites, and Processes

| | TEXTS | | |
| --- | --- | --- | --- |
| | *Primary* | *Secondary* | *Tertiary* |
| *Participants* | Viewers/Fans | Actors<br>Producers<br>Journalists<br>Freelance<br> photographers<br>Publicists<br>Critics | Audiences<br>Viewers<br>Fans |
| *Sites* | Viewership/<br> Spectatorship | Celebrity<br>Fan Clubs<br>Fan Magazines<br>Publicity | BBSs<br>Letters<br>Polls<br>Photos<br>Gossip |
| *Processes* | Subjectivity<br>Pleasures/<br> Gratifications<br>Displeasures<br>Identity/<br> Identification | Intimacy<br>Authenticity | Interpretation<br>Agency<br>Ownership |

soap fans selectively engage its elements. Some do not read fan magazines but gossip heavily with other fans about the narrative. Some never engage celebrity while others don't want to, and still others thrive on it. These differences illustrate the complexity of defining what a soap fan is, despite assumptions by some scholars that engaging in certain activities defines one as a fan.

## Fans, Celebrities, and the Pursuit of Intimacy

"I was almost there. About eight people away. I started shaking. What was wrong with me? I have met so many soap people before and never once did they have this effect on me" (*Springfield Journal* 1992). This fan was describing her wait in an autograph line at a soap event to meet actor Mark Derwin. Many of us have been in her shoes or can empathize with her. Indeed, nearly half (45 percent) of our respondents have never met a daytime celebrity but would welcome the chance. However, while soap fans look forward to meeting actors when they have an opportunity to do so, their own awe — combined with the actor's charisma and fame — can make the occasion unnerving. While celebrity is a central site around which many media-based fanships are organized, in soap fanship it takes a unique form because of ways in which soaps forge close, ongoing ties between actors and their characters.

This happens for several reasons. First, soap actors are tied contractually to specific roles that constrain the time they have available for other artistic projects or commercial activity. At least while under contract, a daytime actor is less likely than actors in other media to be associated with work outside of daytime. (There are exceptions, of course. The popularity of Susan Lucci's portrayal of Erica Kane on *All My Children* has allowed her to parlay her daytime success into prime-time television. Lucci has starred in a number of movies of the week and commercials and has instant name recognition throughout the entertainment industry.) Second, a soap fan sees an actor associated with a particular character (and only that character) for months, years, or even decades. In contrast, actors in other media structure their careers around successive projects that may disengage them from close association with a particular character. Third, because of the subject matter of soaps, actors play characters that develop, have crises, and recover, often in real time, just as individuals do in real life. The characters themselves become vital personalities. Finally, because of the fast pace at which soaps are produced, actors have little time to interpret their dialogue, and, more than in other media, their own personalities inevitably become pivotal to their characterizations.

Fans engage the soap actor/character in distinctive ways. As one daytime actor explained, "With other genres, fans are attracted to the [actor's] 'star' quality, but with serials, audiences are connecting to characters that are 'real' as fictional people." On WCAU's "Local Show" in Philadelphia, May 22, 1993, actor Beth Ehlers (ex–Harley Cooper on *Guiding Light*) compared daytime fans' perceptions of her identity to the experiences of actors in other media: "Being a soap character is different from being a movie actor, you know. You're Jodie Foster, you're Julia Roberts. I'm Harley Cooper, you know, wherever I go. . . . And because [viewers] see me every day, they run up and throw their arms around me, which is not so cool."

Many fans anticipate being drawn in to a character by an actor's presence. One of our respondents says that, for her, getting hooked depends on developing an interest in the actors:

> The combined intelligence of the writers, the actors, and their dialog which centers on banter totally captivated me. I remember saying to myself, "Wow, this is interesting," noting that I suddenly became aware of something undefinable between the actors and characters that made me feel I could not wait to see what happened next. Before that I was an indifferent viewer. What Matthew Ashford and Melissa Brennan Reeves [ex-Jack and Jennifer on *Days of Our Lives*] create as actors playing roles and portraying characters reached out to me in a way that was irresistible.

Fans of any medium are captivated when an actor delivers an authentic, believable portrayal.[5] But because daytime dramas specialize in narratives dealing with personal life and involve characters who develop over extended periods of time, authenticity encourages a distinctive response among soap fans: they merge the character's persona with the actor's by blending the real qualities of the actor with the fictional ones of the character.[6] As a result, fans come to perceive a high level of intimacy between themselves, the characters, and the actors. Perceived intimacy is evident in some of the reasons fans give for wanting to meet celebrities: "Meeting actors makes me feel closer to the characters"; "I become attached to the characters and think it would be nice to meet them in person"; and, "It's fun meeting those people you have watched so long. They are kind of like old friends."

Daytime actors know that this blending of their real personas and their fictional ones is a central aspect of the audience's viewing process. One actor told us that "fans respond to a character as they would to a real person, and then come to see the actor *as* that person." Another feels that

A fan's private collection of photos of her favorite soap actors, which she arranges on her bedroom dresser with selected photos of her husband and children. Used by permission of an anonymous fan.

many fans think they "know" the character/actor because soaps come into fans' homes every day, letting viewers "see [us] do more [emotionally] honest things than they see in real life." Actors also know that the interaction of fans' readings of authenticity, their merging of actors' fictional and real personas, and their perceptions of intimacy contribute heavily to the actors' popularity. For some fans, it is not unusual for an actor to become the sole reason for their attachment to a particular serial, making it risky for a producer to recast a character played by popular actor.[7] Nevertheless, on serials structured more around characters than around the actors who create them, writers and producers care little about fan protest over recasting. Some fans accept replacements without complaint, while others never forget the impact of an actor's predecessor in the role, even if the predecessor was disliked. When actors have made a character so much their own that a recast is all but impossible, some serials prefer to write the character out of the narrative rather than to risk viewer rejection of a replacement. Susan Lucci's popularity as Erica on *All My Children,* for example, ensures that Erica will never be recast, even if Lucci decides to leave the soap.

Actors also know that fan interest can reach such enormity that writers and producers must rewrite narrative history to accommodate widespread fan preferences.[8] One character evolved from antagonist to antihero to hero — Anthony Geary's Luke Spencer on *General Hospital.* Luke Spencer's rape of the show's happily married heroine Laura Baldwin (played by Genie Francis) was retrospectively reinterpreted as a seduction, allowing Luke to be reformulated into an antihero. The overwhelming popularity of the love story that followed between Luke and Laura paved the way for Luke's subsequent transformation into hero. Fans also will follow an actor to another serial. Jack Wagner's enormous popularity as Frisco Jones, the rock star turned singing detective, also on *General Hospital,* guaranteed considerable attention when he announced his move to *Santa Barbara* to assume the role of Warren Lockridge. Undoubtedly his characterization as Frisco affected his fans' interpretations and reinterpretations of the character Warren. Toward the end of *Santa Barbara*'s run, the producers and writers built upon this intertextuality, as Warren became a character with a garage band.

Once fans establish interest in an actor, it is typical for their interest to broaden to other aspects of the actor's career, including previous roles, past achievements, upcoming performances, and personal appearances. More important, fans' interests expand to include information about the actor's private life, particularly aspects of it that fans believe affect dynamics of performance and character development. Soap fans have considerable access to information about actors' real lives through daytime magazines, fan clubs, and actors' personal appearances. It is not uncommon for daytime celebrities to be photographed in their homes with their families or at private social gatherings with co-workers and romantic partners. This publicity locates daytime celebrities in their private settings, mirroring the knowledge fans possess about their characters and reciprocating the kind of information fans often share with celebrities about themselves in fan letters. Although this representation of a daytime actor's real life is a publicity construction to some extent, it contrasts with image-making practices of the entertainment industry more generally, which emphasize revelation of an actor's persona, usually a purely fictional construction (Dyer 1979; Gamson 1992).

For some fans, publicly available information is only a starting point.[9] By successfully cultivating alternative, private sources, and by sharing this new information with other viewers, fans can create ever more informed and elaborate mergers (or separations) between the actor's private life and the public fictional character. Fans' tertiary texts are used for interpretation and reinterpretation of the primary text, the soap itself (Fiske 1987), but some soap fans manage to form what might be considered a fourth text, comprising ostensibly exclusive information or gossip about an actor's real life. The potential ambiguity of the boundary between character and actor provides an organizing focus for fans' construction of this fourth text, and the activity poured into the text is an enterprise unto itself. In part, what makes this activity so elaborate is that fans construct the fourth text while simultaneously checking the accuracy of the knowledge and information that comprise the secondary and tertiary texts. Fans with access to insider sources are privy to information about the "real" reasons behind inexplicable story-line shifts; behind an actor's quitting, firing, unstable health, or divorce; and behind other facts that are used to assess the links between the fictional and the real.[10]

Regardless of how soap fans obtain information, they relish narratives about actors that parallel the narratives of the primary text. Romances between actors are particularly interesting, especially when they occur between performers on the same show who are also playing a leading romantic couple, as occurred on *Days of Our Lives* in the late 1970s, on

Fans' quests for information about the linkage between on-screen characters and actors' real lives extends beyond an interest in romantic relationships. In honor of Father's Day, a magazine portrays actors' relationships with their offscreen families. From "A Father's Day Photo Album," *Soap Opera Magazine* 4, no. 25 (June 21, 1994): 30–31. Reprinted with the permission of *Soap Opera Magazine*.

*General Hospital* in the mid-1980s, and more recently on *Guiding Light* and *Days of Our Lives* (*Soap Opera Illustrated* 1993; *Daytime TV* 1993a; Spencer 1992). Actors' romances considerably expand how the primary (in this case, romantic) narrative can be read, because now a true fusion exists between characters and actors in contrast to an imagined one or one fabricated by a fan magazine or actor's support group. Indeed, for some fans the ultimate pleasure is knowing that the fictional narrative has brought about a real one. Celebrities' real-life pregnancies are another popular opportunity for fans to incorporate the real with the fictional. For example, the pregnancies of actress Kristina Malandro were crucial to development of the Frisco and Felicia story line on *General Hospital* (see *Soap Opera Update* 1990b and *Soap Opera Digest* 1990), as was Melissa Reeves's pregnancy to the Jennifer and Jack story line on *Days of Our Lives* (see *Soap Opera Digest*'s 1992 and 1993b cover stories) and the pregnancies of Katherine Kelly Lang to the Brooke/Ridge/Taylor triangle on *The Bold and the Beautiful*. For some fans, a real-life pregnancy between a real-life couple playing a fictional romantic couple (as has happened on daytime) can be the ultimate opportunity to merge reality with fiction: the pregnancy constitutes public and undeniable confirmation of a real-life relationship acknowledged in the fictional narrative. To those fans, it also suggests a more lasting bond between the actors than just a passing romance between co-workers.

One might assume that the numerous possibilities for blurring the fictional and the real would lead fans to confuse the difference between characters and actors and would distort and exaggerate their preferences for personal knowledge of daytime actors. In fact, fans who play with the boundaries between the real and the nonreal do so quite consciously, and this type of playing is a key element of pleasure. Often fans seek information to help them *distinguish* between actor and character. "I would like to see if the actors differ from their characters," said one fan in our survey, while another says, "I would expect [an actor] to not be like the [villainous] character he plays. I expect him to be warm and friendly because most actors are." Because soap characters are so studied, many fans want to know about similarities or differences in persona between actor and character. This occurs even though fans initially feel affinity with the *actor* simply because they like the *character*'s persona.

Soap fans' awareness of the distinction between actor and character is evident in the reasons our respondents give for wanting to meet celebrities: "I like watching actors go into character"; "I enjoy seeing how much they resemble their character and how they relate in person"; "I would like to see what the actor injects of himself into the character"; "I enjoy seeing how they look off camera." For fans who have met actors, interest centers on how they compare to the characters they play: "I expect to see differences between the actress and her character"; "I am interested in seeing how much actors' mannerisms and personal style are like the characters they play"; "I expect [them] to be nicer in person."

Within soap fandom, viewers' interaction with actors is characteristically layered, developing through repeated contact over time. In many ways, the evolution of a relationship with an actor parallels the revelations that a fan experiences over time with that actor's character. Initial contact with daytime stars can be superficial (such as when one is a member of a large crowd in a shopping mall), fleeting (spotting an actor on the street or in a restaurant), and even indirect (experienced vicariously through another fan's enthusiasm). But it can be personally significant for the fan nonetheless because it establishes not only the separation between character and actor but the embodiment of character-in-actor and actor-in-character.

When actor-fan contact is unplanned and unexpected, fans' familiarity with the character leads them to feel an intimacy with the actor, and they may transfer the fictional character's traits to the actor. In some cases fans see the actor as approachable as a known friend or enemy, and soap actors often find this kind of unsolicited fan familiarity with the soap world amusing. Julianna McCarthy, who has played Liz Foster Brooks on *The Young and the Restless,* told an interviewer for KNXT-TV [now KCBS], Los Angeles, on November 6, 1981, that she was criticized by fans on the street for watering plants incorrectly on the show. In a published interview, actor Mark Derwin said:

> I still get called names for being "Adrian Hunter" [a murderer on *The Young and the Restless*]. . . . Once I went to a restaurant in L.A. and a couple of guys in leather with their women came in. They had their hogs (motorcycles) outside and they sat down and this guy was staring at me. And I was like, "What?" I thought he caught me looking at his girl. He said, "Yeah." And he goes, "I like what you're doin'." And I'm like, "Thanks." He was bigger than me. (Arrigo 1990:142)

One of the actors we interviewed told us how she was spared a mugging in New York by a soap fan who was going to rob her:

> I was in New York City walking to an interview, and was too well dressed for the neighborhood. Suddenly, three men stepped in front of

me, blocking my path, and when I turned around, three more men had moved behind me. They asked for my purse and I started to give it to them when one of them recognized me from the soaps. They gave me back my purse, told me I was in a really bad neighborhood, escorted me back to my interview, waited for me to come out, and escorted me back to a place where I could get a cab. I kept saying to myself, "Thank God, thank God I'm on a soap!"

Daytime fandom differs from that of other media not just in the opportunities for access that fans have to actors, but in the kinds and frequency of access available to them. In other media, unless one becomes a groupie, opportunities for informal, face-to-face encounters are largely limited to unplanned sightings in airports, restaurants, or shops. In contrast, access to daytime celebrities is greatly facilitated by organized events such as mall appearances and annual fan club gatherings that bring fans and actors together on a regular basis. Some soap actors do multiple personal appearances every month. Also unlike celebrities in other media, many daytime actors respond to their fan mail, which furthers the social bond between them and their fans. Fans merge their increased familiarity with the actor with the information and gossip they gather, strengthening the celebrity-fan link. Although it happens rarely, contact can build reciprocally between fan and actor into longstanding friendships. The nature of these layered relationships is captured in one fan's experience:

As a result of [my friend's] fan club for Mart Hulswit [formerly Dr. Ed Bauer on *Guiding Light*] she got to know many of the *Guiding Light* cast members and helped arrange their appearances on *Pittsburgh Today*. . . . On several occasions we picked up [the actors] at the airport and brought them into the city. We later took them back to the airport, so they could catch their planes back to New York. One of these occasions occurred when Jerry verDorn, who still plays Ross Marler on the show, came in for the show. The drive from the airport takes about forty minutes, and we were able to have a lovely visit with him. . . .

I would see Jerry again on two different occasions. A couple of years later, Jerry made another appearance on *Pittsburgh Today*. I was in the audience that afternoon, and Jerry came over to talk to the part of the audience where I was seated. Jerry recognized me and was pleased to see me. About four years ago, Jerry was here to appear at our local convention center. It had been a long time since I had seen Jerry, so I honestly didn't think he would remember me but he did and was pleased that I had come. He also remembered my friend and was upset to hear that she was recovering from a serious illness. He asked me to give her his regards and to get well soon. It meant a lot to my friend that Jerry still remembered her after all these years.

Another respondent has formed a longstanding friendship with actress Candice Earley, formerly Donna of *All My Children*. In 1976, when she was twelve years old, she joined Earley's fan club but never received any of the club's mailings. When she wrote Earley to complain, Earley called her. They have corresponded regularly since the mid-1970s, and she has visited Earley several times; in fact, her parents have met Earley's parents, and they consider Earley a friend of the family. In this case, as in others, the intimacy between fan and actor is genuine and mutual, not a misguided perception based on the fan's knowledge of the actor's personal life combined with affinity for his or her character. In some cases, the actor-fan relationship becomes a narrative built upon actual encounters between the two that become increasingly personal over time. For the soap fans we spoke with, that relationship is organized as a narrative of its own.

Finally, the subculture of soap fans extends beyond the narrative experienced with actors to one shared with other fans. As mentioned in Chapter One, celebrity can become a vehicle through which authentic social relationships develop among fans, and these potentially long-term friendships, organized around intimacy and mutuality, cement the subculture even further. Several of our respondents have established relationships with people met at fan events. Says one fan:

> Over the years, I've had some interesting experiences and met many daytime drama stars, things which would not have happened if I hadn't been a fan of daytime dramas and involved in fan clubs. I've also made some lasting friendships, which are very dear to me, particularly now as I deal with serious family problems. In 1972, I met [my friend] who lived just outside of [my community]. She had gotten my name and telephone number through a "mutual fan club" friend and she called

me one evening. That phone call marked the start of a friendship which is still going strong today. She and I would share many "adventures" as a result of our interest in the "soaps" and involvement in fan clubs. We would also share many personal sorrows.

## How Actors Manage Fans

From the actors' perspective, fans' quest for intimacy is a valuable resource, but one that needs to be managed. Reflecting upon fans, one leading actor remarked that in daytime "you wouldn't have a career if you didn't have those people." Said another, "Fans are fans of the show first, and *then* they become fans of a particular actor." The reality is that actors have been selected by fans from a favored narrative tapestry. Popularity can influence whether actors are written into leading story lines, how much latitude they have in executing a scene, and the extent to which they become core characters on a show. Because the popularity of a character or actor is as important as acting skill to longevity on a serial, managing celebrity with fans is a crucial aspect of working in the soap medium.[11]

The narrative conventions of the soap opera genre shape both the form and content of actors' responses to fans. Particularly important is managing the blurry line between fact and fiction that is so integral to soap fan subculture. With a soap actor's celebrity so intertwined with viewers' attachments to characters and narratives, the cultivation of fans by actors (and by other industry participants) occurs in distinctive ways. In essence, blurring character-as-fiction with actor-as-fact is the primary means through which actors and fans interact and is a key element of fan pleasure. One way in which this is managed in soap fandom is through fan clubs, where an actor can blur self with character in ways that build upon the fan's and actor's mutual interests.

While fan club events may ultimately serve the fan, they are organized to celebrate celebrity. Events provide fans an opportunity to meet actors and show support for their favorite soaps, as well as meet other fans with similar interests. At public sites where formal, organized, and direct celebrity-fan interaction takes place, fan club gatherings not only manage the link between character and actor within the primary text, they also

At a personal appearance, actor Mark Derwin (formerly Mallet on *Guiding Light*) intertextually references himself with a publicity photo of his character. Despite the organizer's prohibition of personalized autographs, Derwin manages to cultivate intimacy by posing with a greeting to a fan who was unable to attend. Used by permission of Beth Stipp.

help elaborate the tertiary text that fans construct around that link. This happens as fans share perceptions of intimacy with each other, trade gossip, make arrangements to exchange resources such as edited tapes and photos, and develop contacts for insider information.[12]

One serial's fan club president says that from the producer's point of view, "the bond between actors and fans is important because it cultivates loyalty, which is essential for the daytime medium to succeed. From a show's point of view it keeps viewers engaged by tuning in every day even if the show hits a lull in the story line." Viewing consistency is important to a soap's overall popularity, and cultivating the bond that sustains it is essential to success in daytime television. In essence, then, producers approve of fan clubbing for its potential economic rewards.

At an annual fan club gathering actress Tonja Walker vamps her character, *General Hospital*'s Mafia princess Olivia Jerome, to the delight of fans who capture it on film. Walker now plays Alex on *One Life to Live*. Used by permission of an anonymous fan.

Some actors feel considerable ambivalence about forming fan clubs, even when repeatedly approached by fans who want to create one. Some up-and-coming actors who regard the soap medium as a stepping-stone to prime-time television and feature films do not want to be overidentified with their daytime character, for fear it will result in typecasting by both audiences and producers. To illustrate the daytime actor's main occupational hazard: one fan did not want to see her favorite actors develop successful careers in feature film because then she would not be able "to know their characters as well" as she could on soap operas.

Actors avoid fan clubs for other reasons. Some feel that a club would intrude in their private lives; one actor justifies her minimal involvement with fans on the grounds that she does not derive her primary identity from acting; still others argue that they are pursuing their art, not celebrity. An actor who considers herself an artist wants to be appreciated for the art she creates through the portrayal of a character, rather than for being that character. She feels that because the daytime format helps break down the boundary between art and artist, fans do not appreciate the art of acting; while this permeable boundary might allow viewers to feel closer to characters, it is frustrating for many actors. This same actor declares fan clubs to be "a business, and I'm not a business . . . the big crowds of fan events are too overwhelming and too tiring. Every fan wants something." At formal events she feels like an object and abhors the adulation. But somewhat contradictorily, she reads all her fan mail, answers some of it personally, enjoys meeting fans on studio tours, and takes the time to talk to fans she meets on the street. Like many actors, she enjoys informal contact much more than confronting fans at formally organized events.

The daytime celebrities we spoke with emphasized that fan response is based on fans' perceived intimacy with them. "Of course fans think they know me as a real person," one actor stated. Managing perceived intimacy requires actors to delicately balance their real persona with that of their character when interacting with the public, especially at organized functions. One fan club president stated explicitly that club events are designed so fans can meet celebrities as a combination of actor and character. In her view, these events are organized this way because fans consider it a privilege to see the actor in "regular clothes" and feel they have seen (and thus know) the real person behind the actor. The actors know (or are explicitly told) not to stray too far from their character and to humor the fans or risk disappointing them. According to one club president, staying in character is "safer" for the actor and relatively easy to manage. Such events are in effect business luncheons — good for actors' careers and good for the show. Yet many actors find staying in character particularly distasteful; one told us she found it "superficial, fraudulent, a mark of insecurity and presenting a false image." She would rather avoid such events than contribute to "that fiction."

Although it is doubtful that many daytime celebrities want to achieve actual intimacy with fans, some are able to cultivate the perception of intimacy better than others. Compared to celebrities in other media, soap actors are typically more adept at anticipating how to reciprocate fans' expectations (see, e.g., Martin 1993). According to an established daytime journalist:

Daytime actors are *the* most patient human beings. They are put upon more often, more closely, more intrusively, and more consistently by fans than any other kind of celebrity. Beyond a doubt they are more patient and more attuned to their specific audience. . . . Daytime actors are more accessible because of publicity through personal appearances, fan clubs, fan club news, and charity events that tells fans where they will be. And, consequently, in dealing with fans, daytime actors know how to conduct themselves better than someone in another medium or genre, because others lack the experience in dealing with fans that daytime actors have. Through the amount of contact with fans, daytime actors gain experience and skill at being sincere.

This facility is clearly demonstrated in that most common of fan rituals, having a photograph taken with the celebrity. Photographs not only provide a vital record of contact with an actor/character, but their usual composition of fan and celebrity side by side or of the celebrity embracing the fan implies familiarity if not personal knowledge shared by actor and fan. One of us has in her office a photo taken several years ago of herself with Anthony Geary. One of her graduate students, who was not a soap viewer, assumed it was a photo of her and her husband, whom the student had never met.

Over time some daytime celebrities do in fact develop personal relationships with fans, occasionally turning to them for insights about their acting or for suggestions about scenes to submit for Emmy consideration, involvements in charities, or operating their fan club. One actor hired her fan club president as her children's nanny, and the late Emily McLaughlin (Jessie on *General Hospital*) actually adopted hers (see *Soap Opera Weekly* 1993). Access of any kind enables a fan to cultivate perceived social intimacy with the actor, but as we discussed in the last chapter,

Fans are welcomed into the *General Hospital* family by actor Paul Satterfield (ex–Paul Hornsby). Used by permission of an anonymous fan.

actors are increasingly aware of the need to maintain an appropriate distance between themselves and their fans, as protection from potentially dangerous (stalker) fans. One actor told us that being a desirable object to fans can be

> a heady sexual thing, but you have to keep it in perspective. Sure, you can play to the audience at personal appearances tweaking it this way or that like in the theater, but afterwards, when you get in your little car and drive away, it ends. You have to tell yourself that they don't want you, its over, and it doesn't mean a damn thing.

Among the burdens placed on daytime actors are the high expectations fans have about celebrity encounters. For one fan, they are "a personal moment of pleasure," for another, "an opportunity to praise [actors] for their performance, and get photos and autographs." Even for one of our respondents who has interacted with soap opera actors for most of her life and has served as a president for several daytime celebrity fan clubs, "meeting stars is a memory to take home." Consequently, soap fans whose expectations are thwarted or dashed can respond negatively to celebrities' desire for privacy from fans. (Similarly, fanships organized around performers who cultivate bad boy or bad girl personas, as rock musicians often do, expect to be mistreated and are disappointed when they are not.) We were given the following account at a fan club gathering:

> On my personal tour of the studio, we hit the makeup room first and [an actor] was in the chair. He was not friendly at all. He was rather rude. He really disappointed me. A friend of mine agreed. She said the actor had an obligation to treat people with courtesy and respect regardless of their mood. He won't have much of a career without them.

Another popular actor drew fan criticism after she said, "I don't want to talk about my personal life to people that I don't know. I don't understand why that is such a difficult concept for the audience to grasp" (Spencer 1992:63).

Despite obvious pitfalls, when managed appropriately, fan club activities can be important sites for promoting celebrities' careers as well as for sustaining the fan subculture. However, success at this endeavor from the celebrity's perspective requires knowledge of and sensitivity to the norms of the subculture.

## How the Daytime Press Fits In

To this point we have examined celebrity as a site of soap fanship in two ways: the pursuit of intimacy by fans and the management of fanship by actors. These phenomena, organized through the formation of personal and social bonds, are largely noncommercial, at least in the ways they are conducted, even though their existence can commercially benefit actors. Another important site of soap subculture is the daytime press, which includes the editors, journalists, photographers, and others who produce fan magazines. These commercial enterprises rely heavily on information crafted by the industry; in that regard they do not differ substantially from magazines that operate as publicity apparatuses in other media (see Gamson 1994). Publicity comes primarily from two sources in the daytime industry: the serials themselves and the celebrities or their publicists. The soaps' publicists emphasize the shows, story lines, and prominent characters more than the actors themselves, so savvy actors (or their publicists) often cultivate direct contact with daytime journalists.

Because daytime magazines contribute to the secondary text through the publicity they deliver, they have traditionally been an important mediating site between the production of soap operas and the audience. As a public site, daytime magazines attempt to align the interests of the industry with the concerns of fans. Fan magazines contribute to the subculture by rendering visible many aspects of fans' private activities, including the personal pleasure around which soap fanship is organized and the expectations for perceived intimacy among viewers. Fan magazines also direct attention to features of the industry that rationalize and legitimate fans' interests. By rendering the subculture visible and accessible both to itself and to outsiders, the daytime press contributes in important ways to defining the boundaries of the subculture and to managing those boundaries.

The first daytime magazine, *Daytime TV,* was founded and edited by Paul Denis in 1970 to reach an unserved market. Denis had worked as an entertainment writer for Earl Wilson of the *New York Post* and knew the industry well. Al Rosenberg, current editorial director of *Daytime TV,* told us in an April 1993 telephone interview, "No market existed at that time for coverage of the daytime industry because daytime performers and producers tended to lead more conventional, private lives. Many were married to professionals and had families. There was no market for coverage of them in other publications because they were not photographed by the industry press." *Daytime TV* cultivated that market through direct contact with the actors themselves, who invited the magazine to "visit the studios, take photos, and do interviews." Denis's efforts were well received by industry participants, and "friendships were established that allowed us to continue returning to the studios. And the magazine sold very well."

Modeled after established industry gossip and publicity magazines such as *Movie Mirror, TV Mirror,* and *Photoplay, Daytime TV* was designed to deliver coverage of the daytime industry exclusively to its fans. However, it differed from its prototypes in significant ways. According to Al Rosenberg,

> While *Photoplay* was tabloidish and emphasized gossip, lurid titles, and sexually oriented coverage, the daytime audience did not want to read anything bad about their favorite characters, even if they were villains. These characters were ones they viewed every day in their homes and identified with. Viewers did not want their fantasy destroyed. We'd get mail saying, "Don't say anything bad about my favorite character." So, there were no blind items or lurid titles in our magazine.

*Daytime TV* began as a quarterly and, once successful, appeared monthly, with occasional special issues featuring serials popular among its readership. By the 1970s its competitors included *TV by Day, Daytime TV Stars, Rona Barrett's Daytimers, TV Dawn to Dusk, Afternoon TV, Daylight, TV Radio Mirror, Soap Box, Soap Opera World,* and *Daytime Stars.* Many of these early daytime magazines were produced by Ideal Publications and Sterling Publications and were almost identical to one another, but *Rona Barrett's Daytimers* introduced "harder gossip, precipitating a shakeout in business," according to Al Rosenberg. The only survivor from that period is *Daytime TV.* A norm of downplaying hard gossip still prevails throughout the daytime magazine industry, but it has been reintroduced in limited ways (such as "blind items" reporting negative information about unnamed actors) following the expansion and diversification of the daytime market over the last decade and competition from the tabloids.

A primary way that early daytime magazines aligned industry publicity with fan interests was to play with the boundary between fiction and reality so central to fans' pleasures. They ran photos and headlines that obscured the boundary between representation and the real; manipulated the codes of actor's dress, expression, and makeup; celebrated the labor and professionalism of actors; and supplemented feature articles on fictional characters and their relationships with actors' biographies (see

# MEMORIAL

Deidre Hall's (Marlena) son, David, shone brightest during his mom's breakfast gathering — especially during the autograph session.

**G**OSSIP AND A GHOST TALE right out of *The Twilight Zone* set the pace for *Days of Our Lives*' 1994 Memorial Day weekend fan festival, when Salem's lot of young talent — Jason Brooks, Christie Clark, Bryan Dattilo, Patrick Muldoon, Lisa Rinna and Alison Sweeney (Peter, Carrie, Lucas, Austin, Billie and Sami) — hosted a Friday night party at the Sportsmen's Lodge in Studio City.

Special guest Peggy McCay (Caroline) stole the show when she recounted an incident that happened on the set earlier that day. "We just started taping scenes dealing with the passing of Tom Horton," McCay explained. (Macdonald Carey, who portrayed Tom, died earlier this year.) McCay was standing offstage as Frances Reid (Alice) was finishing her scene when "suddenly on the monitor I saw this phenomenon — this blue-light aura with pale pink in the middle of it," McCay explains. "I thought it was some terrible special effect. It looked like a poltergeist. Then, we heard somebody in the crew say, 'What is that?' We all got the feeling that it was Mac saying, 'I'm here in spirit.'"

While the rest of the night's fare seemed mundane by comparison, there were a few interesting moments. Rinna explained that her beau, Harry Hamlin, got the nickname Fred when the duo began dating and were keeping their romance hush-hush. Rather than use their real names when they went out, they resorted to aliases. "Harry's assistant nicknamed him Fred and me Larry," explains Rinna. "It sort of stuck."

It was also revealed that Dattilo is the *Days* actor with the most nicknames. Executive producer Ken Corday calls him Skippy, while Brooks has dubbed him Bucky and Wayne Northrop (Roman) refers to him as the Penny-Loafer Dweeb.

Asked which was her favorite fight scene with TV-mom Deidre Hall (Marlena), Sweeney didn't hesitate for a second. "I like the one where I called her a slut," she said demurely.

The next day, Hall hosted a breakfast at Pasadena's Ritz-Carlton Huntington with a special guest in tow — her 20-month-old son, David. As he circled the room with mom, David proved to be a real show-biz baby, clutching his bottle in one hand and the microphone in the other. Proud mama Dee even showed off her son's talent. "What does the librarian say?" she asked him. "Shhh!" responded

Fan favorites (clockwise from left): Jason Brooks, Bryan Dattilo, Roark Critchlow, Patrick Muldoon, Peggy McCay, Christie Clark, Alison Sweeney and Suzanne Rogers (Peter, Lucas, Mike, Austin, Caroline, Carrie, Sami and Maggie).

Scott Groff (Shawn-Douglas) seems happy to be reunited with on-screen mom Kristian Alfonso (Hope).

One potato, two potato...Jason Brooks (right) prepares to play.

Melissa Reeves (Jennifer) looks mighty frisky as she appears at the Pasadena Ritz-Carlton for a celebrity luncheon.

A soap magazine features the annual *Days of Our Lives* Memorial Day weekend fan festival. The article covers actors' accounts of setside activities, captures dynamics of off-set relationships, includes information elicited by fan questions, and describes the participation of actors' families in the events. The coverage

Wayne Northrop (Roman, far left) and Roark Critchlow mingle with their fans during the annual Days luncheon at the Pasadena Ritz-Carlton.

Drake Hogestyn (John) showed off his svelte new physique as he auctioned T-shirts at his gathering.

Paul Kersey (Alan, above left), Thyme Lewis (Jonah) and Roberta Leighton (ex-Ginger Dawson) aboard the Pacific Hornblower.

...ooks (above) helped kick off the weekend festivities ...th his best impersonation of his Days co-stars. ...e following day at the luncheon (right), Brooks ...oked like he wanted just five more minutes to do ...re impersonations, but Eileen Davidson ...risten) wasn't interested.

David. "What does the cat say?" she quizzed. "Meow," he answered.

Fans were treated to home videos, clips of Marlena's best moments over the years, and a reel of outtakes. One in particular — a rehearsal scene where Roman views the tape of Marlena's striptease for Stefano — had everyone in hysterics. As Wayne Northrop geared up to do that scene, the striptease ran on the studio monitor. Ever the jokester, Northrop began grunting, groaning and offering commentary in all the right places. Meanwhile, Hall taped the whole thing off her dressing room monitor. "This is what I put up with every day," the actress quipped.

The second Days of Our Lives Official Fan Club gathering followed Hall's event, with James Reynolds (Abe) as master of ceremonies. The loudest applause went to Kristian Alfonso, Joseph Mascolo and Ivan G'Vera (Hope, Stefano and Ivan). Following McCay's performance of "Addicted to Days," a take-off of the pop hit Addicted to Love, fans began firing off questions to the stars.

Is Alfonso really Hope? "The last time I was on, Ernesto put me in a cage (over a vat of acid). But think about it — if he were really going to kill me, would he have gotten in the cage with me?" mused Alfonso. "Remember, he was a great illusionist."

Northrop fielded his share of inquiries about leaving the show, just as he had at Hall's gala earlier. Diplomatically, he explained that it was not his choice, but rather "just one of those things that happens in this business. There's been mention of my returning to the show somewhere down the road. If it happens, great; if not, I'll go on with other things."

Jack/Jennifer converts praised the pairing of Melissa Reeves' Jennifer and Brooks' Peter. When asked what it's like working with his leading lady, Brooks joked: "Terrible! She's difficult — a real pain, and her husband calls the set 20 times a day! Actually, it's a lot of fun. She's very spontaneous, and she's paying me to say this."

The afternoon's most risqué question ... had been needling Tanya Boyd's constant cleavage action as Celeste, inquired about her style of push-up bra. "Is that a Ball or an 18-hour that you want?" she teased.

Another brazen fan asked G'Vera when Ivan was going to stop fantasizing about Vivian and get some "coochy-coochy" with a real woman.

Continued on page 36

represents the *Days* family to soap fan subculture, legitimates organized soap fan activities, and appropriates soap fandom by selling it back to the fans. From Janet DiLauro, "Memorial Days Delight," *Soap Opera Weekly* 5 (June 21, 1994): 34–36. Used by permission.

Fiske 1987). An actor who was a leading man on a top-rated show in the 1970s and 1980s recalled that daytime fan magazines once identified actors only by character name, implying to readers that actors were the characters they played. Daytime journalist David Johnson, who began writing for *Daytime TV* in 1969 and has written features and columns for numerous other daytime publications since, told us in an April 1993 interview that this practice stemmed from production company demands that only character names appear in daytime magazines: "Actors' names were not to be mentioned." This practice coincided with what was standard procedure until the mid-1970s, not regularly running cast credits for soaps. (Not until the 1976–79 AFTRA contract [the union that represents soap actors] were soap operas specifically mentioned in the collective bargaining agreement and required to list cast credits weekly.)

Although publications continue to manipulate the boundary between reality and fiction, the practice is now far less prevalent as their primary objective. Some magazines continue to serve a traditional publicity function for the shows through "story-line previews" in which preferred readings of the primary narrative are selected and guided by industry participants. However, following the lead of *Soap Opera Now!* many magazines have diversified considerably in the last several years to include news-driven coverage of other aspects of the daytime industry — casting news, breaking industry news and gossip, criticism, and viewer reaction. From the editors' perspective, the greatest competition among magazines is over casting news and story-line previews, both of which require considerable cooperation between the daytime press and the shows. (Mary Ann Cooper, executive editor of *Soap Opera Magazine*, told us in an interview in December 1993 that previews are obtained through confidentiality agreements that protect the serials from premature or overly detailed disclosure of upcoming plot developments.) These developments expand the linkages between fans, between fans and actors, and between fans and other industry participants by bringing viewers inside the industry and behind the scenes. Magazines can now more centrally define and integrate viewer readings that contribute to daytime fan subculture, and their popularity is reflected in their circulation figures (see note 3, Chapter One).

But it is fan magazines' gradual reallocation of space to viewers' opinions that has transformed them into an increasingly important site of fan subculture. Most magazines now include regular forums as outlets for fan perspectives, such as "Letters to the Editor" in *Soap Opera Now!* "Sound Off" in *Soap Opera Digest,* and "Mail Call," "Public Opinion," "A Reader's View," and "Fantastic Encounter" in *Soap Opera Weekly.* Here are two typical examples from *Soap Opera Weekly* of published fan responses:

[*Guiding Light*'s] ratings are flagging because its couples have no charisma. This absence of compelling romantic drama is why Maureen's death caused such a stink — it filled an emotional void. Because viewers haven't warmed to Ann Hamilton's Mindy (maybe they never will), a damper has been put on *GL*'s biggest storyline. Meanwhile, *GL* has made a mess of Harley and Mallet. Mark Derwin won the Soap Opera Award for hottest actor, yet he gets the airtime of a day player. Frank/ Eleni/Alan-Michael is an interesting storyline, but the triangle lacks the magic that makes a romance live or die. Ross and Blake add spice, but lack broad-based romantic appeal. And if *GL* thinks Hart gets anyone excited, dream on. He's such a cliché it's not funny. And Julie is boring. Now would be a good time for *GL* to finally play the Holly/ Roger card. I thought the point of making Holly bitchier was so that Roger wouldn't have to reform in order to be with her. Enough toying with a Holly/Roger reunion during sweeps — it's getting old. Right now *GL*'s most compelling relationship exists between Michelle and Holly — a 12-year-old and her father's ex-wife — and it's not exactly romantic. If *GL* wants to stop the ratings slide it should assess where it's falling short and give the audience what it wants. (1993:41–42)

As a seven-year fan of *One Life to Live,* I must say that I'm appalled at the way the writers have turned Viki Buchanan into a slut. Viki used to be a role model for all women: she had the perfect marriage, a good job and wonderful kids. The writers tried to put her with Tom Dennison, then Roger Gordon. Needless to say, these flings didn't work out because Viki was so loyal to Clint, her husband. Now that Sloan has come along, Viki has apparently become Llanview's newest whore (and she had the nerve to call Dorian one!). *OLTL*, should rethink this story and get Viki back on track before everyone else loses respect for her the way I have. (1993:41–42)

Such commentary reveals how fans engage the text in analytical ways and use their knowledge to challenge the writers' performance. The centrality of fan voices in daytime magazines offers public legitimation of fans' insights and opinions but also opens up increasing possibilities for squabbles among fans, writers, and producers over authorship of daytime narratives (see Chapter Five).

A central feature of soap subculture is fans' shared reactions to a given episode or plot development. Before published forums were available, such exchanges occurred mostly within localized idiocultures of friends, relatives, and co-workers, and they were considered unimportant gossip by most scholars, those in the daytime industry, and nonfans. But with its appearance in print, this gossip is increasingly recognized and legitimated as valid *because* of its publicness, with important consequences for self-perception inside and outside the subculture. Because publication of fan reaction conjoins points of agreement and debate, it may broaden consensus of opinion within audiences, reinforcing even further fans' sense of ownership over a show's history, characters, and story lines.

However, members of the daytime press are not unanimous in their opinion about the contribution of viewer feedback to the industry. Some experienced journalists believe that the trend toward fan-friendly features such as letters to the editor, opinion columns, editorials, and critics' reviews, while generating reader interest, has gone too far. "Who the hell cares what fans are saying?" asks one veteran magazine journalist. "These features generate mail from readers and emotion among readers and encourage fan interaction in fan clubs and between pen pals, but that mail is not indicative of the readers comprising a magazine's circulation, only of those people who write." In contrast, Linda Susman, who has written for the daytime medium since 1976 and is currently executive editor of *Soap Opera Weekly*, observed in April 1993 in an interview with the authors:

The publication of readers' opinions is very important. To not serve the needs of our readers would be cruel. We are a forum, we are a court of last resort. The daytime soaps beg for a forum because of the nature of the medium. Soaps cover intimate material that generates emotions and they have longstanding and loyal audiences, and that creates a unique kind of bonding. So, in addition to fan clubs and hot lines as outlets are the fan magazines. Viewers who have opinions need a place to express them.

*TV Guide*'s soap columnist and critic Michael Logan told us in an interview in December 1993 that magazine editors are sincere in their motivation to devote increased space to fan opinion but can use it for an additional purpose. "There is more of a critical voice [in the magazines], but it is the magazines letting fans do [much of the criticism] so it doesn't reflect badly on the magazines."

Most current fan magazines are not only more diversified in the features they offer to readers, they are also more differentiated among themselves in what they contribute to the market niche for daytime fans. As executive editor Mary Ann Cooper of *Soap Opera Magazine* observed, no other segment of the media supports so many specialized publications. While early magazines appeared as monthly publications, *Soap Opera Digest*, which began in 1975, publishes biweekly. The *Digest*, as it is often referred to in the industry, was introduced prior to the advent of the VCR to satisfy viewer demand for plot summaries for those who could not watch soaps every day. Others publishing biweekly or monthly are *Soap Opera Update, Daytime TV*, and the now defunct *Episodes*, which was published by Capital Cities/ABC. Today, three weekly magazines publish industry news, synopses of the past week's story lines, and upcoming plot developments: *Soap Opera Magazine, Soap Opera Now!* and *Soap Opera Weekly*. They also include publicity, casting updates, and celebrity interviews, although only *Soap Opera Magazine* covers each of the ten soaps in every issue.

Academics and some industry insiders attribute the rise of such magazines mainly to demographic changes in the viewing audience. "For several decades, the audience for soap operas consisted largely of lower-middle-class housewives and upwardly mobile housewives isolated from family and friends in the suburbs. In the late 1970s, a new and younger type of audience was attracted to these shows, consisting of middle-class college students and young college graduates who were unmarried and working" (Crane 1992:45). Mary Ann Cooper of *Soap Opera Magazine* told us in a December 1993 interview that her magazine's target audience includes "women eighteen to forty-nine, college students, those males who comprise 25 percent of the viewing audience, and the older demographic of women over forty-nine." Angela Shapiro, editor of *Soap Opera Update,* notes that "today, the audience is very intelligent. With the advent of the VCR, the soap opera audience expanded to include professional people of both sexes with jobs outside the home and evenings free for a little time-shifting" (Dolan 1992: A1). Linda Susman of *Soap Opera Weekly* counters that the intelligent audience has always been there. The difference now is that "those fans that were once in the closet are now out of the closet. And when they came out, we saw that they included some who were very intelligent, were men as well as women, and were students. And they came from all economic and educational levels, ages, and occupations."

The segment of the daytime audience that is publicly visible is more diverse today. But to equate that diversity with increased audience intelligence not only misrepresents earlier audiences, it risks misinterpreting why fans seek more information from fan magazines. Daytime fans read magazines for many reasons: to supplement their reading of the primary text, to voice their reactions to the narrative through reader mail, and to learn the reactions of other fans. As the magazines' content has become broader and more diverse, they have become contributors to industry gossip. This gossip, in turn, increasingly constitutes viewers' tertiary texts and activities. Thus, fans are able to draw upon secondary texts to augment and promote selected meanings of the primary narrative as well as to contribute to tertiary texts, which they innovatively activate in reading the primary text. In many ways, rather than the fans being more intelligent today, the magazines have simply caught up with their readership. They have discovered the complex intertextual readings fans are capable of creating for themselves between primary and tertiary narratives, and they now offer fans an additional forum for that activity.

This interpretation is supported by respondents' comments about their magazine choices. Not all fans read fan magazines, but many read more than one. Their choices reveal both a clear set of preferences and an acute perception of the magazines' relative strengths. Some read for news of who is joining and who is leaving shows, upcoming celebrity events, and features about favorite actors and actresses. More read for weekly sneak peeks at story developments and information about the production of the shows. Even more read for information about the actors' real lives, in particular the structure and location of actors' work, including their schedules, backgrounds, and activities off-set. This category includes information about the writing staff and their perspective on narratives and characters, the executive producer's vision, the casting director's insights about discovering talent, and so forth.

One respondent told us why she subscribes to several magazines:

> Soap Opera Digest has the best interviews, Soap Opera Weekly has the best current overall information, including news, trivia, opinion sections and upcoming plotlines for the week, Soap Opera Update has the best celebrity photos, and Soap Opera Now! has the best coverage of production and industry news that does not bow to "the powers that be."

Another fan combines Soap Opera Now! because of "its no-nonsense style," with Soap Opera Magazine, which is "more tabloid-like with mostly pictures and scoops." Many respondents repeatedly emphasized the importance of being able to obtain information about actors and shows that was untainted by "hype" or "exploitative writing," or by editorial policies that "kiss up to any one particular soap or star." Daytime TV still satisfies many of its readers by specializing in the blurring of reality and fiction and its ready attention to serials and actors generating the most mail (Daytime TV 1993b:42). Still other magazines are read for more specialized reasons. Soap Opera Illustrated, a trial joint venture between Soap Opera Digest and Soap Opera Weekly, featured exclusive candid and staged photos of celebrities off-set (along the lines of what a lucky fan would be able to capture in an unexpected celebrity encounter), while *Episodes,* published by Capital Cities/ABC, until its demise was an unabashed promotional for ABC shows and offered fans exclusive coverage of ABC's celebrities.[13]

In sum, the differences among publications in their relative emphases organize fans' preferences for what magazines to purchase. From these publications (the secondary text), fans actively weave together elements, building their own story. In doing so, fans incorporate their interests, concerns, insights, and criticisms into a unique narrative (the tertiary text) that they use to reinterpret not only the soaps themselves (the primary text), but even the magazines and the daytime industry as well.

To sustain their presence in the daytime market, magazines must manage the tension between giving fans what they want and serving the commercial interests of the shows and the actors. This tension is exacerbated by the isolation of the daytime medium within the entertainment industry as a whole, which circumscribes what can be included. The small number of subjects (actors, writers, producers, and shows) upon which to focus creates a challenge for journalists, who have to produce new information weekly, year around. As one journalist put it, "Now that magazines are weekly, a lot has to be done to feed the monster." The dilemma affects the magazines' decisions about how to preview upcoming story lines or discuss actors' personal lives, the two areas of greatest interest to fans. Lorraine Zenka at *Soap Opera Magazine* told us in a March 1993 interview that "from the magazines' point of view, there has to be a cooperative effort between fans' and the producers' interests. Magazines have to juggle previewing stories but without killing viewers' anticipation. So, if you'll notice, what is previewed for the week is specific for developments early in the week and vaguer in the latter part of the week." But because of media news, "fans now know whose contract is up in two weeks, who is pregnant, whose scenes are pretaped, or who had surgery, such that it is now very hard to surprise the fans. Freshness is lacking as far as actors are concerned."

But increasing numbers of fans in our survey report that previews do not interfere with their pleasure. "I read your magazine and I'm fairly intuitive where soaps are concerned, so nothing surprises me. Knowing what is going to happen in no way diminishes my enjoyment — and a lot of time it enhances it! I watch the soaps to see how the actors convey their emotions during the crises SPW tells us are happening soon" (*Soap Opera Weekly* 1993:42–43). Another fan states, "I have to say that very, VERY little if anything happens that I don't know about beforehand. Really, the pleasure is watching HOW they'll do what they do, not wondering what's next."

The magazines' resident critics' and editors' columns have established an unprecedented level of candor regarding daytime viewing, among them "Critical Condition" and "Speaking My Mind" in *Soap Opera Weekly,* "Diva von Dish" and "Editor's Note" in *Soap Opera Digest,* "Op-Eds" in *Soap Opera Now!* and the "Soaps" column in *TV Guide.* Daytime journalist David Johnson pointed out in our April 1993 interview with him that predecessors such as his "One Man's Opinion" and Rona Barrett's editorial column, which he contributed to, largely dealt with observations about plot developments. "I had fun with these things. In contrast, contemporary versions of these columns really do focus upon criticism, including performers' acting, appearance, physicality, hair, or wardrobe." Johnson said that it is because magazines have such wide circulation "they now have the power to do this." Daytime critics' perceptions of their own power are revealed in a recently published anecdote in *Soap Opera Digest.* Apparently daytime actor Tom Eplin responded with verbal hostility to a benign comment about his hairstyle made by a *Soap Opera Digest* editor at a party preceding the 1993 Emmy awards. Warned the magazine in its piece covering the incident: "Our advice to Mr. Eplin: Lighten up. And don't mess with the press" (*Soap Opera Digest* 1993d:95). Changes in magazine content and format over the years have elicited very different reactions among daytime journalists and actors. Fans, however, relish the inclusion of (and, indeed, focus on) backstage gossip, eagerly incorporating it into their readings and rereadings of primary narratives.

Managing fans' interest in personal detail about actors and other participants entails more complicated considerations. *Soap Opera Update*'s editor Angela Shapiro states her policy as follows: "During an interview, actors will say they're a recovering alcoholic, or they hate the storyline, all kinds of things. We won't print it. Reporting negative things is not our image" (Dolan 1992:A1). *Soap Opera Weekly* has a policy of not covering personal information about celebrities unless it comes from the actors (or other participants) themselves. "We won't deal with who is sleeping with whom. We have features 'with' people but not 'about' people," Linda Susman told us in an April 1993 interview. *Soap Opera Magazine,* even though owned by the *National Enquirer,* also manages revelations carefully. As staff journalist Lorraine Zenka explained to us in an interview in March 1993, "Daytime is too small a market to reveal personal stuff or story lines too early. Besides, fans don't want the dirt, and if they do, the tabloids cover daytimers. Soap magazines don't 'out' people, and unless the actors themselves talk about personal things such as romances, health status, or sexuality, the information we may have is off limits."

The tension between the daytime media and fans' interests can escalate around this issue, stretching the boundaries of what Zenka described in our interview as the "reciprocal courtesy not to offend anyone" that exists between daytime magazines and those they write about. On the one hand, the small and relatively isolated daytime industry prevents journalists from becoming too critical. According to *TV Guide* columnist and critic Michael Logan in our interview in December 1993:

> Soap journalists are in constant interaction with those that they are covering. A journalist may say something in print one week and the very next week have to call the show's [executive producer] or publicist [for another story]. Being a soap critic is not like being a film critic, because Siskel and Ebert don't rub shoulders with the people that they review. They are not talking with them on a daily basis on the phone. We are in constant interaction with the very medium that we're critiquing, and that is very different, and is also another reason why you don't see a whole heck of a lot of [criticism] in soap journalism.

On the other hand, "if it's out of their mouth, it's out of their mouth," claims another journalist. Daytime fans, like audiences of other entertainment mediums (Gamson 1994), are knowledgeable about the entertainment business. Inevitably journalists know more than they print, and they manage that information carefully. As one explained, " 'FYI's' are submitted as side notes to magazine editors, and are monitored to see if a trend emerges. This kind of stuff doesn't help fans or the actors to see [that kind of] news in print. It's the kind of stuff you want to talk about but not see in print [as a feature article]." This information, when it does appear, shows up as blind items or trade secrets or in eavesdropping columns.

While blanket courtesies exist, fans are savvy to how magazines implement those courtesies differently and are often able to glean information through multiple sources. As one fan told us, "The way to figure out what is really going on is to read across *all* the magazines and even everything within a given issue and compare the information that may be only hinted at in one but photographed in another." Magazines go through cycles of greater or lesser disclosure, depending upon who is on staff and the relationships individual staff journalists have with industry participants. Celebrities' willingness to do feature articles or go on record often depends upon their belief they won't be misrepresented by a particular journalist or magazine editor. Savvy fans recognize this variation and track it accordingly, spreading word on the best sources for information.

Sharp-eyed fans seeking personal detail also can draw upon the photos that all daytime magazines print. As one journalist pointed out, daytime magazines are increasingly photo driven rather than text driven, although some publications, like *Soap Opera Now!* remain primarily text. While some photos result from assignments (for example, photos of celebrities in their homes or in costume on the set taken to publicize a plot development), many are produced by free-lance photographers who attend as many events as possible to capture celebrities off-set. Actors who would otherwise not merit mention in a magazine know that photos offer a route to inclusion. A recurring dayplayer commented to us at a charity event, "I'm not stupid. I know how these things pay off for me. I get my picture in the magazines, this gets fans to like me. And my volume of mail increases."

Although contributors to the media, freelance photographers are free to cultivate their own connections to industry participants, and while their association with journalists is cooperative, they sometimes know or capture more than journalists can or choose to put into print. One freelancer described to us how this works. On one occasion, he was the only one from his corps who went to an out-of-town daytimers event. Warned by colleagues in the print media that two celebrities in attendance whose budding romance had not yet been made public through the media were inaccessible to the press, he pursued them anyway. Indications were that a relationship existed, and the two acknowledged in response to a query from the audience that they "were going together." They allowed him to take photos, knowing he would try to sell them to daytime publications. His photos from that event appeared in print, as did photos of other photographers at subsequent events, until the couple finally went public in a feature exclusive a few months later. Until that time, fans were strategically piecing together photographed records of the couple's joint public appearances, relying on nonverbal indicators of intimacy captured in the photos and the cleverly worded captions that accompanied the photos. Another free-lance photographer explained that the demand for photos is greater when news such as a romance is still unconfirmed. After a relationship goes public, "the need to capture it on film dies down and the photos are less in demand. But at least when there is still ambiguity about the relationship, at least ambiguity in the public acknowledgment of the relationship, that's when the photos of couples are at their hottest."

When publicity is poor, the press is uninterested, or an actor is reticent to contribute information to the media, fans will construct their own textual collections from multiple and informal sources. We excerpted the following quote from one idioculture's interaction on an electronic bulletin board:

> Thanks sooo much for the inside scoop! . . . As for [the actors], I feel like I'm playing some kind of detective game trying to figure this situation out. If they aren't "friends" what was she doing there in the first place? . . . OK all you sleuths out there let's pick apart [the] clues and try to guess what's going on!

This idioculture's data consisted of an extensive collection of personal photos of the actors and their friends and relatives; tapes of one of the actor's songs and of concerts, plays, personal appearances, and radio interviews; and information gleaned from the actors' publicists, personal managers, and fan club presidents. This information is reread against the information that is officially presented in the secondary texts and against clues gleaned from dialogue and nonverbal behavior in the primary text. For the most part this collective activity remains within the realm of the secondary text, since what is not evidenced in their interaction together is how fans then use the information privately within their own tertiary texts (which may in turn be used to reread once again the primary text).

Thus, the text and photos that make up fan magazines, legitimated as publicity about celebrity, mediate between the private activities of fans. This renders some important activities public by giving dimension and reality to fans' private pleasures and linking fans with others whose opinions can be evaluated within one's immediate circle of friends. What is unique about the soap opera audience is how intertextually and variably constructed its fanship is. Whereas the publicity arm of the larger entertainment industry must craft fictional personas as real, the publicity of daytime has a fictional narrative already in place on which to draw. It is no wonder that daytime fans seek information that not only penetrates the narrative but undercuts and reconstructs it. What is perhaps more important is how that narrative is read back into the primary narrative, an issue we will discuss in detail later.

Finally, the increasingly institutionalized site of criticism from viewers and critics alike merits attention for its visible contribution to daytime serial subculture. *Soap Opera Weekly* runs a critic's column, "Critical Condition," in every issue as well as other columns, including "Hit or Miss," "Freeze Frame," and "Dress for Success," on a recurring basis. As a biweekly, *Soap Opera Digest* has the time to develop entire feature articles like "Report Card," which critically evaluates each serial's performance on the dimensions of stories, acting, continuity, couples, humor, and recasts. *Soap Opera Now!* includes "Op Ed" and "Managing Editor's Corner" in which staff debate their differences of opinion. Features like these introduce another layer of narrative to the secondary text.

Television critics have traditionally been the spokespersons for their audiences, verbalizing the consequences of programming and viewers' likes and dislikes that cannot be expressed in ratings (Lang 1958). By the late 1950s, the role of the prime-time television critic had evolved from interpreter of the meaning of program narratives into advocate for audiences in their search for entertainment; however, a comparable institutionalized role for daytime television did not fully emerge until much later. *TV Guide*'s soap columnist Michael Logan told us in our December 1993 interview that the critic's role in the soap medium is currently more ombudsman than advocate, making viewer preferences known to the industry. In contrast, some journalists see themselves playing a more active role in shaping viewer preferences. Mimi Torchin, editor-in-chief of *Soap Opera Weekly,* asks in one of her weekly columns, "Do the opinions of critics—with no personal agendas—carry no weight with the viewers? What will it take to entice you to sample a show so many agree is the best? This matter confounds me!" (1994a:4). Still others see no need at all for critical analysis in the magazines. For Mary Ann Cooper, executive editor of *Soap Opera Magazine,* only two opinions matter, "those of the people in the magazine and those who read the magazine." As an editor, she said in an interview with us in December 1993, she believes her opinion does not count, because "it is no better than any other fan's. Some fans are more in tune than I am . . . and *they* are the informed ones."

Given the diversity of views among journalists themselves, it is not surprising that fans question critics' loyalties. One fan writes: "I was beginning to wonder if you were on the *Guiding Light* payroll because you have been praising it so much. But you redeemed yourself in the January 10 issue with your response to a letter" (*Soap Opera Now!* 1994:6).

In the absence of critical journalism, daytime fans themselves, usually within idiocultures, traditionally fill the role of advocate/interpreter/critic for the subculture. As initially conceptualized (Fiske 1987), the tertiary text was constituted by gossip, primarily about the primary narrative. But as we shall see later, it also incorporates analysis, debate, and commentary among fans. With many fan magazines now providing a forum for fans to speak knowledgeably and critically to one another, why are critics even necessary? Moreover, if these critics speak for their audiences in terms already understood by members, to whom are they really speaking? We suggest two possibilities.

First, the role of columnist/critic emerged as the daytime press came to recognize the diversity and sophistication of the soap audience as a resource. With so many kinds of daytime viewers now out of the closet and soap fans increasingly savvy to the industry, the daytime press has found an audience for critical perspectives on issues within the medium. Some editors, as did Linda Susman in our April 1993 interview, advocate a philosophy of "recognizing the level of viewers' viewing, readers' reading, and the civilians' view of the industry. . . . [We do that by] servicing the readers and servicing the industry. . . . There is a kinship between our readers and those of us daytime journalists who are professional watchers." Furthermore, columnists, critics, and editors increasingly monitor the boundaries of the subculture, taking issue with commentary that fails to rise above outsiders' stereotypes of the subculture. For example, editor-in-chief Mimi Torchin took the *New York Times* to task for being "condescending to our industry" (1993a:4).

Second, the presence of critics, in conjunction with published fan opinion, increasingly mediates the quality of soaps' pleasures to those outside the subculture, a particularly important contribution because the daytime medium is so denigrated within the entertainment industry.[14] Journalist Lorraine Zenka observed in our March 1993 interview that "daytime television isn't represented anywhere other than daytime publications. It is still ghettoized within the entertainment industry by press agents, casting directors, and producers." Consequently, increasingly successful incursions of daytime events into prime time, such as the *Soap Opera Digest* awards, the daytime Emmys, and prime-time specials of daytime serials, are regarded as accomplishments pivotal to legitimating the medium to outsiders.[15] The daytime press recognizes that such productions must be well crafted to engage nonfans. For example, in reviewing *Guiding Light*'s prime-time special, Marlena De Lacroix, *Soap Opera Weekly*'s resident critic says:

> If you want to know *le vraiment* (that's Swiss for the truth), I'm sure the people who put together this "special" had nothing or very little to do with the stellar writing and production teams at the afternoon show. . . . But absolutely the worst part of the show was the abysmal writing. Is the prime-time audience really at the third-grade level? . . . Soap opera anniversary shows are a family affair which should be produced in daytime for the daytime fans who have loved their shows for so long. (1992:38)

Writing that is too "sharp, sarcastic, or snide," noted Lorraine Zenka, is considered inappropriate because it does not take the medium seriously.

For example, Mimi Torchin criticized the production team of the 1994 Daytime Emmys for the way "daytime was falsely represented to a prime-time audience as a mindless, sexist, sleaze-driven, tacky industry" and praised as "unsung heroes" the actors from *As the World Turns* who "sacrificed the show's only onstage appearance because they refused to participate in the egregiously distasteful segment they were to be part of." She went on to note that if others would follow their example, "perhaps the image of soaps could be elevated a little. No, soaps aren't Shakespeare, but they're not burlesque either. It's time to take a stand" (1994b:4).

Ultimately, success at spanning boundaries between the daytime medium and outsiders depends on legitimating and institutionalizing the sophistication and diversity of the daytime audience with those who produce the serials. "We have industry executives, writers, and producers paying attention to *Soap Opera Weekly* for insight. They are interested in fan feedback. They are happy at the praise and they smart at the criticism," says Linda Susman. Their presence, however, contributes to the longstanding battle between audience and producers over creative authorship of serial narratives; the advocacy they provide the audience intersects with the contested terrain over authorship.

Meanwhile, as soaps struggle for legitimacy outside the medium and critics struggle for recognition within the fan subculture, fans remain sensitive to being stigmatized and are quick to recognize gratuitous efforts by the daytime press to relabel them as more intelligent or sophisticated. A case in point is the negative reaction elicited from fans by the feature article "Look Who's Watching: Forget the Stereotypes, Soap Watchers Are a New Breed" (*Soap Opera Digest* 1993c). In a BBS discussion about the article one viewer remarked, "Although I probably fit SOD's idea of an 'atypical' viewer, I was bothered by the implication that 'typical' viewers (homemakers) can be stereotyped and that anyone who wears a suit and watches a soap on his/her VCR at night is by definition a more intelligent viewer than someone who watches while doing ironing." Critics and journalists in the daytime press face two challenges. The first is to recognize the diversity and intelligence of the soap audience. The second and more difficult challenge is not presuming to speak for an audience that is capable of speaking for itself.

# Chapter Three

## Becoming and Being a Fan

About six years ago, Sandra and her family bought their first VCR, and Sandra started regularly taping *Days of Our Lives*. A few years into watching the show, she became captivated by the budding romance between blue-collar Patch and girl-next-door Kayla. By her own description, the show took over her life. She says that at her "worst" she spent about ten hours a day watching specially edited videotapes of Patch/Kayla scenes. During the morning, before the day's episode aired, she sat in front of her television, remote control in hand, trying to catch commercials featuring Patch and Kayla, which she would then transfer to a special videotape. Sandra spent hundreds of dollars on postage, phone calls to the NBC studio, and fan magazines, all of which her family "definitely could not afford." She was able to keep most of the expenses secret from her husband, because she spent her tips from work. She completely ignored her children during this time and barely spoke to her husband. "It was almost like I was cheating on him." She went "wild" when the phone rang because it meant interrupting her viewing, and family members knew never to enter the bedroom when she was watching tapes. In Sandra's view, her attachment to the characters was both psychological and physical: "When the story line was up I was up, when the story line was bad I would cry, vomit, [and I] could not sleep. I was horrible to my family in the sense [that] I only did what I had to do. I would watch tapes all day and all night."

Phyllis tells a similar story. In her words, the Patch/Kayla romance "destroyed my life." She made hundreds of edited videotapes and spent her days watching them repeatedly; spent money on magazines, phone calls, and postage that the family needed for other things; and ignored responsibilities to family and friends. When the story line was going in a direction Phyllis didn't like she became physically ill, with headaches, weeping spells, and general depression. Her family was so alarmed that Phyllis began hiding her activities from them.

Both women stopped taping *Days of Our Lives* when Stephen Nichols, who portrayed Patch, left the show in 1990, but Sandra still has not been able to bring herself to watch the final scenes in which Patch dies (although, in typical daytime fashion, a mysterious coffin switch at the end of the episode leaves the door open for the character's return). Both women are relieved that they no longer watch, and both feel their personal lives have improved as a result. When asked about persistent industry rumors that Stephen Nichols might reprise his role as Patch, Sandra says: "I am scared to death that it's going to happen again. . . . It absolutely terrifies me. . . . I'm going to be hanging over the toilet bowl. . . . It's going to mean a lot of pain." Sandra compares her past behavior to that of an alcoholic, while Phyllis says her own was like a drug addict's.

We interviewed these women after one of them contacted us, having seen the advertisements for our study. How typical are their tales? The image of fans drawn in either the popular or academic press suggests that Sandra's and Phyllis's stories are not unique. *All* fans are addicted to their shows; *all* forms of fanship are potentially (self-) destructive. On the other hand, while cases such as these exist, a whole range of normal fanship has yet to be described and understood. In this chapter, we investigate what it means to be a normal fan of soap operas.

Earlier we described the variety of activities engaged in by viewers and fans of daytime dramas, such as watching soaps, buying magazines, and attending luncheons. As we pointed out, most research on media fans defines fanship almost exclusively in terms of such activities (Bacon-Smith 1992; Jenkins 1992b; Penley 1992), so to participate in fan activity is to be a fan. We believe that this conceptualization of fan as doer obscures an important dimension of fanship, the acceptance and maintenance of a fan identity. One can do fan activity without being a fan, and vice versa.

Fanship is not merely about activity; it involves parallel processes of activity and identity.

## Becoming a Viewer, Becoming a Fan

Most viewers have initiation stories that explain how they got involved with soap operas (Seiter et al. 1989:234). Entering the serial world happens gradually, through the kind of activities Becker (1963) describes as "side bets" associated with entry into behaviors and subcultures marginal to mainstream society, initially without commitment or purpose, that become increasingly significant over time and only retrospectively are understood as important to one's identity. Because of the complexity of the soap genre, some of the boundaries to the viewer/fan world can be forbidding. *Soap Opera Weekly* editor-in-chief Mimi Torchin suggests:

> Sit down to watch your favorite daytime drama with an "outsider." Then try to explain what's going on. By the time you've described just a tiny portion of any storyline you'll have a better understanding of why the uninitiated make fun of soaps. If you don't follow the form, soaps can seem absurd. (1993b:4)

Novice viewers have to negotiate a "hump factor" before they can become regular watchers (Whetmore and Kielwasser 1983). Due to the intricate networks of character relationships with complicated histories (Allen 1985), it takes time before a naive viewer can understand what is happening on a daytime drama. As one respondent said, "It's not like 'Matlock.'" Ruth Rosen notes:

> The inexperienced viewer is "positioned," in a sense, like a newcomer to a community. When one moves into a new town, it takes time to ferret out relations and events that older residents might prefer to forget. . . . Gradually the viewer is drawn into the circle of insiders. (1986:54–55)

Most watchers depend on more experienced viewers to help them make sense of the unfolding narratives, and people must be patient enough to overcome their initial confusion before they can become regular soap watchers. This process of learning the daytime world can take many years and indeed may never be fully accomplished. One of the authors of this book has been watching *All My Children* for thirteen years yet is still confused by some of the characters occasionally referenced in an episode.

Initiation stories vary. Some people are introduced to daytime television by a relative or family member, and the watching of serials is gradually integrated into the family's shared history (Brown 1987:9; see also Whetmore and Kielwasser 1983). Our respondents say:

> I have been watching *General Hospital* since 1964. My mother watched it, and after I graduated in '64 I started watching it on a daily basis.

> I'm turning 14 in a couple days, and unlike most all my friends, soap operas happen to take up a large part of my life. I come from a family of soap watchers. My mom used to watch *General Hospital*. My sister, who is now in college, watched *Santa Barbara* for a couple years before switching to *The Young and the Restless*.

Others are introduced later in life through roommates, spouses, or co-workers; virtually any person that one has regular contact with can act as an initiator. Other viewers find (or rediscover) serials by themselves during an illness, parental leave, or at-home time spent with children. One of the authors, who had not watched soaps for many years, was reintroduced to them after repeated proddings by her students. Individuals with flexible work arrangements—part-timers, professional athletes, consultants, students, and the self-employed—are also likely to be exposed to soaps. Still others find serials serendipitously and become captivated by the genre. A common element of these introductions is the luxury of time: novice viewers must invest enough time in watching if they are to overcome the hump factor. But people no longer need access to the private realm during the daytime hours to become soap watchers. Given the popularity of VCRs, flexible work schedules, and televisions in office lounges, most soap watchers are not home-bound in the way they were even a decade or so ago.

BECOMING AND BEING A FAN / 89

Most people can remember clearly who introduced them to soap operas and how old they were when they first started watching them. One respondent began watching when she was four and remembers seeing a beautiful wedding scene and bursting into tears. Her worried mother assured her that what was happening on the screen wasn't real. She told her mother that she knew it was fictional, but "it was just that the acting was so good." Another respondent, fourteen at the time of our contact with her, says, "I have been watching *Santa Barbara* since its premiere in 1984. I must confess that I was the only third grader I knew who rushed home from school to catch the latest plot twist." Another young woman's early viewing experiences have merged with her childhood memories:

> When I was younger my grandmother used to baby-sit me, and she watched *Guiding Light,* so I guess you could say I got hooked at a young age. Although then, I probably didn't really like it, I probably just watched it. It's funny though, when people mention names from the past and I have some recollection of them. Like Kelly, for instance. I remember him, but I don't. It's kind of freaky!

While viewers are usually introduced to soaps by another person, different access points (Whetmore and Kielwasser 1983:111) within the genre hook the viewer: actor, character, writing, story line, costumes, or some other identifiable feature. Some respondents follow favorite actors, writers, and directors from show to show; others are loyal to a specific show and its familiar community of characters. The idea of different access points is important in part because it is central to differentiating viewers from one another. Fans who scrutinize acting skills, for example, can become frustrated with viewers who are "hung up on story," and those who are loyal to the entire fictional community of Genoa City, Corinth, Llanview, or Bay City are aghast at others who can pick up or drop a program seemingly at will.

Most of our respondents first began watching soaps in a supportive environment, surrounded by others with similar interests. What happens when those private interests come under public scrutiny? Some viewers are "remarkably open and secure" in their viewing habits (Seiter et al. 1989), despite public derision of soap operas. Others feel guilty and defensive about their television preferences (Derry 1985; Rosen 1986; Whetmore and Kielwasser 1983; Williams 1992), usually because they fear taking too much time away from family members or being ridiculed for enjoying such a disparaged cultural form. The viewers we studied are very aware of the negative stereotypes. In their own words, a soap watcher is "part idiot," "someone whose brain has turned to mush," "a bored housewife," "crazy," "a couch-potato," or someone who is "unemployed, fat, lazy, and not up-to-date on current events." The title of a recent scholarly piece on soap watching, "Confessions of a Soap Opera Addict," implies something sinful or embarrassing about enjoying soaps (Levin 1993). Since one's self-perceptions about being a fan are fundamentally affected by the reactions of others, the power of those stereotypes clearly affects some viewers.[1] A sample from respondents:

I'm sort of embarrassed to admit that I like soaps.

[Soap viewing] is, indeed, a strange phenomenon. I must admit that for many years I was a "closet" viewer and was embarrassed to admit I had succumbed to the inexplicable appeal of soaps.

## Fans Manage Stereotypes

In order for viewers to sustain their interest, stereotypes must be managed. Viewers argue that negative stereotypes exist because nonwatchers are ignorant of the genre; serials are a joke only for those who don't understand them.[2] Despite their narrative complexity, soaps can indeed appear both simplistic and wildly unrealistic on the surface, and their appeal is usually incomprehensible to nonviewers, who are unable to read their unique coding devices. In fact, even loyal daytime viewers find each others' favorite programs questionable: "I love *Santa Barbara* because it is something special, not just another show. I have watched other soap operas (just to see if they are all the same) and I found them dull, dreary, and *dumb*."

Public scorn contributes to viewers' ambivalence about watching and enjoying daytime television (Seiter et al. 1989); thus, it has consequences for how they evaluate their own involvement as viewers. Viewers find the

genre intensely pleasurable but are uncomfortable knowing that it is belittled by others. Some viewers downplay their own viewing habits; others
report they have "tried to stop watching" but could not; still others know
people who watch daytime television but "pretend not to." As mentioned
earlier, we were told of loyal soap watchers among fundamentalist Chris-
tian organizations who keep their viewing secret because they think that
watching defies the teachings of their ministry. Awareness of public derision is also evident in the case of a longtime *General Hospital* viewer, an
attorney who during one job-hunting phase refused to watch *GH* because
she didn't want people to know she was at home without anything "pro-
ductive" to do. Once she found a job, she resumed watching.

Ambivalence also results from viewers' convictions that they are manipulated by the soap format. As Ellen Seiter and her colleagues discuss in
*Remote Control* (1989), viewers frequently talk about and criticize the
people who act in, direct, produce, and write for daytime dramas. They
are keenly aware of the constructedness of the genre, are savvy about
production details, and often believe that they know the show better than
those who create it. The following quote from a BBS illustrates a fan's
sophistication about production constraints on daytime story telling:

> I have a theory that the actress who plays [Dominique] . . . really isn't
> leaving "General Hospital." . . . I'm beginning to suspect that the [pro-
> ducers] started the rumor on purpose to pull us into the [story line]. . . .
> The main reason I think they're pulling this on us is because it's been
> such a long time since they originally said the character . . . would be
> leaving. . . . My bet is that we're all being had!

Viewers' ambivalence about watching is reflected most clearly in their
frequent and vehement complaints about lack of narrative and character
consistency — an inconsistency inevitable given the turnover of writers,
directors, producers, and actors in the daytime industry (Allen 1985) —
and about having their "intelligence insulted" by poorly conceived story
lines. Most viewers can readily recite what they dislike about daytime,
including superficial characters, bad dialogue, amateurish acting, and out-
landish plots. *One Life to Live*'s Wild West and Eterna story lines of the
late 1980s are oft-cited examples of the latter. In the Wild West debacle

several of the major actors simultaneously played their regular characters as well as pioneers from the 1800s. One of the more incredible story lines had townspeople trying to prevent a character from marrying the woman who was destined to be his grandmother. Frustration with narrative inconsistency and lack of realism is articulated by respondents:

> What will cause me to stop watching is a show that has a person in authority who dislikes the daytime serial format and despises the viewers. They show it by idiot plots, formula dialogue, factual errors in stories because they haven't taken the time to do simple research (i.e., having characters recover from *viral* diseases because they were given *antibiotics*) and gross ignorance of the history of the characters (i.e., a brother reminds his sister how she held his daughter as an infant when the viewer remembers the family didn't know of the baby until the child was 5 years old). I am very alienated by the story that stumbles and blunders along first one way then another because the *show* can't decide how it should end. That's when I bail out of soap viewing. I don't have time for people who insult my intelligence so grossly.

> Basically, soap operas drive me crazy. I would *like* to enjoy watching them . . . but the writers' failure to devote intelligent attention to the plotlines and factual development is infuriating. I am often disgusted by the simple lack of *effort* expended in getting things right. The writers and producers demean the viewers by assuming that we do not care if characters do completely ridiculous things or fail to do perfectly obvious things. It is okay to have dramatic and unlikely scenarios — that is what makes the "stories" fun. But I am tired of watching a show and thinking "that's completely absurd, how does this person spring on the scene and successfully masquerade as a competent doctor when they're really a psychopathic trombone player" — doesn't anyone check references?! Also, if soap operas are going to focus on legal or medical subplots, then the writers should consult with experts so that what is presented is at least close to accurate. Again, the viewers are smart enough to know when the characters are spouting information that is way off base. And does everyone have to show up in the courtroom in leather miniskirts and spring forward from the back of the room to

storm the witness stand and give rambling speeches? Have the writers ever been *near* a courtroom?? I don't mind jazzing things up a bit, but when developments don't ring anywhere near the truth it is just offensive.

A similar view is articulated by Jason, an unemployed man in his mid-forties who was watching all eleven network serials airing at the time of our contact with him. While Jason believes that writers ultimately create the characters, his own viewing pleasure is invested in the actors' ability to interpret and develop them. If the quality of acting is poor, character and narrative lose credibility. Like others, Jason's main complaint about soap operas is their lack of internal consistency. He accepts the story-telling efforts of writers and producers as long as they are believable and credible within the premise of the show. For example, aliens were the premise of the now defunct prime-time show *Alien Nation,* so alien characters were acceptable and credible. In contrast, *General Hospital's* late 1980s introduction of Casey, the alien from the planet Lumina, was not credible because it did not fit the basic premise of a contemporary metropolitan hospital-centered community. Jason calls this sloppy story telling and is frustrated because "it would be so easy to do it right."

Given such ambivalence and frustration, why watch? One woman responds, "This is a question I wrestle with myself because I am painfully aware of [soaps'] faults . . . yet I still get hooked from time to time. Sometimes the actors and the characters blend into a believability so strong you almost feel you're eavesdropping on real lives and it is fascinating." This quote centrally addresses the issue of fan pleasure, particularly the pleasure of merging the boundaries between real and fictional that we alluded to earlier. Even long-term viewers and fans must wrestle with the inconsistencies and drawbacks of the genre in order to negotiate the hump factor and find pleasure in watching.

If soap viewers face negative stereotypes about their viewing habits, what stereotypes are directed at soap fans? In general the public sees fans as "foolishly obsessed, lacking education and critical distance" (Brower 1992:163), and thus to speak as a fan is to accept a culturally belittled identity (Jenkins 1992b). Perhaps the most persistent negative stereotype is that fans cannot tell the difference between fiction and reality. Some scholarship, our own included, shows that most fans, far from being deluded, *consciously* play with the boundary between the fictional and the real; nevertheless the image still holds that fans are "not able to tell the difference between the character and the actor in which she or he is embodied" (Brown 1987:9). The stigmatized persona of the fan can be described as follows:

> Were I to call myself a fan, I would imply that I am emotionally engaged with unworthy cultural figures and forms, and that I was risking obsession, with dangerous consequences. I would imply that I was a psychologically incomplete person, trying to compensate for my inadequate life through the reflected glory of these figures and forms. My unstable and fragile identity needs them, they are a "therapeutic crutch," a form of "para-social relations," functioning as "personas" in my life. I must have these relationships because my lonely, marginal existence requires that I prop myself up with these fantasy attachments to famous dead people, and these alliances with abstract, imaginary communities. (Jensen 1992:23)

Because of these negative stereotypes, media fans do not enter fandom lightly (Bacon-Smith 1992:87) but make conscious and sometimes difficult decisions to do so. People either keep their fan identity secret or "risk the stigma that comes from being a fan" (Lewis 1992:1).

Our respondents are as knowledgeable of the poor image of fans as they are of the stereotypes of soap watchers. In their words, fans are usually seen as either "lunatics" or "swooning teeny boppers," and some of the dedicated viewers we spoke with support this negative image. The attorney who refused to watch serials when unemployed said, when we asked if she wanted to meet a daytime celebrity, "No, I [would] feel like a jerk letting people I don't know and who care nothing about me think they mean something to me, let alone how much. I'd feel like a freak." A graduate student among our respondents carefully manages her identification as a fan when she interacts with soap actors:

> I could never engage in the idle chitchat other fans seem to have no trouble doing. I still have this problem. I find I have no idea what to say

to an actor other than to compliment his or her performance. I have no shared experiences with these people other than how they act on a show I watch. I find that it's easy to slip and address an actor by his or her character's name, and I hate doing that because I want the actor to understand that I understand that he or she is a person separate from the character. I hate being thought of as an unintelligent soap fan who is divorced from reality. When I attend appearances, I often like to wear political buttons (such as feminist, pro-choice, and pro-gay rights buttons) to indicate to the actors and to everyone else who sees me that I am interested in something other than the soaps.

Another woman finds public interest in media celebrities sad, because celebrities are "no better than us . . . it's sad that we have to reach out to something false." One respondent says she will never join a fan club because clubs are for people who "don't have lives" and are trying to live out a vicarious fantasy life through superficial contact with celebrities. She refuses to attend celebrities' public appearances because she cannot imagine that it's the "high point" of an actor's day to be "surrounded by screaming women." A woman who joined clubs for both *The Young and the Restless* and *The Bold and the Beautiful* specifically to attend fan luncheons said the one event she attended was "enough." In her view, the mostly female fans acted as if the characters rather than the actors were present and went "absolutely nuts" over them. The actors, for their part, seemed to be simply humoring the fans. She concluded, "I can't sit in a room with people who think it's real . . . [it was] very uncomfortable."

While most viewers do not condemn fanship as readily as these respondents, they reveal ambivalence about public or even quasi-public fan activities. An aspiring journalist in her mid-twenties justified attending her first fan event by assurances that the proceeds were being donated to charity. Enthralled by the Jack/Jennifer characters on *Days of Our Lives*, she sometimes asks herself, "Why am I doing this? Why do I care so much?" but has decided there is no point in questioning her involvement since it brings her pleasure and "it's not hurting anybody" (except, as she admitted, her budget). She hosted a party at her house to celebrate the twenty-fifth anniversary of the show with a cake and a specially edited videotape but did not attend the officially sponsored event because she did

not want to be a "lookyloo." Another fan who questioned her own behavior offered a justification a moment later: "I'd never written a fan letter
to anyone before. . . . You feel sort of stupid, don't you. But when you see
them five times a week on TV, you feel like you know them."

In contrast, other fans feel little ambivalence about their activities. They
might not advertise or publicize their involvement in soap fandom to
nonfans, but neither are they apologetic or defensive about the pleasures
they derive from daytime television. Some explicitly self-identify as fans;
others consider themselves fans but do not present that identity openly.

## From Viewer to Fan

What does it mean to say someone is a fan of a popular cultural object?
For some scholars, fans are "the most visible and identifiable of audiences," with a high level of textual competence and involvement in all
forms of media interactions (Lewis 1992:1, 139). Fans "not only 'follow'
a program, but . . . are invested in its *continuance*" (Brower 1992:168).
Most researchers see a fan as someone who interacts with a community of
people with similar interests and who creates new products derivative
of the primary narrative (Bacon-Smith 1992; Fiske 1992; Jenkins 1988,
1992a, b; Penley 1991).

One four-part model of fanship and fandom incorporates activities as a
central component (Jenkins 1992a). First, fans "adopt a distinctive mode
of reception" to a cultural object in that they translate reception into other
activities. Second, fan communities are organized around shared interpretive activities. Third, fandom constitutes a particular "art world," a site of
collective activity where cultural works are produced and consumed
(Becker 1982). Finally, fandom "constitutes an alternative social community" defined through shared consumption of cultural objects (Jenkins
1992a:209–213). Creating a fan community is thus articulating specific
shared pleasures and engaging in activities around those pleasures. The
consumption of one text leads to the production of new ones.

Soap fans recognize the importance of fan communities and shared
interpretative activities. One respondent, a fan of both Jack Wagner's
music and his soap opera characters (he portrayed Frisco Jones on *Gen-*

*eral Hospital* and Warren Lockridge on *Santa Barbara*), responds to some of Wagner's other fans about his concert appearances:

> What great experiences to be able to recall! I've been to a couple of Jack's concerts at the Universal Amphitheater, but the show was the only entertainment. I don't have any before, during, or after memories to cherish. It sounds like members of his fan club were once very familiar with one another and that when he was most active, you were just the right age to get maximum enjoyment out of it all. It probably wouldn't be as thrilling an experience this time around as an adult. . . . I remember in 1984, I saw Michael Jackson in concert 11 times in Detroit, Chicago, Pennsylvania, and Los Angeles, but I didn't have nearly as much fun as it sounds like you had with Jack's plays and concerts. Of course, the fact that you had so many people to share the adventures with made all of the difference.

As this fan illustrates, there is more to being a fan than simply participating in collective activities. An intense affective experience contributes fundamentally to her fan identity.

Being a fan requires not only participation in activities but the adoption of a particular identity that is shaped through subjective and affective experiences.[3] More than just an active consumer of cultural texts, a fan relates to a text through emotion, affect, and ideology (Grossberg 1992a:56). "I got so into the scenes today that I fast forwarded through everything else! Now that they've started bringing the romance back. . . . I WANT MORE!" wrote one fan. In simplest terms, a fan is someone who has made an affective investment in something that matters to him or her and who holds strong beliefs that legitimate the investment.[4] As fans make such emotional investments, they "divide the cultural world into Us and Them" (Grossberg 1992a:58). Incorporating the identities of viewer and fan into one's self-concept distinguishes the self from nonviewers and nonfans in a meaningful way. A fan asked about a memorable scene featuring a favorite actor responds: "I knew there was some reason I liked you. When I heard your question I knew that was the scene that stirred the most emotion in me." Another fan experiences the division between Us and Them as follows: "You have me watching golf! Never in all my years would I try it. But since [actor Jack Wagner] may be in the lineup, I do. ABC, ESPN, etc. . . . . my other half thinks I have lost it."

Individuals differ in the ways they organize their fan identity. The way we perceive our own self, our self-concept (Westen 1991), can comprise any number of things, such as age, gender, ethnic/racial affiliation, level of education, and economic class. People order and rank these aspects of self in hierarchies. For example, one person might place the educational category of "college graduate" as central to his or her overall sense of self while another might see gender as particularly salient to personal identity. In other words, individuals differ in the categories that comprise their identity and the relative importance they give them, as we can see in what fans choose to disclose about themselves to others who share their interest. Some fans draw upon experiences salient to their identity, such as having a physical difference, living a single life-style, being a teenager, or becoming a parent, as the basis for interaction with others about soaps. On the other hand, many fans who interact regularly never discuss or even disclose anything about themselves beyond their immediate mutual interest. They choose to compartmentalize their identity as fan and relate to others on that basis alone, as this respondent suggests: "I don't know many other fans, and I am selective in who I get involved with. Of those I know, I know them only because of our mutual interests. I don't care to know other aspects of their personal lives."

Some aspects of the self are visible to observers, others are invisible; some are voluntarily chosen, others are not. Moreover, the desirability or undesirability of an identity influences the degree to which it will be proclaimed or hidden (Deaux 1991:79). Thus, we can expect dedicated soap viewers to differ in how they construct their identities as fans. We explore the construction of fan identity by considering how it varies along two dimensions: degree of privatization and degree of centrality.

Given its routine stigmatization (and thus its undesirability), the visibility of fan identity in one's self-concept can vary greatly and thus influence the degree to which fans keep their identity private. Some fans overtly self-identify, such as this fan who describes his reaction to ridicule about soap viewers: "I won't go into detail, but I also get sick of the abuse (because it is NOT good natured). I take it because I watch a soap and am not ashamed to admit it." However, most fans' identities are more privatized, like those of the following respondents:

> I don't consider myself to be the "gaga" fan type either. I tend to be very shy, so I'm really surprised at myself that I had enough nerve to ask a question [of the actors at a fan event].

> I live in a small community, so I used to buy soap magazines out of town. The first time I bought one, I sent my friend's son in since my son would be recognized and therefore I would be found out. Now I subscribe in my cousin's name.

Fans might not conceal that they watch soaps, engage in fan activities, and adopt the "affective sensibility" of a fan (Grossberg 1992a, b), but neither do they publicly advertise their fanship. Some are willing to reveal their fan identity only when they know they'll be supported by others. Others choose not to disclose their identity because they do not want to waste their time dealing with criticism from nonfans.

Equally important to such revelations, however, is the intensely personal pleasure fans may derive from soaps. As one of our respondents told us, fans find each other and connect if "they care as much [about something]" and "they know they are thinking about the same things all the time." Sharing pleasure thus implies sharing emotions in a way that many find potentially difficult or even painful. We mentioned in Chapter One that most people prefer to view serials alone, primarily so they can feel free to engage emotionally with the events unfolding on the screen. The pleasure of viewing requires privacy; hence for many the pleasure of fanship is also experienced privately.

Fans also differ in how central their fan identity is in their lives. According to one scholar, "For some, being a . . . fan can take on an enormous importance and thus come to constitute a dominant part of the fan's identity. . . . For others, it remains a powerful but submerged difference that colors, but does not define, their dominant social identities" (Grossberg 1992a:58–59). Being a fan can assume such salience in one's hierarchical organization of identities that other identity categories are pushed

A quasi-public display of a fan's private pleasures. In responding to our question-naire, a young viewer included a photo reflecting her identity as a fan. Like all fans, she also has other identities and interests; hers include UCLA. Used by per-mission of Tassie Anna Deppert.

to the background; the object of fanship is treated as central to the self (Hirt et al. 1992:725). For those individuals, being a fan of something means more than simply considering it a hobby — it is to have something matter to the extent that other things matter less (Grossberg 1992a). One soap fan states, "I see my fetish for my show as the equivalent to my husband's all-sports fanaticism." Others literally identify themselves as fans. One woman signed her letter to us "[Susan Morrison,] Dedicated Soap Opera Fan," and another signed off "[Lisa Hartford,] I Love Jack Wagner."

Other soap followers consider watching their shows and engaging in fan activities less central to who they are. Many compare their engagement with soaps to friends' and family members' devotion to Monday night football or garage sales or weekly bowling. Soaps are simply one thing they enjoy, the way that other people enjoy other things. These are the fans for whom watching soaps is taken for granted as part of their lives. One explained, "I have been watching *As the World Turns* for over 37 years, and *Guiding Light* for only 15." For her, soap viewing is neither an extraordinary nor an unimportant part of her life.

Somewhere in between lie viewers who find themselves increasingly aware of the importance of soaps in their lives, and who are thinking through and articulating to themselves and others how fan identity fits with their other central life interests. One middle-aged female respondent told us, "I realized I had to get to [an actor's] personal appearance, even if it was a five hour drive. I brought my husband with me. When I finally met him, I told him I felt like a total idiot being there, that I was so embarrassed, and that I was much too old for this."

If being a fan entails an identity rooted in emotion and affect, how are we to understand fans who are perceived to have lost control of their emotions? Nothing has shaped perceptions of fans more sharply than the widely held image of the lunatic/loser fan.

## Excessive Fanship

The two common images of the excessive fan are the fan as loser and the fan as lunatic. Familiar pictures of the loser fan include the hysterical starstruck teenager, the lonely housewife, and the delusional wanna-be. For example, A. L. Greene and Carolyn Adams-Price discuss adolescents' "secondary attachments" with celebrities, defined as fantasized relationships projected onto media stars: in romantic attachments, adolescents fantasize about having a romantic relationship with a celebrity; in identificatory attachments, they imagine being or being like a star (1990:336). Bacon-Smith (1992) implies that fans are marginalized individuals in search of a community, however stigmatized. Some research explicitly labels all soap fans as losers, saying that daytime serials supply fantasy social networks for lonely people to imagine themselves a part of. As one scholar put it, "Soap operas . . . are ways of extending and peopling a sparse social universe" (Fowles 1992:58).[5]

Regarding the other common image, that of the fan as lunatic, both the popular and academic presses persist in portraying *all* fans as potentially desperate and dangerous stalkers of media celebrities and other public figures. This image has received extensive notoriety since the early 1980s from the widely reported incidents involving daytime (Andrea Evans, Ricky Paul Goldin), prime-time (Rebecca Schaeffer, David Letterman), and feature-film (Jodie Foster) celebrities. According to criminologist Park Dietz:

> There are many thousands of individuals inappropriately fixated on Hollywood figures who have greater access to their potential victims than is desirable. Only a small proportion of those potential public figure assassins are known to their most likely victims. (King 1991:6)

Or, in the words of a *Time Magazine* article discussing the tragic shooting death of Rebecca Schaeffer, "The words 'obsessive fan' cause a premonitory chill among celebrities these days. Increasingly they have seen that the most fervent admirers can turn into crazed attackers" (Ostling 1989:43).

Both of these images of the pathological fan imply a thin line between normal and excessive activity that is crossed if and when fans can no longer distinguish between fantasy and reality (Jensen 1992:18; see also Fine 1983; Ostling 1989).[6] Is it true that many viewers "genuinely experience soap opera characters as perfectly real" (Fowles 1992:168; also, see Rosen 1986:43)? Is abnormal fanship characterized by the inability to distinguish reality from fiction? At what point does fan behavior become excessive or problematic?

The people we spoke with, including fans, actors, fan club staff members, daytime magazine journalists, and serial writers and producers, believe in the existence of a "lunatic fringe" (as one actor put it), but none feels that most fans fit this description. Actors report receiving letters from seemingly out-of-touch fans, indicated (as Joli Jensen predicts) by the fact that the letter is written to the character they portray rather than to the actor. A fan club president explained, "Some address the envelope to the actor, care of the fan club, so I'll open it. But the letter is written to the character. And then they expect the character to solve their problems. It's scary." One actor who plays a nurse on a popular serial has been asked where she attended nursing school, and another actor who has played both a secret agent and a police officer regularly receives fan letters warning him about the actions of evil characters on the show. In Chapter Two we mentioned some widely reported incidents where actors were assaulted on the street by fans who intended the assaults for their characters. Daytime actors say they are regularly called by their characters' names rather than their own when approached by fans in both informal and formal contexts. While this close identification between actor and character is understandable given the nature of daytime television, many actors believe these fans are unable to tell the difference between what is real and what is not.

When one of the authors of this book appeared as a guest on Lifetime's *Jane Pratt Show* along with four popular daytime actors and suggested that fans do in fact know the difference between fiction and reality, the actors disagreed, pointing out that they are often called by their characters' names. A male audience member shouted, "But that's all we know you as." He felt that calling the actors by their own names would be presumptuous, given that he is familiar with the characters only. (Unfortunately, the actors did not get a chance to respond to his comment.)

Other types of behaviors are also perceived as evidence of widespread fan delusion. According to one scholar:

> Whenever a favorite [character] gets "married," the network will be flooded with congratulatory cards and letters, and when another "dies," telegrams and sympathy cards pour in. Thousands upon thousands of letters warn the heroine of impending dangers, give straight-from-the-shoulder advice, praise good behavior, goad action. . . . According to CBS, poor characters on their soaps had to be eliminated because too many CARE packages kept arriving. (Fowles 1992:168)

While we cannot vouch for the veracity of any specific claim, clearly there exists a minority of viewers and fans who do not understand that the events portrayed on the television screen are fictional, and whom the industry perceives as potentially troublesome.

Most actors we interviewed are quick to point out that few fans fit the lunatic image. One estimates that less than 1 percent of the letters she receives or the fans she meets approach the "lunatic dimension," while others give estimates ranging from 15–30 percent. Actors know that some fans *are* potentially dangerous. Indeed, Andrea Evans, who portrayed Tina Lord on *One Life to Live,* was forced to quit her job and remain in hiding for several years as a result of one fan's efforts to harm her. As one actor commented, "Any type of notoriety or fame puts you in jeopardy . . . there's just real kooks out there." Another well-known actor only feels comfortable meeting fans if she is attending a formally sponsored fan event or is introduced to a fan by someone she knows. The prospect of meeting fans on the street frightens her. In most cases, however, actors we spoke with feel that the fan-as-lunatic stereotype harms fans. Says one well-respected actor, "Fans as a whole get a reputation for things that are really individualistic characteristics . . . fans are as different as people are."

Writers of daytime serials and fan club staff members we interviewed agreed that few fans present real physical danger to daytime celebrities. They also define the out-of-touch fan as one who writes letters to characters rather than actors or who seems unusually immature. One writer says that "you know . . . when you get the letter [from an adult] written in pencil on the ruled paper." Fans can be problematic. Some fans become hysterical at fan club luncheons (termed "screamers" or "groupies" by one fan club staff member); corner celebrities and ignore harried event organizers; become overly persistent in trying to track down a celebrity's home address, phone number, or work schedule; and send birthday and holiday gifts to characters. But these represent only a small minority. Writers and fan club staff resent the bad press given to soap fans and say most are "quiet, behind-the-scenes people who see actors as other everyday people" and are "so nice and so normal." One fan club secretary has become sufficiently upset over the deprecating coverage of fans in soap-oriented publications to write complaining letters to the editors. A staff member of the National Association of Fan Clubs says that one of the group's explicit goals is to improve the public image of fans and fan clubs.

Fans themselves, equally aware of the lunatic stereotype, deny its general validity. Our data support their claim, if lunacy is indeed measured by fans' misperceptions that soap operas are real. Only 2 percent of our respondents report having written fan letters to the character rather than to the actor, and many were amazed (if not insulted) by the question.

> These are actors portraying their characters. I can't believe the people that actually write to their characters and don't differentiate between the person playing the role and the role.

> It's the actor who brings the character alive!!!!! People who do not appreciate great acting and write to the character are out of touch with reality.

> [I would] feel stupid writing to a fictional person and the actor should feel stupid receiving [a] letter on behalf of one.

> Why write to the characters? They couldn't answer (unless the writers sat down and made an answer up).

And in response to the widely reported cases of fans sending cards and gifts to characters, one fan comments in a letter to a fan magazine:

> You had an article on the 42 arrangements of flowers, fruit baskets and candy jars that [actor] Drake Hogestyn received at the "Days" studio recently from fans. I would like to clarify one point: The fans did not send these arrangements to "John Black" in sympathy over "Isabella's" death; they were sent to Drake personally to compliment him on the outstanding performance that he gave throughout the entire storyline. (*Soap Opera Update* 1993c:15)

Most serious scholarship agrees that fans do not lose touch with reality but rather come to see fictional characters as simultaneously real and constructed (Brown 1987; Jenkins 1992b). Fans realize that they are watching something fictional; but they are able to approach and read the characters as real people, which contributes to the pleasure of viewing.

Like members of other subcultures (see Fine 1983), daytime fans implicitly agree to bracket the real world when gossiping about the fictional world:

> [Soap] fans are quite playful when they talk about characters as real. . . . [Most fans do not really] believe that the characters are "real," but most are willing to speak of them as if they were, discussing them, for example, on a first name basis, and speculating at length on future directions on the show. (Brown 1987:15)

Without question, excessive fanship does exist. But what is meant by "excessive"?[7] Sometimes it involves considerations of time, energy, and money fans devote to their interests. Fans can spend hundreds of dollars on magazines, videotapes and sophisticated video equipment; invest considerable time and money in trips to celebrity appearances; maintain video libraries containing hundreds of tapes; create scrapbooks of celebrity photos (one respondent is currently working on her seventh); and make frantic requests to strangers in other time zones to videotape for them during national emergencies or feared cancellations (the emergence and popularity of electronic bulletin boards has greatly facilitated this videotape exchange network). One woman told us about a co-worker who "hasn't had lunch in years" because she drives home every day during the noon hour to make sure her VCR is taping properly, and about another friend who strolls by the local appliance store window when she knows all the television display sets will be turned to *Days of Our Lives*.

If fans' personal investments can easily reach a level nonfans would label excessive, where do fans themselves draw the line? One respondent reasons, "If it doesn't hurt anybody, I can afford it, and it's something I want to do, why not do it?" When it comes to how a fan allocates personal resources, the line is often viewed as the point at which their activities are injurious to themselves or others or are no longer a source of pleasure. To these fans, their activities are excessive only because others label them as such.

For fans whose interests lie in meeting or observing celebrities in everyday settings, drawing the line entails recognizing a boundary between acceptable behavior and stalking. One fan among our respondents is quite explicit about the boundary:

The other activity I have become involved with is what we jokingly refer to as "stalking": we will stand outside the studio and wait for the stars to come outside during their lunch break. I guess our use of the word "stalking" comes from our ambivalence about what we are doing. I know that I am not dangerous or obsessive, but I wouldn't blame the actors if they thought I was. I have done this only a few times, and never alone.

But as an indicator of excessive fanship in our data, talk about stalking behavior is rare. Much more frequent are fans' characterizations of their own viewing habits as obsessive or addictive, as these responses show:

I believe I'm addicted to soaps, days' and nights'. I record all of CBS and record all of NBC and watch ABC when I can. My life is revolved around soaps. I stay up until 3:00 A.M. watching soaps and get upset if I miss one day.

I haven't missed *Days* in 1 year! Not 1 day! And I never will. It's not like a soap opera to me, it's more like real life; I cry with them, also laugh and screech! I've shared their goods and bads, ups and downs, and births and deaths.

I am absolutely addicted to them. I realize that they are unrealistic, yet I cannot keep from watching them. . . . I would go nuts if I missed [them]. If I didn't work I probably would do nothing but sit around, watch soaps, and get fat.

I am the most crazed person I know. I buy every soap magazine on the market. . . . I play my favorite episodes over and over again until they are firmly embedded in my memory. . . . I have structured my existence around *Santa Barbara*. . . . I shudder to think of the harsh reality of cancellation. I would die.

Another fan wonders why she continues to watch *Days of Our Lives* despite her frequent complaints about "all of its flaws":

I don't know, it's that t-i-n-y glimmer of hope that they will somehow manage to pull it all together and be good again. It has become a marathon thing now — how many months of bad story lines and unappealing characters can they manage before I finally give up the ghost. . . . I used to watch *Another World* by default because my sister did, but really only wanted to see *Days*. Now the shoe is on the other foot. I "suffer" through *Days* to get to *AW* which has . . . lots of interesting characters and story lines right now . . . B-U-T, at the same time, I can't quite stop watching the drivel in the preceding hour. I guess that's what it means to be hooked!

Can soap operas, or any form of television for that matter, really be addictive? Research suggests not. A recent study (McIlwraith et al. 1991; see also Finn 1992) examined whether television watching could be addictive according to the clinical model of addiction put forth by the American Psychiatric Association. The authors responded to research claiming that television use might fulfill up to five of the criteria for addiction (see Kubey 1990):

(1) Substance often taken in larger amounts or over a longer period than the person intended;

(2) The person realizes that substance use is excessive and has attempted to control it but has been unable to do so;

(3) Important social, occupational, or recreational activities are given up or reduced because of substance use;

(4) With heavy and prolonged use, a variety of . . . problems can occur and are exacerbated by continued use of the substance;

(5) With continued use, characteristic withdrawal symptoms develop when the person stops or reduces intake of the substance. (*Diagnostic and Statistical Manual of Mental Disorders-III-Revised* 1987, quoted in McIlwraith et al. 1991:106–107)

After reviewing a wide range of evidence, the authors found no difference between self-proclaimed addicts and nonaddicts in terms of their uses and responses to television and concluded that there is little evidence to suggest that people can become clinically addicted to or obsessed with any form of television, including soap operas (McIlwraith et al. 1991:118).

Most fans who talk about being obsessed by soaps do so in a humorous and self-deprecating manner. They laugh about bewildered spouses, children, co-workers and friends who don't understand the pleasure they get from daytime television. One BBS subscriber revealed:

> I used to just give my husband dirty looks when he commented on my infatuation with this thing, and then one day I decided to challenge him with something like, "You, the guy who runs around after little white balls, talking about hooks and bogies and subscribing to five, count them, five golf magazines, SHOULD understand about hobbies."

Most fans are comfortable with their choice of soap watching as a leisure activity, even though they might not express it openly. Only a few seem truly concerned about their investment in daytime serials. One respondent who initially questioned herself about her interest in the Jack and Jennifer romance on *Days of Our Lives* decided that her self-doubt was unwarranted since she was enjoying herself so much. Another woman who has met a number of daytime and movie celebrities sometimes worries that she fits the lunatic fan image: "I literally have to control myself . . . so I won't act [crazy]." When we asked why she likes to meet celebrities, she got very excited and said, "Just that [you find out] they're real, they really ARE real, and you can TOUCH them." She laughs and says she's glad she doesn't have time to attend many fan events, because she doesn't want to find out that she "really *is* crazy."

Some scholars believe that merely being a popular-culture fan indicates psychological disturbance, some even arguing that soaps are so real to fans that "psychotherapists are finding [them] to be a convenient point of entry into the minds of troubled patients" (Fowles 1992:172). Both the academic and popular presses have characterized celebrity-fan relationships as instances of erotomania, a psychiatric disorder in which someone has a delusional and idealized romantic fixation on another person (*Diagnostic and Statistical Manual of Disorders-III-Revised* 1987:199). In most cases, the erotomaniac is a female with low self-esteem who mistakenly believes that a man of higher social status (such as a celebrity) is in love with her (Dunlop 1988; Meloy 1989). In a recent study of celebrity-fan erotomania, a criminologist reported on 214 people who wrote to

CHAPTER THREE / 110

celebrities. In his analysis, 16 percent had erotomaniac delusions and 5 percent (eleven people) actually believed they were married to the celebrity (in Meloy 1989:479). (It is important to note that even among people diagnosed as clinically erotomaniac, only 5 percent ever become violent [Meloy 1992:22], a finding that disputes the widely held assumption that all fans are potential stalkers.)

While scholars seem to be backing off from widespread characterization of celebrity-fan relationships as clinically erotomaniacal, a condition called "borderline erotomania" is increasingly being used as a framework for analyzing some forms of excessive or unusual fan behavior. Borderline erotomaniacs are not delusional but often have distorted interpersonal attachments. Rather than actually believing that the fictional is real, they intentionally (and consciously) blend reality and fantasy (Meloy 1992:29).

As a possible example, consider the experiences of Sandra and Phyllis described at the beginning of this chapter. Despite their excessive involvement with *Days of Our Lives,* the "idealized romance" that the women invested in was *not* between themselves and the actors (as would be the case with an erotomaniac), but rather between the actors and the characters they portray. Both women, captivated by the romance of Patch and Kayla, wanted the actors who played them (Steven Nichols and Mary Beth Evans) to become romantically involved offscreen. They felt that Evans and Nichols had such incredible chemistry together as actors that it only "seemed right" that they be a couple both on and off camera. To that end, Phyllis and Sandra joined a *Days of Our Lives* support group that functioned in part to initiate false rumors within the production industry and the fan community that the actors were indeed dating, all in hopes of having the fictional romance come true.

While these fans' attachment to *Days of Our Lives* is intense, it does not indicate erotomania. At no time did the women confuse fiction with reality, either unconsciously (as in clinical erotomania) or consciously (as in borderline erotomania). They stated emphatically that they knew at all times the difference between Evans/Nichols and Kayla/Patch. More important, however, even if they had intentionally and consciously blurred reality and fantasy, isn't such behavior a common element in many forms of textual consumption and the activities that surround them (see Brown 1987; Jenkins 1992b)? In other words, borderline erotomania suggests that blurring the boundaries between the real and not real indicates psychological disturbance. Given that most (if not all) viewers and fans play with these boundaries, are we all borderline erotomaniacs?

This zone that borders the real and the fictional is a key site not of mania but of pleasure for consumers of soap operas (and of all other texts). The daytime industry is well aware of this, and, as we have already shown, secondary texts in particular orient to and play with this transitional zone of experience. Both Sandra and Phyllis blame the daytime industry for their excessive fan behavior and claim that the soap format causes viewers pain. According to Sandra, "I think they really want to hurt people. . . . [They] set fans up by saying 'always' and 'forever' but never follow through on the promise." An inevitable component of daytime television, broken promises are especially likely in stories involving what the industry has termed Super Couples. These were a mainstay on *Days of Our Lives* in the 1980s during the height of the Patch and Kayla story line; while popular with viewers, Super Couples complicate story telling:

> Because the couple's relationship is perfect and neither one would ever do anything to jeopardize it . . . the characters cannot move with the stream of other characters in looping and intersecting plotlines which are always essentially about the process and progress of relationships. The producer then has no story for the most popular couple on the program. (Reep 1992:99)

By idealizing Patch and Kayla as a romantic couple with unshakable love between them and destined for a future of unbridled happiness, producers and writers boxed themselves into a corner and disappointed viewers. Sandra and Phyllis feel that producers should be more aware of the intense involvement people have with fictional characters and more consciously avoid causing viewers and fans emotional anguish.[8] According to Phyllis, producers do not understand how soaps "can make you ache and hurt and how your life can be affected." Both women suspect that there are other viewers who are as intensely involved with soap operas as they were with *Days of Our Lives.*

## Normal Fans and the Viewer/Fan Continuum

While most scholars agree on what an abnormal fan looks like (a desperate loner or psychopathic stalker), there is little understanding of what constitutes normal fanship. According to most accounts, to be a fan is to be abnormal: the normal fan is a lunatic fan. While this presumption is especially strong in terms of soap fans, it holds true for all forms of media fans, including fans of prime-time television and feature films. Consider, for example, the letter-writing campaign waged by Viewers for Quality Television (VQT), a generally well respected viewer advocacy group, to persuade network officials to renew the low-rated *Cagney and Lacey*. Rather than simply dismissing VQT (a common response to fan campaigns), the show's producer supported members' efforts by defining the letter writers as *atypical* fans: "These [letters] were not the traditional fan letters written in Crayola by people saying, 'I kiss my pillow every night thinking of you.' They were affluent, well-educated people. There were petitions from working women and college students" (Brower 1992:170). Only as "nonfans" could they and their efforts be legitimized. *Twin Peaks* fans who waged a similar campaign were also granted legitimacy by the show's producers, who saw them as different from (better than) most fans. Both cases illustrate the industry's perception of the (abnormal) fan of daytime television and the (normal) fan (or, rather, nonfan) of prime-time and feature films.

If daytime fanship is inherently abnormal, how can we conceptualize a normal fan? Some say that "as long as the fan shows 'good common sense,' remains 'rational' and 'in control,' " then he or she is normal (Jensen 1992:18). Yet no one studies normal fans; our most basic assumptions about fans have not been examined. Scholarly literature depicts fans as members of marginalized subgroups (e.g., Bacon-Smith 1992) or, more often, treats normal fans as a known category, using them as reference points for a discussion of excessive fanship (e.g., Schickel 1985).

The inability to conceptualize normal fanship seems largely a result of the dichotomization of fan and nonfan. Scholars assume a clear-cut boundary between the two, "strongly marked and patrolled" (Fiske 1992: 34–35; see also Grossberg 1992a; Jenkins 1992b; Jensen 1992). Fans and nonfans alike know that the boundary exists, and both are invested in its maintenance. Nonfans want to avoid the "taint of fandom" (Fiske 1992:35), and fans want to ensure that only those with similar tastes and interests enter their community. Self-identifying as a fan creates an Us versus Them distinction in fans' minds (Grossberg 1992a). This is clearly illustrated in the science fiction filking (song) community, whose members relish creating songs that poke fun at the presumed ignorance and lack of creativity of nonfans (Jenkins 1992a). The scorn nonfans hold for fans is returned.

Yet, this distinction between fan and nonfan seems too clear-cut. The dichotomy makes sense if fanship is defined solely in terms of participation in fan activities (so that the question becomes merely, Does she participate or doesn't she?). However, when fanship is conceptualized as incorporating parallel processes of identity and activity, the distinction based on participation falls apart. We thus argue instead for the existence of a viewer/fan continuum, marked on either end by the categories of nonfan and abnormal (excessive) fan, with involved viewers and normal fans as points in between. There are several ways in which individuals could be located on a viewer-to-fan continuum. Our proposal is not intended to be a complete guide to all points of the continuum; rather, it serves to illustrate the nuances of viewership and fanship that are largely overlooked.

As we talked with respondents about why they watch soap operas and what they enjoy and don't enjoy about their favorite shows, there emerged a difference between what we call "breadth" viewers/fans and "depth" viewers/fans. Breadth respondents are loyal to the serial genre as a whole rather than to a specific program, actor, or writer. They drop in and out of daytime communities: one day they might watch *As the World Turns,* the next day *Another World,* and the following day the entire CBS lineup. If a show is not sufficiently entertaining or they are bored with a story line that drags on interminably, they simply pick up a new program. One woman told us she cannot understand how people can watch the same show for years. She compares soaps to novels: just as she stops reading a novel when it becomes boring, so does she switch to a new program during slow story lines. Others say that it does not bother them if they misprogram their VCR and tape a different show than intended; they will watch it anyway. It matters more that *a* soap is watched than that a *specific* soap is watched. Breadth viewers' loyalty lies with the soap genre as a whole.

For depth viewers, this behavior is incomprehensible. Depth viewers tend to be loyal (*very* loyal) to a specific show and cannot imagine dipping in and out or simply dropping one program for another. They may become interested in other soaps, but they do not discard their favorite. As one respondent declared, "I'll *always* watch *All My Children*." Depth viewers have patience during sluggish weeks (or months or years), because they have faith that the show will eventually improve. Longtime depth viewers can easily replay a serial's history in their minds and talk of entire months and years when a soap was "up" or "down." They evaluate a show in terms of long-term cycles, in contrast to breadth viewers for whom immediate gratification must be in sight or the show will be abandoned. Gratifications in watching serials can be immediate (such as switching channels and stopping to watch an attractive actor), short-term (watching the resolution of a subplot), or long-term (watching long-projected story lines unfold [Kielwasser and Wolf 1989]). Long-term gratifications are generally only available to depth viewers.

A second factor that helps locate a person on the viewer/fan continuum is orientation or position of access (Whetmore and Kielwasser 1983). As we mentioned earlier, people are oriented to a wide range of factors when watching serials: the acting, dialogue, character or story line development, direction, set design, lighting, and so on. Viewers engage a serial through a potentially infinite number of access points, and the element(s) to which they are attuned help define and shape their viewership/fanship.

Many of our respondents focus on acting and writing skills and are unconcerned over story/character development as long as the quality of the acting and dialogue remains high. As one woman said, bad acting can make "any story line unbelievable and unwatchable." These viewers often have little patience for watchers unappreciative of the talent displayed on the screen. Others, invested entirely in character and story line, care little about the nuances of writing, directing, and acting as long as the story unfolds in a pleasurable way. They are loyal to a specific actor only in his or

her portrayal of a favorite character. This group of viewers complains bit-
terly about recasting efforts, equating loss of actor with loss of character.

This difference in orientation creates a subtle barrier between viewers
that is often overlooked by those in the production industry but is highly
significant to those viewers for whom soaps are intensely personal. One
female viewer oriented to quality of acting finds it difficult to talk with
other viewers because so few are attuned to the same things as she. For
her, talking with most fans is like talking on different levels or different
tracks; "we all see everything differently." She finds it uncomfortable and
emotionally painful to talk with other viewers because it is distressing
when they fail to read the show the way she does. The difference in orientation blocks communication, even between viewers equally devoted to
the same show.

A third factor that helps locate viewers and fans on the continuum is the
particular show(s) they watch. Those with little understanding of (or interest in) the serial genre see no difference between viewing one show and
viewing another: one is simply a soap watcher (Derry 1985:87). For
insiders, however, different shows excel in different ways and thus are
known to attract different types of viewers and fans. *Days of Our Lives,*
for example, was known for its glorification of the romantic Super Couple,
while *General Hospital* introduced science fiction elements to the genre in
the early 1980s and is widely credited with attracting increasing numbers
of male viewers to soaps.[9] Some serials have the reputation of being solidly
family oriented (such as *Guiding Light* and *All My Children*), while *Santa
Barbara* was known for its eccentric story lines and characters.

Because different story emphases attract different types of viewers,
within the industry, which show(s) a person watches is considered indicative of the type of fan one might be. For instance, viewers and fans of *Days
of Our Lives* have a well-known (and disparaged) reputation within the
industry for being excessively loyal to (and vocal about) *Days* actors,
characters, and story lines. While the show is neither top rated nor critically acclaimed, *Days* fans are the most publicly devoted of all soap fans.
For example, *Soap Opera Digest* regularly reports on which program
elicits the most letters per two-week period, and *Days* tops the list vir-

tually every time. For these viewers, Nielsen ratings or critics' opinions matter little: *Days* is number one to them.

Some respondents use *Days* fans' reputation as a reference point for interpreting a range of viewer and fan activities. The editor of a fan publication told us that letters from *Days* fans "rant and rave" about story line or character treatment but lack sophistication and a focus on constructive solutions. Fans of *The Young and the Restless,* on the other hand, write quality letters revealing knowledge of production intent and suggesting resolutions for story-line complexities. This editor found it easy to spot *Days* fans by their one-dimensional letters concerned only with defending the show. Other fans characterize *Days* viewers as more likely to be out of control at organized events than fans of other shows. Having such a reputation, *Days* fans are often put in the unenviable position of being the yardstick against which all other fans are measured.[10]

In addition to breadth versus depth, direction of orientation, or difference in program(s) viewed, viewers and fans can be distinguished from each other in innumerable ways. Do they save videotapes or reuse them? Do they watch scenes or programs more than once? Do they self-identify as fans yet participate in no formally recognized fan activities? Do they stockpile magazines or give them to friends? Do they buy magazines at all? Do they scour fan and trade publications for inside information and story-line scoops, or would they rather be surprised by events as they air? Do they post urgent electronic mail messages when a program has been preempted or could they not care less? Answers to such questions can provide clues as to where someone might be located on a continuum of viewer/fan activity and identity.

Clearly, engaging in fan activity does not by itself define one as a fan nor does not engaging in fan activity define one as a mere viewer or nonfan. The dichotomous relationship between viewer and fan (and fan and nonfan) that is repeatedly posed in the literature obscures the richly complex differences among serial followers. The difference between viewer and fan is not marked by a single point; rather, viewership merges into fanship along the dimensions of activity engagement and identity management. To fully appreciate what it means to be a fan, we need to recognize the possibility of the viewer/fan continuum.

## The Public/Private Continuum

Rethinking the distinction between viewer and fan requires that we also rethink the distinction between private and public activities. Viewing is usually considered an activity located in the private, domestic sphere, while to be a fan is to publicly declare one's loyalty to a cultural text. We have argued, however, that fanship is a process of activity *and* identity: one can privately self-identify as a fan without openly engaging in fan activities and can participate in activities without considering oneself a fan. To call viewing private and fanship public is an oversimplification. Private forms of culture are not necessarily private in the usual sense of being individual or personal; rather, they are also shared in a social community (Johnson 1986/87:50). They might have limited general accessibility but are embedded in consumers' everyday lives. Understanding private and public as end points on a continuum is the logical extension of the viewer/fan continuum. Just as viewership merges into fanship, so do private uses of cultural objects merge into public ones.

Recent work on the social impact of electronic media by Joshua Meyrowitz (1985) offers clues for how to reconceptualize the public and private. Different modern media forms, including television, have rearranged social life so that "where we are physically no longer determines where and who we are socially" (115). Television has weakened the relationship between social situation and physical space and collapsed social spheres that were once distinct, merging "formerly private spheres into formerly public ones" (93). As the distinction between public/private becomes increasingly conflated, we can conceptualize two new spheres of experience: the private/public and the public/public. The private/public realm includes events that involve public actions but are isolated in a specific time-space frame, while the public/public realm encompasses events carried beyond the time-space frame by electronic media (287). Each sphere encompasses a unique relationship between action, time, and space.

These concepts can be adapted to the distinction between viewership and fanship. We suggest that viewer/fan activities located in the private/public sphere include those that take place in the domestic arena (such as individual or family viewing, gossiping with friends or family, or creating a scrapbook), are enacted individually although in a public setting (such as buying a fan magazine or exchanging videotapes through an advertised network), or engage a public institution but remain invisible to the general public (such as writing letters to those in the production industry). Private/public activities are publicly accessible but perhaps not publicly recognizable or noticeable, such as attending a fan club luncheon. In her work on homoerotic science fiction fandom, for example, Camille Bacon-Smith (1992) tells a story of several women at a science fiction convention monitoring a table outside of the convention hall who are approached by a man asking what is happening inside. The women smile sweetly and report (falsely) that it's a meeting of a ladies' literary society. In this case, the convention is taking place in a public setting, but its meaning remains private.

Finally, public/public activities include those forms of fanship open to public scrutiny and public condemnation (such as celebrity mall appearances, fan appearances at on-location tapings, or the occasional celebrity stalker) and falsely believed by most to constitute the entire range of media fanship. While most enactments of viewership and fanship are located in the private/public sphere, the visibility of public/public activities contributes to the continued misunderstanding and stigmatization of soap viewing, fanship, and fandom.

# Chapter Four

## Entering the Wild Zone

One longtime fan speaks eloquently about the various pleasures she finds in soap operas:

> Sometimes the actors and characters blend into a believability so strong you almost feel like you're eavesdropping on real lives and it is fascinating to watch them work through their problems and their relationships. That's when viewers remember dialogue, action, great detail from those scenes. That is the best reason for watching a serial. Even when a serial is done badly I may watch it in hopes it will recover and provide more of those great moments. Great moments are rare. Then there are the lesser pleasures. Chatting with a friend about a soap has the satisfaction of gossip without the guilt because the people aren't real and can't be hurt or betrayed by what one says about them. The challenge of guessing which direction a plot or character will be taken can cause endless speculation and fun. The private lives and career patterns of the actors, directors, producers, and network people can be more interesting than what goes on the air . . . often full of intrigue, drama, and passion. In this case the gossip goes with a little dash of guilt because these *are* real people, but people far removed from us or our circle of influence. . . . It can be fun to keep track of props — sheets that were on the heroine's bed turn up on someone else's bed. China moves from newlywed's apartment to villain's Greek villa. . . . Sometimes there is the reassuring familiarity of a long-running soap — no matter where you are or what's happening in your life there's good old Tom and Alice Horton or Rachel Cory or whoever are the anchor char-

acters of your favorite show proving that people do survive grief, pain, sorrow, poverty, betrayal, separation, or whatever and continue to have moments of love, fun, satisfaction, and triumph. Then there is the nagging curiosity to see what will happen next.

The pleasures of soap watching are complex, and the value of these pleasures — as with all leisure activities — remains a focus of debate. While the pleasures derived from some activities are socially acceptable, those from popular culture are always suspect. Why do we play video games or go to movies or read comics or get hooked on daytime television? What do we get out of them?

Criticism directed at soap opera pleasures dates back to soaps' radio days, with attacks coming from psychiatrists in scientific journals and from the popular press. Even to informed observers, soap operas are an enigma. In his bemused analysis of daytime serials, James Thurber (1948) put considerable effort into capturing their complexity, while social scientists resorted to psychological tests of a group of female listeners to ascertain "what the daytime serial is as a symbol system, and how its symbols functioned in the public and private lives of the women who listened" (Warner and Henry 1948:7). In more recent work, soap opera's pleasures have been explained in a number of contradictory ways. Some researchers locate viewers' pleasure in psychological identification with and fantasy about characters and narratives (Ang 1985; Brown 1987; Kaplan 1986; Walkerdine 1986). Some argue that repetitive consumption of traditional feminine texts provides a means of resisting or coopting patriarchal discourse (Brown 1987; Hansen 1991; Modleski 1983; Press 1991; Radway 1984; Seiter et al. 1989). Some believe that pleasure is rooted in familiarity and ritual, as daytime serials become integrated into the rhythms of women's daily lives (Brown 1987; Brunsdon 1989; Modleski 1983). Finally, some scholars suggest that pleasure is built into the generic structure itself: the gradually unfolding narrative provides layers of gratifications for viewers (Barthes 1975; Kielwasser and Wolf 1989).

Each of these perspectives assumes that the pleasure of consumption serves some extrinsic need. Why not pleasure for pleasure's sake? Instead of treating pleasure as something to be explained away, can it be understood on its own terms (Csikszentmihalyi 1975; see also Ang 1985; Press 1991)? We adapt the term "wild zone" from Elaine Showalter (Williams 1985) to refer to the realm of intense pleasure surrounding both viewership, where pleasures have been extensively documented, and fanship, where pleasures remain a mystery.

We should emphasize at the outset that the pleasure can be so intense that it almost cannot be articulated by those experiencing it. We were struck repeatedly in our interviews and informal conversations with fans by the strength of their passion for, devotion to, and sheer love of daytime television, to an extent often beyond their own comprehension. These pleasures are nearly as elusive for analysts who risk converting them to rational and intellectual experiences, leaving enjoyment itself unexplained (Walkerdine 1986). Feminist film and literary theorists successfully anticipate the space between text and viewer in which fantasy resides, but they underconceptualize viewers' experiences with pleasure.[1] Furthermore, their insights might be inapplicable to soap opera viewing, which is more complex in its textuality and subjectivity than most media forms. Soap operas simultaneously engage and distance the viewer, juxtapose fiction with realism, and create characters that are both the objects of spectacle and our emotional representatives (Geraghty 1991). Soaps refuse single-character identification by positioning the viewer in the process of the narrative instead of capturing the viewer within it (Brown 1987; Kaplan 1983). In addition, soap viewing takes place within the context of an industry that intentionally blurs not only the boundary between reality and fiction, but also that between private and public interests. We must remember that soap opera pleasures are socially as well as psychologically constructed phenomena, based upon satisfaction from viewer presence in the text as well as absence and engaged through active reader positions as well as passive ones (Brown 1987).

Because females have historically made up the soap opera audience, much of the existing literature on soap pleasures focuses specifically upon female pleasures. Our discussion is thus constrained by that. However, in our own exploration of fans, we focus upon both men's and women's pleasures, seeking to integrate these in our perspective on contemporary pleasures.

Dimensions of Pleasure: Identification, the Familiar,
Resistance, and Genre

## IDENTIFICATION AND FANTASY

Some consumers of feminine texts find pleasure through a process of
psychological identification. Pleasure is rooted in the ability to fantasize,
and through fantasizing to identify with some aspect of the narrative: the
heroine, the love story, or the life-style in general.[2] This is especially likely
in terms of character identification. The ability to imagine the characters
as real people and to identify with them is a necessary precondition for
engagement in serials and an anchor for viewer pleasure (Ang 1985:30).[3]

Soap operas thus succeed because they fulfill the psychological needs of
female viewers looking for fantasy and escape from their everyday lives. A
fan told us, "Of course, I watch soaps for entertainment and escapism!
They provide hours of enjoyment and relaxation, especially at the end of a
hectic day!" The element of fantasy is intricately tied up with that daytime
staple, romance. Almost half of our respondents (42 percent) prefer love
stories to all other kinds of narratives, and some use fictional narratives as
a way to make sense of their own relationship choices (Press 1991:70;
Seiter et al. 1989:236). One single woman in her late twenties interprets
her romantic life in light of that of her favorite on-screen couple (the
actors are also married in real life):

> I just find it intriguing, like a storybook actually, that two such attrac-
> tive people really do exist in the real world as in the soap world. It's
> like there is romance in life as well as in fiction. A love like Heathcliff's
> and Catherine's might really exist out there somewhere and it makes
> me think [of] my own life. Like do you settle for a guy you get along
> with real well or do you wait for someone who scintillates you? If I
> didn't think couples could really sizzle, I would settle for someone I
> just liked, but because couples like this make me think real passion can
> be found, I think twice.

Viewer identification extends beyond a simple identification with character or narrative to an almost transcendent emotional one. As does reading, soap viewing lets viewers "experience intense emotions unashamedly,

granting temporary release from the emotional limits of everyday life" (Rogers 1991:12). Similarly, soap viewers identify with the subjective and emotional experience of the fictional world, with the "structure of feeling" embedded in the narrative (Ang 1985:45). Like those of most melodramatic texts, soaps' main effects are to evoke emotions and to glorify and exaggerate the emotional meaning of everyday life. Making the ordinariness of life special dissipates viewers' own dissatisfactions, at least temporarily (Ang 1985:80).

The emotional pleasure of soaps comes through most clearly in respondents' explanations of why they would rather watch their shows alone than with company:

I usually prefer to watch alone. With others one must constantly comment or seem unsociable and that distracts from "falling into" the action.

If the episode is a good one . . . I prefer to watch undisturbed which usually means alone so I can get lost in the story as one does with a good book.

It makes for a better cry when a cry is called for.

I can react any way I like and not be considered weird or too involved with the characters.

A voyeuristic quality to witnessing the unfolding of intimate and emotional details from another's (albeit fictional) life is evident. What Sigmund Freud and others have termed *scopophilia,* the pleasure of looking, is the "fascination of watching without being watched, seeing without being seen" (Whetmore and Kielwasser 1983:112). Conceptualizing the female viewer as voyeur draws on Laura Mulvey's seminal article "Visual Pleasure and Narrative Cinema," in which she argues that Hollywood films perpetuate gender inequality by positioning the women as object of the male gaze; even female film viewers who take the active stance of the voyeur experience the passive stance of "to-be-looked-at-ness" (1975:11), inherently objects for other (male) spectators.

Mulvey has been criticized for making it difficult, if not impossible, to conceptualize the female viewer in any other way but as an absence. As Miriam Hansen (1991) asks, does aligning a desiring look with the position of the female rather than male viewer allow for an alternate perception of female pleasure? Hansen studied female fans of Rudolph Valentino and argued that his films' focus on the gaze itself as an erotic object (rather than on the source or object of the gaze) defeated the masculinization of the spectator position. Rather than signaling defensiveness about their viewing choices (see Williams 1992), soap viewers' preferences to watch their shows alone might indicate the active stance of the voyeur, not a passive object position. If we accept undistracted and concentrated viewing as the mode associated with (male) power (see Brunsdon 1981), we need to recognize female soap watchers as one of the only groups of television viewers who purposively and consciously adopt this mode.

Viewers who enter the fan world also find pleasure in fantasy and identification. As we have shown, a central site for creating the daytime subculture is celebrity, particularly the blurring of fiction and reality, character and actor. The soap industry, actors, and fans themselves have an investment in treating the fictional world as somehow real. The pleasures that viewers experience are incorporated into the fan's world, which helps explain why many fans treat the actors at formal events not as themselves but as the characters they portray. Indeed, many actors cooperate with fans' fantasies (and producers' requests) by being in character at public functions. This example of the collective or shared fantasy that is central to the creation of media and gaming subcultures entails an implicit agreement among participants (here, actors and fans) to manipulate the boundary between the real and the fictional (Fine 1983:183).

Despite fantasy's centrality to participants, its function has been oversimplified and misunderstood. We tend to think of fantasy as a simple process by which one places oneself in a narrative to escape the humdrum of ordinary life (Kaplan 1986). In this sense, fantasy bridges the distance between the (pleasurable) absent and the (unpleasurable) present (see Ang 1985). But fantasy itself is ridiculed, and fantasizers are often derided for spending time doing "unimportant" things (Fine 1983:5). This is especially true for women, whose engagement in romantic fantasy is considered particularly troubling. But fantasy *as such* is neither good nor bad;

it's simply part of human life (Kaplan 1986:153). Fantasy neither compensates for empty lives nor provides temporary flight from them but rather adds a crucial dimension to life in providing a setting for desire (Kaplan 1986:150). Why can't we take fantasy seriously as a reality in itself (Ang 1985)?

## THE PLEASURE OF THE FAMILIAR

Besides identification and fantasy, pleasure in viewing and fanship is rooted in viewers' familiarity with the genre and the integration of soap operas into everyday life. Every television genre implies a certain order and framework for expectations (Cawelti 1976; Fiske 1987; Kaminsky 1985). If we turn to a soap, we recognize it as a serial and know to anticipate a certain range of pleasures; we find emotional security in familiar formulas (Cawelti 1976:9). But while viewers recognize formulaic television, they are not passively sucked into the generic structure. Rather, they often object to and struggle with formulas as they generate meanings and interpretations of cultural objects. "Viewers develop a critical viewpoint that allows them to define a social space of their own" (Lembo and Tucker 1990:105).[4]

As mentioned earlier, the romance genre or formula on both radio and television is structured to correspond closely to women's lived experience, to the rhythms of women's lives (Modleski 1982). Indeed, the range of pleasures it offers is tailored to female viewers, and the genre itself is structured to facilitate women's (rather than men's) engagement with it. Elements such as the fragmentation of story lines, emphasis on domestic concerns, multiple narratives, and a unique camera style are designed to enhance women's viewing pleasure.

Part of the formula of serials—and a source of intense viewer pleasure—is that they offer daily involvement with fictional characters and communities. Through weeks, months, and years of watching daytime television, viewers come to feel that they know characters intimately (Bielby and Harrington 1992; Brunsdon 1989; Seiter et al. 1989), sometimes better than they know their own friends or family members because they have access to the most personal details of characters' lives. As one respondent explains:

I like soaps because they air *5 times* a week, instead of just once a week like night-time shows. This allows viewers to get a full understanding of [the] characters *gradually,* over a long period of time. I like the fact that many of the best actors on daytime stay on their shows for several years (sometimes decades!) which makes them like a "second family" — these characters have great familiarity to long-time viewers and give their show continuity.

Another respondent says that in watching soaps, she can witness a variety of people (characters) exhibiting a range of intensely personal emotions. In her own life, she rarely sees such emotional displays because they are reserved for only a few intimate friends and relatives. In addition, she says that real people often apologize for their emotional displays afterwards, whereas expressiveness is treated as a normal and acceptable occurrence in the soap world. Most viewers find it comforting to turn on the television daily and enter the familiar world of Salem, Port Charles, Oakdale, or Springfield. College students, for example, say that regular visits to their favorite soap world forestall homesickness. The viewer-character bonds that emerge through engagement with a familiar and pleasurable genre create a community of people coming together through shared interests.

## PLEASURE IN RESISTANCE

Another research perspective suggests that women find pleasure in conservative and potentially disempowering texts through readings that emphasize a feminist subtext chronicling women's resistance (Press 1991; Radway 1984). A diverse group of women can thus engage with texts that on the surface would seemingly *not* appeal to them. Resistance is revealed in part by women's decision to claim time for themselves: for reading a romance novel or watching a favorite daytime show rather than cooking or cleaning or taking care of others' needs. Many women refer to their leisure activities as something they have earned and are unapologetic in their decision to enjoy themselves. Some women are ambivalent about the conflict between work and leisure demands and their conscious choice of leisure over work, but for most the choice is guilt free (Seiter et al. 1989:230). Reading romances or watching soaps is thus a form of silent protest against the constraints of everyday life in a patriarchal culture (Radway 1984; see also Scott 1985).

A second type of resistance engendered through traditional feminine texts is personified in the women-centered community that emerges around them. Women engage with feminine texts "in a private, domestic space which is often characterized by the absence of men" (Seiter et al. 1989:244) (although, as mentioned earlier, the preferred setting for most viewers is not the absence of men but the absence of *everybody*). Central to the viewer/fan community and to the validation of feminine culture is gossip, which both reflects a denial of male-defined pleasure and serves as a source of independence for women. Through gossiping about soaps, women construct their own discourse as "a type of affective resistance to dominant ideology." This pleasure can be subversive because "the audience has taken into its own hands the power to use soaps as a resistive form" (Brown 1987:1–3, 10).

Women construct pleasures and meanings to be shared with others through a genre whose purpose (along with most forms of television) is to encourage viewers to adopt the passive role of product consumer:

> Soaps which are designed to reinforce existing social practices which
> isolate women and encourage them to buy as a source of pleasure, in-
> stead promote a women's community which gets pleasure from it-
> self. . . . [Women] then create their own discourse and their own
> pleasure from the text. (Brown 1987:10)

While female viewers might recognize the dominant discourses in serials and the focus placed on them as consumers (most of the commercials aired during the day continue to be for household products, emphasizing both women's roles as consumers and their traditional status as domestic laborers), they are still empowered through their interpersonal bonds with other women. Viewers thus have the dual capacity to participate in both patriarchal and feminine discourses (Showalter in Williams 1985).

Some say that women can play freely in the wild zone, but others argue that they pay a high price for attempting to resist patriarchal ideology. In her study of romance readers, Janice Radway (1984) argued that the pleasure women get from reading romance novels is largely compensatory. Romance reading provides women with imaginary solutions to real structural problems and is a poor substitute for real life. If women don't experience real pleasure in reading, but merely an illusion of pleasure (see Ang 1988:186), the time and energy invested only divert their collective attention from the real structural barriers that block their route to empowerment.

In addition, the resistant discourse women might create for themselves is silenced by the dominant culture through its stigmatization of feminine texts and their consumers. Women themselves participate in the silencing by keeping their identities and pleasures private: "The opportunity to produce meanings and pleasures by engaging with a discriminated popular text is 'paid for' by women's willingness to conceal these pleasures and meanings whenever the dominant discourse is spoken in a social setting" (Seiter et al. 1989:244). Female viewers and fans are thus caught in the classic double bind: do we reveal our pleasures and risk public derogation, or do we deny our identities and thus participate in our own oppression? To extend the earlier anecdote about female fans' reactions to a curious male onlooker at a science fiction convention held in a hotel ballroom:

> The community is open to anyone willing to participate, but closed to anyone who might jeer, or worse, blow the whistle. A man in a ten-gallon hat approaches and wants to know what is going on. There is a gleam in his eye: he sees only women about. . . . They all return his bravado with suspicion. Lois, in her late forties and looking very prim, looks up from her place at the registration table and smiles the smile of PTA mothers everywhere. "It's a meeting of the ladies literary society," she answers very properly. "Mighty nice," the ten-gallon hat responds. As he walks away, another voice at the table whispers: "And terrorist society." (Bacon-Smith 1992:3–4)

While Lois and her friends have managed to create a women-only space to experience and share what they find pleasurable, their readiness to conceal their activities from the ten-gallon hat permits the continued derogation of women's texts, and the disempowerment of those who find pleasure in them.

PLEASURES OF THE GENRE

Finally, viewer pleasure can be embedded in the narrative structure of daytime serials (Geraghty 1991). The relationship between the viewer and the content of a television program is similar to exchange relationships between real people, specifically the implicit agreement to maintain the relationship if enough rewards are received (Kielwasser and Wolf 1989: 112–113). Soap operas engender extreme loyalty and devotion in viewers at least partly because they maximize both quantity and quality of rewards over time. Pleasure is also embedded in the meaning of narratives themselves. While narratives entail an unveiling of the truth, the pleasure of the text lies less in the actual unveiling than in the *hope* of seeing truth unveiled. It is the relationship between what is shown and not shown that creates pleasure (Barthes 1975:11). Christine Geraghty (1991:19) observes that "the establishment of the truth, the aim of most narratives, is, in soaps, subject to conventions which quite overtly postpone resolution, making us aware that fiction is not the inevitable and uninterrupted revelation of the truth." Delays in resolution lead viewers and fans to enthusiastically and gleefully second-guess story lines. While fan gossip can function in different ways, collective speculation about upcoming events takes up the bulk of time spent talking about soaps and indeed seems most enjoyable to participants (Bielby and Harrington 1994; Harrington and Bielby 1995).

In fact, narrative speculation provides so much pleasure that viewers wrestle with whether or not to buy fan magazines, call information hot lines, or read newspaper synopses that reveal upcoming story lines. Although desperate to know what will happen next, some fans refuse to seek out readily available information to the extent of muting the television set and closing their eyes when commercials depicting upcoming events are aired. Fans argue among themselves about whether it is better to be surprised by events as they air or to know what will happen in advance. A recent *Wall Street Journal* article reported that even the staff at fan publications considers knowing about future plot twists a potential drawback of the job. Says one staffer, "It kind of ruins it for you" (Dolan 1992:A5).[5]

Fans also experience pleasure in the routine organization and structure of fan events. While each event provides its own unique pleasures, they are structured so similarly that fans are able to emotionally anticipate and gear up for certain portions of the program. We have attended or viewed videotapes of fan club luncheons for shows on all three networks, and the structure is virtually identical to our description in the first chapter: celebrities are introduced one by one to wild cheering, a lunch is served, entertainment of some sort follows, zillions of photos are taken, and an autograph session closes the event. The routine of fan activities, much like the familiarity of a formulaic narrative, allows fans to find pleasure in the anticipation of events.

While we have chosen to discuss separately these various bases for pleasure — identification and fantasy, resistance to dominant ideology, familiarity and ritual, and the generic structure — people experience pleasure in multiple ways, like the fan quoted at the beginning of the chapter. And there are other pleasures beyond those discussed here; for instance, some fans derive pleasure from a more detached relationship with the soap medium, which tends to be expressed as a preference for self-parody, excess, or camp within the narrative. It is in part pleasure's complexity and multifocality that make it so difficult for fans and analysts to articulate. It is not just that different audiences receive different pleasures, but that individuals experience a range of pleasures in soap operas. Does this imply that we ought not to worry about the abstract notion of pleasure because it is indeed so varied (Morley 1989)? Can a more general understanding of pleasure encompass these more specific pleasures? We are convinced that considerable value lies in understanding pleasure abstractly. While empirical studies have demonstrated the extent to which pleasure can be differentiated not only between individuals or social groups but also between each subsequent encounter with a cultural object, the pleasure experience itself is unifying. In other words, regardless of what people are engaging with or how that engagement is modified by social characteristics such as age, gender, class, or ethnicity, the affective experience is similar. Pleasure is pleasurable, regardless of how and why it is felt, or who is feeling it.

## Having Fun Is Fun

Instead of looking at enjoyment as something to be explained away, we should try to understand it on its own terms. An intrinsically rewarding experience, or "flow," produces a transcendent inner state "so enjoyable that people are sometimes willing to forsake a comfortable life for its sake"; in a state of flow, people make little distinction between the self and the environment, between stimulus and response, or between past, present, and future (Csikszentmihalyi 1975:37, 36). To be in flow is to be in harmony with one's deepest desires: to be, in fact, in ecstasy. In terms of experiencing ecstasy in fictional narratives, we draw on the work of Victor Nell, who studies pleasure in reading. Nell describes pleasurable or ludic reading as totally absorbing; it stands outside the boundaries of everyday life. Ludic readers prefer books that increase their "trance" potential, or the extent to which they can become "a temporary citizen of another world" through the power of the narrative (Nell 1988:77). The best vehicle for ludic reading is formulaic fiction such as westerns, detective novels, or romance novels. Just as the formula of soap operas structures possible viewer/fan pleasures, formulaic fiction permits the anticipation of enjoyable reading experiences, for readers familiar with the structure know they can get lost in the story.

Central to Nell's work is his belief that novels offer us alternative realities only because one gives them explicit permission to do so. The notion of control is crucial. One opens a novel (or turns on a soap or plays Dungeons and Dragons) because one *chooses* to, and the time spent playing in fictional worlds is subject to one's own will. Although Nell argues that television viewers aren't allowed the same control over the pacing and structure of programs as readers have over books, the emergence and popularity of VCRs has allowed viewers increasing control over how a show is watched; for soap viewers, the ability to fast-forward through commercials or uninteresting story lines and to replay favorite scenes is a key element of pleasure. Unlike most media theorists who posit a barrier between subject and object, we believe that soap watching (like reading or fantasy gaming) is simultaneously a spectator and participant activity. It is participatory in that the story and the alternative world do not exist until we consciously and actively engage the text (Nell 1988:3); it is a spectator activity in that we necessarily adopt a bordered position to the fictional world. The pleasure resides in the conscious decision to bracket the real and enter the fictional. Viewers can thus approach texts from an emotional position of aesthetic distance that allows them to be both observer and participant in the action. "At aesthetic distance, there is a balance of thought and feeling. There is deep emotional resonance, but also a feeling of control" (Scheff 1979:64).

This dance between realms of experience — between living only in the present and simultaneously experiencing the past, present, and future; between being grounded in the real world and having the freedom to live in multiple worlds — creates space for the wild zone of pleasure. As television viewers negotiate with cultural texts, they create free spaces where "novel types of cultural creation, communication, and self-understanding may develop" (Lembo and Tucker 1990:103). Ronald Lembo and Kenneth Tucker (1990) suggest a link between the concept of free spaces and psychoanalytic theories of development that focus on infants' capacities to experience the real and the fictional simultaneously and unproblematically. While they refer to this linkage only briefly and do not explore how it might apply to adult experiences, they have pointed to what may be a key element to understanding this form of pleasure.

Earlier work had begun to consider how fantasy, pleasure, and controlled distance are associated with soap opera viewing. Ien Ang's (1985) initial work on viewers of *Dallas* established that they are well aware that their pleasures come from playing with the boundary between reality and fiction in a state of "controlled self-delusion." In later work, Ang (1990: 83) tied pleasure to the "large *emotional involvement* which is invested in identification with characters of popular fiction. . . . [The characters] do not function as role models but are symbolic realizations . . . with which viewers can identify *in fantasy*."

In a modification of these findings, others suggest that a source of pleasure is based upon

an implication with characters which is more complicated than identification. An implicatory reading would imply that the audience chooses a reading position which recognizes discursive possibilities in character types — the villainess, the ingenue, the good mother — but at the same time is intensely involved with the characters. Implication as a reading strategy, then, is audience controlled and there is active pleasure. (Brown 1987:19)

Active engagement contributes to viewing pleasures; gossip and other social aspects of the oral culture surrounding soap operas are an important means through which viewers engage and control their fantasies (Brown 1989). Familiarity with the conventions of the genre creates pleasure by facilitating "the ability of the audience to distance itself from the programmes, to step back and comment on how the fiction is created" (Geraghty 1991:19).

While these ideas about pleasure suggest some avenues for further theorizing, they do not themselves provide a unified approach to understanding what contributes to soap opera pleasures. They focus on pleasure as an entity and largely ignore the *process* by which pleasure is created by fans. We offer three proposals concerning that process: that a key form of pleasure is rooted in activities and experiences that allow individuals to challenge the boundaries between internal and external realities; that viewer and fan pleasures are linked to specific affects, particularly limerence, the feeling of being in love (Tennov 1979); and that several aspects of contemporary society help explain the particular pleasures enjoyed by soap followers.

## Soap Operas as Transitional Phenomena

Following other researchers (Lembo and Tucker 1990), we draw on a branch of psychoanalysis called object-relations theory, which is broadly defined as

attempts within psychoanalysis . . . to confront the potentially confounding observation that people live simultaneously in an external and an internal world, and that the relationship between the two ranges from the most fluid intermingling to the most rigid separation. [Object-relations theories are] concerned with exploring the relationship between real, external people, and internal images. (Greenberg and Mitchell 1983:11–12)

How do individuals manage the relationship between internal and external worlds? D. W. Winnicott (1971) proposes three realms of life: inner reality, external life, and an intermediate area of experiencing that keeps the inner and outer worlds separate yet interrelated. The intermediate realm is "another area of experience which is neither inside nor outside, but in between" (Rayner 1991:60). Winnicott links this realm to a specific stage in which infants first develop the capacity to perceive of the self as both subject and object. This stage, which occurs between four and twelve months of age, is characterized by the appearance of transitional phenomena. These are material objects to which an infant becomes attached (such as a blanket), yet which the infant does not fully understand as belonging to external reality. "The transitional object is *not an internal object* (which is a mental concept) — it is a possession. Yet it is not (for the infant) an external object either" (Winnicott 1971:9). These phenomena gradually lose meaning for the infant as development and maturation proceed.

Most important for our purposes is Winnicott's assertion that even though transitional objects are primarily associated with a specific stage of infant development, people never stop negotiating the boundaries between objective and subjective, real and fictional, even as mature adults: "No human being is free from the strain of relating inner and outer reality. . . . Relief from this strain is provided by an intermediate area of experience . . . which is not challenged" (Winnicott 1971:13). Regardless of age, the links to creativity are explicit. "Play, artistic creativity, and appreciation are the direct, natural successors to the early good transitional objects; all require the capacity for creative 'magical illusion' " (Deri 1978:53).

Yet children and adults experience and use transitional phenomena differently. Children can become attached to virtually any object and have it function as a transitional object, while adults are granted legitimacy to experience the intermediate world only in overtly creative realms of social life such as the arts or religion (Winnicott 1971:2). Additionally, while

infants are granted the freedom to fully experience objects as simultaneously real and not real, if adults were to insist that their transitional
phenomena are real we would call them crazy, despite the naturalness of
these phenomena in adulthood (15). As adults we are expected to know
the difference between internal and external realities even if we do manipulate the boundaries. The fear of being labeled crazy leads us to hide our
engagement with intermediate realms from others; instead, we experience
them privately (14).

Lembo and Tucker (1990) suggest that television might serve as a transitional object for adult viewers, evidenced at the most basic level by the
fact that people watch an astounding amount of television yet routinely
deny its centrality in their lives. We agree, and we propose that soap
operas are uniquely structured to function in this manner. As we have already discussed, the nature of the soap genre lends itself to intense viewer
attachment and involvement, more than any other televisual form. While
many genres aim at fictionalizing the real, serials are uniquely situated to
offer a fictional community to viewers who then, quite knowledgeably,
bounce the real off the fictional and the fictional off the real. If television
programs can act as transitional phenomena, then soaps are the easiest
type of programming for us to use in this way. (The new boom in television talk shows and reality programming, which are explicitly in the business of serving up real life as entertainment, raises interesting questions in
terms of object-relations theory.) In addition, because soap viewers are
offered a new installment of the fictional text daily, they feel little need
to construct alternative fictional texts with which to interact. Due to
soaps' narrative structure, then, soap viewers quite literally have a different point of departure from other media fans in their access to this form
of play.

How socially acceptable is this transcendent function of daytime television? As Winnicott (1971) said, we make distinctions between what are
and are not acceptable transitional phenomena. Artistic and religious efforts are okay. National sports teams seem okay, as evidenced by the
socially legitimized and unapologetic national fervor over the Super Bowl
and the NBA playoffs. But explicitly fictionalized sports, such as professional wrestling or "American gladiators" or monster truck mashes? Not

okay. (We will ignore for the moment the credible argument that events such as the Super Bowl are highly fictionalized themselves.)[6] Consider games. Chess is okay because of its presumed link to intellectualism. Fantasy games, such as Dungeons and Dragons, are not so okay, evidenced at the most basic level by the cultural stereotype of gaming fans: geeky, socially inept males. In terms of television, news shows are the only type of programming that it is sort of okay to be a fan of (see Alasuutari 1992: 563), even though they can be constructed and fictionalized (the 1993 scandal involving *Dateline, NBC*'s rigging of a crash test for a General Motors pickup truck being one vivid example).

What, then, divides what is acceptable as a transitional object from what is not? Is it whether or not the activity is explicitly fictional? Alasuutari says that soap operas receive the most degradation of all generic forms *because* they are regarded as the least realistic type of television program: "the way in which people talk about realism in connection with soap operas . . . explains why [they] occupy the lowest position in the moral hierarchy [of television]" (1992:570–571). (In England, where the realist tradition is highly valued in the media, soaps are an "object of scorn" precisely because they offer an aesthetic experience that contaminates realism with light entertainment and melodrama [Geraghty 1991: 35].) Certainly, this view explains the low status of professional wrestling, for while everyone on the industry side of the sport insists that it is unstaged, fans and nonfans alike widely accept its fictionalization (Jenkins forthcoming). Others suggest that the acceptability of transitional objects depends less on their fiction/nonfiction status than on whether they are culturally designated highbrow or lowbrow. Television is considered lowbrow (including news shows), while opera, a fictionalized drama, is deemed highbrow and is thus presumably acceptable in terms of its transcendent potential. These dimensions of fiction/nonfiction and highbrow/lowbrow intersect in complex ways, making it difficult to reach only one conclusion as to why some forms of play are socially acceptable while others are not. By all accounts, though, soap operas are both lowbrow and fictional. Fans use them as transitional objects, even though it is socially unacceptable for them to do so.

## Inhabiting the Wild Zone

I thought it was so romantic when Frisco and Felicia first made love and she said, "I love you, I love you, I love you . . ." and I thought that he might not want to hear it and he said, "No-o-o-o. I adore you I just ADORE you." That was the best part of the whole show for me.

—Soap fan on a BBS

Consider again viewers' declarations that "love stories" are their greatest source of pleasure, their idealizations of their favorite couples, their passionate attachments to characters and actors, their unceasing speculation about what will happen next, their personal happiness being tied (to greater or lesser degrees) to events befalling their favorite couple, their intense pleasure in something not real, and their distress when their expectations for the couple's happiness are not realized. A fan's inability to articulate why he or she is hooked on a soap couple is likely to sound similar to that person's inability to explain why he or she is in love with another in real life. It is not that fans are infatuated with or in love with fictional characters. Rather, their emotional recognition of the pleasures of infatuation allows them to embed themselves in the love stories they see unfolding on television. Fans fall in love with a couple's state of love for each other. One usually thinks of limerence, the feeling of being in love, as something that happens between two people, one person falling in love with another. But we believe that the emotional state of being in love might apply to people's attachments to broader cultural phenomena: fans fall in love with the love they see on soap operas.

A key aspect of limerence is feeling uncertain about the other's feelings for you. Your own degree of hopefulness about the relationship is based less on objective reality than in reality as you perceive it (Tennov 1979: 57). While people acknowledge that being in love is a source of intense pleasure, its expression is generally taboo. Infatuated or limerent people are routinely ridiculed for not living in the real world, and the newly married are often warned that their infatuation with one another will wear off. The pleasure of limerence is thus predicated (in both the fictional and the real) in part on its distance from the real. However, Dorothy Tennov observes that most people in a state of limerence are "fully functioning, rational, emotionally stable, normal, non-neurotic, non-pathological members of society" (1979:89).

Scholars who study these kinds of fan pleasures analyze them as identificatory emotional involvements prescribed by and contained within the boundaries of the fictional narrative. Ang, for example, discusses how viewers at this stage "identify in *fantasy* . . . fantasizing obviously affords the subject pleasure, which . . . has to do with the fulfillment of a conscious or unconscious wish" (1990:83). From this perspective, a viewer's involvements, while embedded within the lovers' fiction, are experienced as escapism. Viewers' pleasures exist as a *byproduct* of watching.[7]

We think that fans' embeddedness is a more complex form of involvement than identification located in fantasy. When limerence is satisfactorily portrayed between the lovers in an on-screen romantic couple, fans engage the couple and their affect as a transitional object: they embed themselves within that limerence. Fans become coparticipants in the fictional couple's dynamic as it reflects and refracts the experience of limerence that viewers know exists in reality. Here, a fan describes her involvement with the romance between the characters of Harley and Mallet on *Guiding Light* wherein their pairing overtook her:

> I have always liked the character of Harley. She is gorgeous, straight-to-the-point, and funny. Mallet was one of those characters about whom I felt neutral, but when the writers put Harley and Mallet together . . . sparks flew. The chemistry between them sizzled. . . . Unlike many story lines on soaps, there are no hidden agendas between these two. They are both passionate and have integrity. My addiction has reached the point where even a fantastic movie cannot stop me from thinking about Harley and Mallet. Even when I'm at the opera . . . I'm still thinking about Harley and Mallet well into the second act (and I'm sitting in a fifty dollar seat!). (*Springfield Journal* 1993:7–8)

Another important aspect of being in love is its onset through the process of discovery. The "relative admiration you feel for your [love object] as compared with others may be based on peripheral, even trivial factors, which, however, like the moment of initial interest, tend to be remembered. The question 'What did you especially admire in ——?' or 'What particularly attracted you?' generally yield[s] a definite and specific response" (Tennov 1979:27). For example, after Harley and Mallet first made love, an event that offered proof to fans that their perceptions of this couple's limerence were true, some fans recollected for each other significant moments when it occurred to them that the characters could become a couple, even before it was apparent their story line would draw them together. Labeling their recollections "first times," these viewers also shared memories of the onset of *their own* embeddedness within the fictional couple's limerence. One fan noted, "It was when he threw her over his shoulder and carried her off to the Spaulding yacht that I said to myself, 'Aha,' " while another shared that "it was when he stared at her legs in the garage apartment, after she helped him after the beating, that I knew they had potential to become a couple." Through this activity, fans recall seemingly minor events from the couple's past and attribute significance to them as important markers of the onset of the couple's current state of love (and fans' pleasure). In addition, these recollections indicate a heightening of fans' pleasures as they anticipate possibilities for both the couple's future and their experience with it.

In fact, there is yet another layer to this limerence — the fictional representation of Mallet's limerence, included as part of the narrative in a dream sequence well known to his fans. In that scenario, Mallet has an erotic dream in which he focuses upon the shoulder and back of an unidentified woman. Not until she turns in his bed to face him do we see her and learn simultaneously with him that the shoulder and back he possesses are Harley's. As if this fan/fiction interplay was not already sufficiently multilayered, in a public statement many months later, the actress revealed that the taping of this dream sequence figured in the onset of her real-life relationship with the actor (Sloane 1993:72).

An even more elaborate exploration of the boundary between reality and fiction becomes possible when the actors portraying the couple become romantically involved in real life. In the absence of a real-life ro-

mance, the actors merely embody the limerence of their characters' relationship. But when real-life involvements occur between actors, the potential exists for fusing the actors' real narrative with their fictional one.
This fusion opens up rich opportunities for fans to track the real within
the fictional, and its perceived impact upon the fictional. As one fan observed, in these instances "people combine reality with illusion; it's a romantic notion to find parallels between the two." Another remarked that
"knowing they are involved makes a difference in how I watch and care
about them. I get to ask how much of this is acting and how much of this is
real."

For these fans, seeking the blurred boundary between the real and the
fictional provides considerable added pleasure, with these pleasures now
*guiding* their viewing. One fan recounted for us her perception of the real-
life relationship of Mark Derwin (Mallet) and Beth Ehlers (Harley) on
*Guiding Light:*

> It was the looks they gave each other in the police academy storyline,
> even before they actually got together in real life, that told me some-
> thing was really happening between them in real life. And, it was the
> way Mark reacted to her when as Mallet he was supposed to be angry
> with her. Mark's reactions exceeded the intensity needed for the scene,
> and that suggested to me something was going on.

Indeed, it may be that these fans receive the most intense pleasure in the
transitional realm and engage in the most complex form of viewing as they
ascertain how markers of real-life limerence transcend how it is usually
acted, directed, or represented within the medium. This pleasure is reinforced by rewatching favorite episodes and scenes where they began to
notice evidence of the real, and by splicing scenes from the couple's story
line together onto special tapes to isolate and heighten their experience
with the evolution of the romance. Some fans pursue it further by acquir-
ing scripts for use in rewatching an episode in order to document how
departures from the script (such as actors' ad-libs, looks, touching, laugh-
ing, and so on) reveal evidence of a real-life relationship.[8] As one fan
elaborates, "I usually tried to get scripts for not the most romantic or
eventful shows like a wedding or something, but for shows where little

stuff like that happened, that caught my eye. I'd wonder if it was an ad-lib and then I'd want to see for myself."

This activity is not unlike detective work. Fans pick up information, share hunches, and challenge each others' interpretations within the context of a shared understanding of how limerence is manifested in real life. In this example, they share excerpts on a BBS from a sequence of observations that ultimately uncover a real-life relationship between actors:

> I am getting so invested in [the characters'] storyline. Have you been noticing the increasingly responsive looks on [the actor's] face when he looks at [the actress], especially during their love scenes? Makes me wonder what's going on there despite other fans' opinions.

> Did you happen to notice at the very end [of a prime-time special celebrating the soap's anniversary] — when [the actors] were saying goodnight — that she was standing behind him and had her hand on his shoulder??? Maybe I'm just being extra sensitive to everything they do, but it really makes me wonder if there might actually be something going on between the two of them. I would not be at all surprised if something was going on given that they are publicly signaling SOMETHING!

> WELL, WELL, WELL. What is going on between those two? I noticed the very same thing during the taping of the prime-time special. . . . Did you also notice no one else in the group touched each other at all, and as they walked off the set they were arm in arm. I am wondering what is going on between [the actors]. She was not wearing her wedding ring for the special, she rubbed his shoulder as they sat with the cast, plus there are the photos of them in magazines, the report of visiting relatives on a weekend, their proprietary stance about their storyline, and a blind item about a marriage that has fallen apart, all making my "radar" active. I am waiting for more data from the Emmys, when they co-present. . . . I have noticed photos of them in "more than just co-worker" poses.

For these fans, the evolution from insight to discovery and finally to confirmation of the actors' real-life relationship is uniquely pleasurable, as disbelief in their initial perceptions gives way to fulfillment. A full year later, after the actors publicly acknowledged their relationship, the real was readily incorporated by many fans as they engaged the couple's story line. By this time, the characters' relationship had progressed to planning a wedding, and fans readily drew on the real along with the fictional as they considered, via BBS, the impact of that pending event upon the actors' real-life relationship:

> I can't help but wonder with [the actors] going together in real life, and all this talk about marriage on the show, do you think that would have any influence on their real lives? Maybe they will be thinking along the same lines. Did anyone think that while watching them the last few weeks?

Another fan remarked:

> I was wondering something along the same lines. On the show they are professing their eternal love for one another and saying that they want to spend the rest of their lives together. What if their real relationship hasn't progressed that far? Would what they say and do on the screen push them forward or make some things awkward?

The ultimate vehicle for fans' play occurred with the emotional on-screen wedding of the two characters. Even other actors on the show commented on the blurring between the real and fictional. "Both [actors] cried real tears throughout the ceremony," reported one actress, and another said, "It's a scripted storyline make-believe wedding, but love is love, and we do have the subtext of [the actors] being in love" (Vine 1993).

Clearly, limerence has a central place within soap opera viewing, and fans can become quite invested in it as a source of viewing pleasure. Because actors usually do not stay on one show forever, their career moves disrupt the continuity of fans' play with them as transitional objects, and fans experience an emotional loss as this site of pleasure disappears. One fan's letter about the departure of *Guiding Light*'s Harley and Mallet captures this affect:

> I recently learned Beth Ehlers and Mark Derwin will be leaving their roles of Harley Cooper and A. C. Mallet in the fall. I think this is a dev-

astating blow to *Guiding Light*. Harley and Mallet have their own unique niche and having them absent for a month this summer has really driven the point home. No other couple in daytime can match their chemistry, wit, or realism. Since recasting is out of the question, I hope they can make frequent visits to Springfield. Absence doesn't make your heart grow fonder, it gives you heartache. I hope *Guiding Light* gives them the wedding they deserve. (*Soap Opera Update* 1993a:14)

And another fan comments on a BBS:

Beth and Mark's moving performances left me weak. Yesterday's payoff to the Harley and Mallet storyline will linger in my memory long after they've left Springfield. . . . They will be sorely missed.

Both responses suggest the importance that satisfactory resolution of fictional limerence has for viewers, and this is recognized by those in the industry who create it. In the case of Harley and Mallet, Beth Ehlers, who played Harley, and *Guiding Light*'s executive producer and head writers publicly expressed interest in resolving the characters' story line in a way that provided fans emotional satisfaction. In a cover story in *Soap Opera Digest* (Kahwaty 1993) just before Harley and Mallet's wedding, Beth Ehlers stated that "the show always knew they had to marry [the characters]." The executive producer, Jill Phelps, added that "if they (Derwin and Ehlers) weren't leaving, we wouldn't be marrying them now, because Harley and Mallet already feel married to each other. This is a reward for the audience." And in an interview with *Soap Opera Now!*'s Joanna Coons, *Guiding Light*'s co-head writer Nancy Curlee reassured fans that their wishes would be met. "And speaking of THAT inimitable super couple, H&M fans take heart," Coons reported. "There is no way, no how Nancy Curlee would give this pair anything other than a happy ever-after ending!" (1993a:6).

For fans consciously engaging evidence of real-life limerence, certifying the satisfactory resolution of the relationship between actors can also be central to the conclusion of a fan's own pleasures. Fan activity organized around seeking this kind of closure is usually triggered when the fictional no longer provides ready access to the primary text for context, and the support from fan magazines, industry publicity, and other outlets within the secondary text is no longer readily available. For example, there was considerable activity among a group of *General Hospital*'s Frisco and Felicia fans after Jack Wagner, the on- and offscreen love to Kristina Ma-landro's (now Wagner) Felicia, decided to leave the show. Fans' concerns included how the actors' real-life relationship shaped a satisfactory out-come of their characters' relationship, and whether the actors happily resolved their real-life relationship. Fans also teased one another via a BBS over their own emotional attachment to the characters/actors.

> With the last month of Frisco and Felicia, even though the powers that be knew that Jack was leaving, had already signed a contract with NBC, they still had F & F fighting over whether or not Felicia should join the police force. F & F were supposed to have these knock down drag out arguments, which never materialized. The fact that they had a personal relationship kept the couple from breaking up as Gloria Monty [the executive producer] had planned for them to do. When they wouldn't (or couldn't) play the fight scenes, then SUDDENLY Frisco said it was o.k. for Felicia to join the police force and F & F stopped fighting. His last week was bad, but I know if they hadn't been together in real life, then Felicia would have flirted with [another character] or F & F would have broken up earlier in 1991, because of excessive fight-ing. Also, I don't think the [characters' last scene] in 1987 would have been as effective if they hadn't been sorry to part in real life. [Actress Kristina Malandro] spoke of the "realism" that was going on when they were crying and holding on to each other at the time.

In trying to ascertain the consequences of the actors' subsequent real-life breakup following Jack Wagner's departure from *General Hospital,* one fan assesses the situation as follows on a BBS:

> What I think is UNtrue about the tabloids' characterization of Jack is that I feel he cares for Kris a lot more than his detractors want to notice. He's never had another long-term relationship and working with her constantly as he did, mere physical attraction would have died

long ago, if that's all there was. By the time Pete [their son] became a twinkle in his eye, he'd already known the woman 5 tumultuous years. I think there's got to be an awful lot of feeling and concern.

A friend responds:

WHOA!! It seemed like you needed to get a bit off your chest! I know you like J & K together. If I can't have him, I want her to have him too. Just kidding. I love Jack, but I'm not and never have been IN LOVE with him. I have done some stupid things but I'm not that disillusioned!

The first replies:

Given [*Soap Opera Update*'s] comments, now I really think the poem in [Kristina's fan] newsletter about long-lasting love that weathers storms, is never selfish or demanding, and survives during times of "despair" is about her and Jack. . . . I still think it was her way of telling her fans that they were back (or still) together.

Another fan adds:

Another thing about [a *Soap Opera Update* interview]. He thinks she's "more beautiful than ever, both on television and personally." Well, if there was any doubt in anyone's mind about their offscreen status, it's gone. I'm glad. If I can't have him, I want her to.

Finally, *Soap Opera Digest* steps in:

Okay, all you Frisco and Felicia fans, this one's for you. YES, Kristina Malandro and Jack Wagner showed up at the party together. YES, they were holding hands. YES, they spent the evening smiling and chatting with their many friends from Port Charles. And NO, we don't know if they are back together. Here's what GH's Joneses would like you to know about their offscreen relationship: They are happily co-parenting their two-year-old son, Petey, and anything else that may or may not be happening between them is private. (1993f:33)

But the matter is hardly concluded for these fans. In response to this item, one fan remarks via BBS:

I got a good laugh out of that one. As much as I would love to hear that they are back together — from them — I love the fact that they want to keep that part of their life personal. No telling how many problems it has caused that we don't know about — let alone what we do know about!

And when at last Jack Wagner and Kristina Malandro are seen together in public with their son, a fan comments on a BBS:

They were always smiling at each other. . . . It looked so DOMESTIC, like a couple that's been married for some time. . . . I loved seeing the little family together and thought of you when I watched them, because it would warm your heart as much as it did mine.

Following a surprise announcement in December 1993 that Jack and Kristina had married in a small, private ceremony, fan interest remained high. In their efforts to unravel the significance of the timing of the marriage, this group of fans weighed all the information they had at hand — the absence of family members at the ceremony, rumors of a second pregnancy, and most important, whether Jack and Kristina married for love.

Actors know that fans engage in this kind of play, especially when the real and the fictional appear so closely aligned. While it can create challenges for them in its public management, actors don't dismiss this activity as "stupid." In a *Soap Opera Update* interview, Kristina Malandro says:

When people see us out in public, like at a golf tournament, to them it's like Frisco and Felicia live. . . . To them it's a romantic notion that something that worked pretty well on-camera might actually be going on off-camera to some degree as well. But to me it's like, oh boy, I don't know if I like living a real life and fake life together. I think Felicia and Kristina are *very* different. (1993c:59)

Whether fans' play has a beneficial impact (in terms of popularity) or a detrimental effect (because it complicates actors' lives), real-life couples differ in how they accommodate that play. Melissa Reeves (Jennifer on *Days of Our Lives*) states that she, her husband and fellow soap actor, Scott (Ryan on *The Young and the Restless*), and their daughter, Emily, keep themselves open to the public: "We're really honest and open with our fans. People have basically seen us grow up on television, and because they support us, I feel there's a certain responsibility to share part of our life with them. We're really, really normal and I think people like to see that" (*Soap Opera Update* 1993a:61).

Not all actors are as agreeable, however, and many prefer to keep their personal lives unentangled with their fictional ones. *Soap Opera Digest,* for example, was unable to woo known real-life couples to pose for the cover of its 1993 Valentine's Day issue, even though they were willing to pose for covers featuring their story lines (1993a:112). Entwining actors' fictional and real personas can significantly complicate their lives, because some fans may feel entitled to access to the real along with the fictional. As actress Beth Ehlers notes, fans "take it personally" when changes in actors' lives occur (Spencer 1992:63).

## Limerence and Social Bonds

Being in love can be as fraught with insecurities as with pleasure, both because we are rarely convinced that our love is fully returned, and because we're blind to our lover's imperfections. Completely secure relationships where the needs of both parties are balanced are difficult to achieve because they are based on deep mutual knowledge and acceptance. Secure relationships are in "attunement," with perfect balance between emotional distance and emotional closeness (Scheff 1990).

When we are blinded by love, the relationship is inherently insecure. We long for a person we really don't know, or who we think we know isn't real. Our limerence blocks our ability to understand what is real and renders us incapable of anything more than idealization (Scheff 1993: 163). In the same way, some fans lose perspective in their embeddedness in fictional others' limerence and come to idealize characters and actors. For example, consider how a fan of Stephen Nichols bids farewell as he departs his role as Patch on *Days of Our Lives*:

> Women all over the country felt that Steve "Patch" Johnson was misunderstood. If only *they* could change him. . . . They rooted for [Kayla

Brady, played by Mary Beth Evans] to influence him, love him, and do what women always fantasize doing with a man of dubious character — change him. . . . The skillful acting of Stephen Nichols always allowed him to portray Steve Johnson with such honesty, that millions of people felt that they knew him. . . . I was a fan before a friend [of the actor's] and Stephen Nichols filled the void that the actor James Dean left in my youth. (*Soap Opera Update* 1990a:10)

A respondent we described in detail in Chapter Three, Phyllis, says that "we see [Patch] as attractive because we see him through Kayla's eyes. . . . There is something in us that needs something outside of ourselves to worship." According to Thomas Scheff, "infatuation casts an irresistible aura over its target" (1993:163).

Infatuation is almost inevitably accompanied by heartbreak from a breakup. This would account for the intense reaction of some fans when their desire for blurring the fictional and the real is denied, for instance, when actors whom fans want to be a couple in real life (because of their effective portrayal of fictional limerence) are not romantically involved with one another. Well known to the soap world are the extensive and persistent efforts of *Days of Our Lives* fans to unite the actors Stephen Nichols and Mary Beth Evans off the set through rumors that they are a couple in real life. Efforts by fans to reunite the actors/characters on *Days* (complicated not only by Nichols's departure from the show but also by Evans's decision to join the cast of *General Hospital*) elicited reactions from the soap press, as in managing editor Michael Kape's column titled "Patch & Kayla Fans Bash So I Bash Back" in *Soap Opera Now!* "And now here's a third wave of people coming at me. This time it's the Patch & Kayla people who somehow want [*Days*] to force [*General Hospital*] to negate its contract with Ms. Evans, then bring back Stephen Nichols from the hinterlands where he's doing dinner theatre" (Kape 1993:2). Failing that, fans pressed for Stephen Nichols's addition to the cast of *General Hospital,* as in a letter to the editor entitled "Will GH Get Smart?": "Boy, Mary Beth Evans (Katherine) goes to 'General Hospital!' I just hope GH shows more smarts and gets Stephen Nichols (ex-Steve, *Days of Our Lives*) to join, too. . . . Again things would be perfect with Stephen Nichols at *General Hospital*" (*Soap Opera Now!* 1993a:2).

While some fans' attachment to actors and characters is clearly based on idealization and infatuation, other fans' engagement of soaps as transitional phenomena is based on their understanding that soaps are fictional ("not real") and transcendent. This is revealed in fans' self-awareness of their attachments to soap operas as shown through humor, reflection, and disbelief. How can fans' relationships to fictional texts and characters ever be secure? How can one experience mutual attunement and respect with a fictional object?[9] Our data suggest that many fans *are* able to position themselves within fictional narratives in an emotionally secure way. Undoubtedly, soap fans are arrayed along a continuum of ability to achieve secure bonds with fictional narratives, and individuals change positions on that continuum as they encounter different phenomena and experiences. Scholars' insights about relationships and infatuation help us make sense of the considerable variation in fans' experience of limerence in the intermediate realm (Scheff 1990, 1993; Tennov 1979). The excessive fan behavior described in Chapter Three that seemed so inexplicable is now partly comprehensible.

Moreover, these insights about insecure bonds account for an altogether different type of soap viewer who constantly criticizes and denies his or her pleasure in viewing but insists on watching regularly. Theory suggests two types of insecure bonds: in an engulfed bond, the individual is underdistanced from feeling, is incapable of sufficient thought, and sacrifices the needs of the self for the needs of the other; in an isolated bond, the individual does too much thinking and not enough feeling and allows the needs of the self to supersede the needs of the other (Scheff 1990).

The stories of Phyllis and Sandra that we told earlier illustrate the engulfed bond, where both women "sacrificed" themselves for *Days of Our Lives*. What about the isolated or alienated fan who has a bond to soap operas but denies the feeling? Alienation and displeasure can arise for any number of reasons and reflect the denial or negation of a fan's desire for the development or resolution of a narrative. While pleasure is routinely assured through television's incremental stasis, continuity, and repetition, displeasure is felt by fans when those elements are noticeably disrupted or absent (Mellencamp 1990). Consider the following from BBSs:

> OK, everybody. I'm a pretty liberal gal, right? So why did the scenes with Vinny make me cringe?

> [Responding to another fan's word-play with the character of Victor on *The Young and the Restless*]: "Victurd" hahaha. I like that. Anyways, I had a revelation. . . . Ya see, for the past week I watched Y&R and a deep hate for Jack formed. I couldn't believe the way he was acting about the V-man's "death." But now I see the error of my ways!! Jack is not to be loathed. I love the way that he can see what a greedy S.O.B. that Victurd is. Jack is god. DOWN WITH VICTURD!!!!

> If we can see this then why can't [the writers]? I just don't get it. [The actor] really is gross. He tries to sound so sexy by talking soft. It is so obvious he is putting the goods to that poor innocent Hope. What a troll.

As long as such displeasure is juxtaposed with pleasure from other aspects of the narrative, and in these examples through the process of sharing mutual distaste with other fans, these fans' bond with the narrative, characters, or actors remains intact, albeit unstable. They are united in their alienation, creating a community organized through sarcasm as a form of play. However unstable their relationship to the narrative may be, it is hardly tenuous. If these fans were truly alienated, they would reject watching altogether, assuring isolation from each other and the show. Moreover, even in alienation, they participate in the wild zone just as do those seeking pleasure: by assessing the validity of fiction through its juxtaposition with what is credible in reality.

> Although Victurd was given away by his mother and put in an orphanage and became a self-made millionaire he doesn't need to hold that grudge forever and continue to hurt other people. This bit about the orphanage will be coming up and then we are all supposed to feel sorry for Victurd all over again. This is no excuse to be so bitter and continue this dominance thing he has.

Please, tell me she won't have that ugly clown outfit on tomorrow. "Please, I'm on my hands and knees begging [the producer]. Please, Oh Please, take that ugly, ugly, outfit off of Jill! Don't you realize there's pregnant women and women trying to get pregnant watching your show and when they see Jill wearing those ugly getups, they'd prefer wearing their regular clothes and taking out the seams. . . . Consult with one of your women fashion designers and dress her better . . . !"

Displeasure can be understood only in relation to or as a counterpart of pleasure (Mellencamp 1990), and future work on attachments with televisual narratives would do well to consider "unpleasure," as Patricia Mellencamp calls it. But as we have seen in our exploration of fans' pleasures, it is perhaps more important to understand the *forms* displeasure can take. Fans are not simply dissatisfied; even when they are isolated, television assuages loneliness by assembling audiences who can have fun together: social bonds are maintained.

## The Social Context of Play in the Wild Zone

We believe that playing in the wild zone is becoming increasingly visible in contemporary society for a number of reasons. We agree with other scholars that a wide range of pleasures is available to soap viewers and fans and that viewers and fans experience multiple pleasures from soap opera. However, virtually all of the literature (including our own reliance on object-relations theory) implies that pleasure is a purely psychological and emotional phenomenon and gives little attention to the social or historical *context* of specific pleasures. (A notable exception is some of the literature on women's pleasure in resisting and coopting traditional feminine texts, which explicitly links pleasure to struggles against structural oppression [see Brown 1987; Press 1991].) We are not suggesting that pleasures simply come and go with historical or economic shifts or that the affective attachments that people have today to soaps differ substantively from those felt twenty-five or thirty or even five years ago. Rather, we propose that, for several reasons, it makes sense that *this* type of pleasure — playing in the wild zone — is increasingly visible in *this* particular time period.

First, we refer back to Chapter Two and some of the industry changes noted there. An ongoing controversy in the soap industry is the increasing voice given to fans: fan magazines are allotting more and more space for viewer letters, complaints, editorials, and advice. This transformation offers readers the illusion that they can participate in creating the fictional narrative. In addition, as celebrity-oriented secondary texts (which are in the business of offering readers behind-the-scenes information and details of actors' private lives) become more successful economically, greater numbers of consumers are implicitly invited to step out of the world of consumption and into the world of production. Both of these changes break down the barrier between the fictional and the real by fostering an illusion of intimacy between celebrities and fans (see Gamson 1994) and create space for this form of play to flourish.

A related reason for the increasing visibility of this type of pleasure/play is based in technological advancements. One of the booming modes of communication between fans of all sorts of cultural objects (movies, soap operas, comics, etc.) is electronic bulletin boards. Subscribed to by millions, these boards provide forums for fan communication and gossip and put fans in contact with others who share similar interests and pleasures.[10] They give soap fans access to others who find pleasure in the same things and play in the same way. There is considerable differentiation among viewers/fans in terms of what they enjoy about soap operas, and many times that pleasure is so personal as to prevent two people from being able to connect with one another, even though they might be equally ardent about the same program or actor. The wild zone play we have focused on in this chapter is engaged in by a fairly small subset of fans, and the emergence and popularity of electronic bulletin boards both affords these fans access to one another and renders their play more publicly visible.

Next, we emphasize that the category "fan" has to be understood historically. We have always been fans of things, because we cannot exist "in a world where nothing matters." But whereas fans historically related to things like politics or religion or labor, today they relate primarily to popular culture. There is no clearly identifiable reason for this, but "it is certainly the case that for the vast majority of people in advanced capitalist societies, this is increasingly the only space where the fan relationship can take shape." Fandom can potentially be a site of optimism and empowerment "in a world in which pessimism has become common sense" (Grossberg 1992a:63, 65).

Similarly the "popular" is not a static category but rather a historical process (Levine 1988; Ross 1989). Cultural objects are popular at different times for different reasons, and popularity has as much to do with the context of the times as with the object itself (Ross 1989:98).[11] As cultures undergo transformations and the popularity of cultural texts ebbs and flows, so too do the forms of pleasure and play that surround them. Playing in the wild zone, while not a *new* pleasure is a newly *visible* form of pleasure.

# Chapter Five

## Story Struggles and Meaning Making

I've noticed that most of you in the business of reporting on the soaps have decided that John Black will be put back with Marlena on "Days of Our Lives." Maybe because the show is unable to come up with new ideas. But shouldn't we, the viewers, get a choice? Everyone I've talked to about this doesn't want this to happen. . . . This past year or so, the show has decided who should be with whom and has shoved them all at us no matter what. Let's face it, many of the show's decisions didn't work and still don't. . . . Give us all a chance to see what works best and is most enjoyable.

— Letter to the editor, *Soap Opera Now!*

Soap fan subculture is not defined merely by geographic location or even shared activities, but by emotion and feeling: fans create mattering maps (Grossberg 1992a, b) — affective investment portfolios — that grant salience to pleasure. Scholars assume that the creation and sustenance of pleasure is unproblematic for fans — that they can freely construct mattering maps with pleasure as the central dimension and effortlessly maintain it. In contrast, we argue that fans must actively struggle to locate and sustain the pleasure they find in soap operas. These struggles are made visible through fans' moral claims to authorship. Fans have always believed that, given the chance, they could tell better stories than do the writers and producers because they feel they know the characters and the fictional community more intimately. In the past fans either kept their feelings private or shared them only within localized idiocultures (Ang 1988; Fiske 1992; Hobson 1982). They had little public space in which to air their grievances. But in the daytime industry fans' private struggles are beginning to go public, as illustrated in the 1992 letter quoted in the epigraph. This trend has important consequences for fans' relationships to cultural texts and their abilities to manage and control their own pleasure. Their public claims to authorship have emerged in two arenas: the public arena of the daytime press and the quasi-public arena of electronic bulletin boards. While in each of these forums fans make claims to meaning and interpretation that are crucial to their maintenance of pleasure, their success in the struggle depends on where, how, and to whom they voice their claims.

## Who Owns Soaps' Stories?

At the heart of all relationships between producers and consumers of media texts is a struggle over meaning, or authorship. Does the author of a text have complete authority to determine the range of meanings available within it, or does the consumer have freedom to determine meaning? While this debate began in literary and media theory, the issues raised are relevant to popular cultural texts as well.[1] In our research we were struck repeatedly by the overt struggles over authorship within the daytime industry. Head writers speak of hours of creative brainstorming over long-term story projections. Associate writers and directors talk about shaping those projections and finding a way to put their own creative stamp on the narrative. Actors point to their unique contributions to the story-telling process and speak of bringing their characters to life. Viewers and fans criticize producers, actors, and writers who are not telling the story "correctly" and lament their own lack of control over the writing process. Who is telling daytime stories? Whose stories are they?

The question of authorship has at least three overlapping layers: who legally owns a cultural text (its owner), who creates or authors it (its actual author), and who morally owns or authors it (its moral author).[2] (We use the term *moral author* to refer to a person who feels that a soap opera is morally or emotionally theirs, regardless of who might have actually written the text.) Creative authorship, like all artistic work, whether highbrow or lowbrow, is collaborative.[3] The production of any piece of art depends on a complex division of labor and is the work of an art world or art community rather than a solitary artist (Becker 1982). Despite the fact of collaboration, highbrow or elite art is characterized by the image of a solitary artist who is revered for his or her unique creative genius and control over what is produced (Fiske 1992; Gans 1974; Levine 1988). For example, auteur theory (Sarris 1981) designates the director of a film as the creative genius, despite the inherently cooperative nature of film production. The talent guilds representing directors and writers have been at odds with each other for years over the director's right to claim possessory credit ("A film by . . .") (Cox 1994). Similarly, a painting or novel is falsely assumed by most consumers to be the product of a single artist or writer.[4] These myths allow the boundary between the artist and the consumer to remain sharply drawn, with their respective statuses indisputable (Fiske 1992), and they facilitate the aesthetically distanced positioning of the elite consumer.

Television, along with other lowbrow texts, has largely failed to sustain an authorial myth, thus reducing the aesthetic distance between producer/consumer and text/consumer. Indeed, some suggest that traditional views of authorship are irrelevant for television (Reeves 1990:148). In the commercialized world of television production, industry members fight as intensely as high-culture artists for creative control of its products (Gans 1974) and know who is responsible for creating each textual element, but that information is lost when the product moves "outside the creative community into the consumer public" (Bacon-Smith 1992:57). Historically, viewers have tended to perceive television as unauthored because they had little knowledge of the backstage battles over authorship or of the various participants' functions in the production process. This perception is changing, however, due partly to increasing viewer sophistication about backstage maneuverings, which are widely publicized in both print and television gossip forums and trade publications. It is also changing in terms of television series' creation, where questions of authorship are gradually becoming more relevant. On a series, the executive producer is considered the author, and his or her name is used in marketing (Reeves 1990). For example, David Lynch's series *Wild Palms* was marketed as a David Lynch creation. Indeed, an executive producer's reputation is the main factor in network programmers' decisions about prime-time scheduling (Bielby and Bielby 1994).

The authorial myth may confer highbrow status on a cultural text, but it obscures issues of interest to sociologists: it ignores both the collaboration necessary to produce any cultural text and the impact of intertextuality on cultural production, and it mistakenly implies that the meaning embedded in a text is the result of purposive intent by a single artist (Barthes 1977; Becker 1982; Gaines 1991; Gans 1974; Uricchio and Pearson 1991). The single-author myth can also create tension between industry participants and fans. In his work on prime-time and film fandom, Henry Jenkins describes battles over authorship and textual meaning. While some producers are sympathetic to fan activities (such as fanzining and songwriting) and occasionally use fan texts to their advantage, others treat them "with contempt, suggesting that fan efforts to protect favorite aspects of fictional texts infringe upon the producer's creative freedom." As examples Jenkins points to film producer Tim Burton's casting of Michael Keaton as the lead in the movie *Batman* over vehement fan protests, and William Shatner's public ridiculing of *Star Trek* fans whose textual readings are, in Shatner's opinion, outrageous (what Jenkins calls the "Get a life!" critique). Shatner adopts the position of exclusive textual author and "takes on himself the right to judge what meanings can be legitimately linked to the program and which are arbitrary or false" (Jenkins 1992b: 30). In a 1993 seminar on popular culture, Jenkins (1993) described how *Star Trek* creator Gene Rodenberry was so outraged by fans' original interpretations that he employed a "fan liaison," whose primary duty seemed to be to attend fan conventions and inform fans that they were interpreting the show incorrectly.

The claim to exclusive authorship rights leads industry participants to dismiss fan interests and to attempt to control fan-produced texts. Lucasfilm, for example, has tried to block production of fan products based on the *Star Wars* series, claiming that they infringe on issues of copyright and threaten their own officially sponsored fan products. Angry fanzine editors responded "in favor of a readers' right to free play with the program materials" (Jenkins 1992b:31). In these examples, the legal ownership of texts gets confused with the moral question of authorship, as legal owners "also attempt to enforce *what* the popular form means" (Gaines 1991:229).

The soap opera poses uniquely difficult problems of authorship because, unlike any other cultural text, its very success *depends on* its appearance of unauthoredness:

> Its world and characters cannot bear the mark of a particular creator. . . . If the character is not to be perceived by the audience as schizophrenic, idiosyncratic differences in dialogue writing styles must be eliminated; the character must speak with a single voice. . . . [Different directors'] styles must be indistinguishable, since if viewers were aware of directoral interventions, their attention to the events unfolding in the soap opera world would be distracted. (Allen 1985:56)

Soap operas aim for authorial seamlessness. They must appear autonomous and self-generating, as if the fictional worlds they create were quite literally different worlds existing alongside that of the viewer (Allen 1985). To achieve such seamlessness, the individual styles of those involved in creating soaps are muted and suppressed rather than valorized, and "the soap opera production process has long been viewed as inimical to artistic expression of any sort" (Allen 1985:15).

As in all forms of cultural production, however, many authors contribute to the daytime narrative, and heated backstage battles occur over authorship. While the original creator of a series is revered within the community, she or he often has little to do with the day-to-day story telling on the show and is rarely considered by insiders to be the show's author. (The active participation by the Bell family on the two shows it has created, *The Young and the Restless* and *The Bold and the Beautiful,* and Agnes Nixon's with *All My Children* are notable exceptions.) According to the production hierarchy, head writers are perhaps the true authors of daytime narratives (Cantor and Pingree 1983; Rouverol 1984), since they are responsible for coming up with long-term story projections and often write some of the dialogue.[5] But many other participants play greater or lesser roles in creating daytime narratives. Associate writers are responsible for writing much of the dialogue but often have little or no control over character or plot development, and their unique stylistic talents are deliberately muted by head writers (Rouverol 1984). One associate writer told us that the most frustrating thing about her job is having her creative abilities stifled by the production process: "[I would] love to express my own ideas without having to go through ten people."

Writers also negotiate authorship rights with the networks and production companies, executive producers, directors, and actors, among others. Executive producers in particular are increasingly involved in daytime story telling since Gloria Monty's unprecedented success with *General Hospital* in the early 1980s. This move is viewed with dismay by many soap writers, including one associate writer who told us, "There are a lot of people [in the business] who think they can write but they can't. . . . Producers should produce, writers should write, and actors should act." Another key author is the director, who is typically responsible for one or two shows per week but must make his or her style as indistinguishable as possible to maintain the naturalistic flow of the fictional world.

Making differences between backstage collaborators invisible to viewers results in a unique role for secondary texts and soap critics, who patrol the borders of daytime television. Secondary texts function to perpetuate a particular authorial illusion for serial viewers: they "preserve the possibility in the mind of the viewer that characters are, in part at least, products of the volition of the actors" (Allen 1985:56). In order to mask backstage story-telling changes and preserve the illusion of seamlessness, secondary texts have historically colluded with the soap opera production staff in offering a false image of the *actor* as creative initiator. This is ironic because, of all the authors of the soap opera text, actors probably have the least control over the direction of the characters they portray.[6] They might suggest elements of character development or specific dialogue to the producer or head writer, but ultimately, story-line decisions are not theirs to make. Actors acknowledge their relative powerlessness. Anthony Geary, who reprised the character of Luke on *General Hospital* after playing Luke's cousin Bill Eckert for several years, is one of the most powerful actors in soap opera, yet he must continually negotiate and fight for the characters he portrays. On *Pure Soap,* E! Entertainment Television, on November 11, 1993, Geary talked about the on-screen demise of Bill Eckert:

I'm the first one to tell you it's been hell for two and a half years to be Bill Eckert. . . . I did everything I could within my power, which was at times formidable and at times impotent, to twist this guy into something I could believe in. . . . The creative team decided that because Bill wasn't home he was therefore a bad dad and they could get mileage out of that. I kicked and screamed all the way down that road but I lost. . . . I'm very sorry to see Bill go because Bill was one of my favorite characters I've ever done in twenty-six years of acting. Maybe it's because I've fought so hard for him.

Even though actors do not control their characters, they still participate in the struggle over authorship, and their portrayals are often central to the success of soap operas. A gifted actor can make a poorly written character appealing to viewers or create magic in a character or romantic couple that transcends the confines of the writing and directing, thus improving his or her popularity and chances of employment longevity. But to say that actors *create* their characters is misleading. In fact, actors' attempts to put a unique imprint on the narrative through misinterpreting dialogue or ad-libbing considerably frustrate writers and producers, who say such efforts work against the success of the narrative. (One associate writer told us that her response to actors' suggestions about character development is "listen and ignore.") As daytime critics point out, actors *must* follow the rules in order for soap operas to function effectively:

Daytime drama is a highly structured genre. Before stories are approved, they are carefully scrutinized by a whole committee. . . . By the time they get into the actors' hands, they're ready to go as written. At this point for an actor to refuse to deliver the lines because "my character would never say that" is taking a liberty that is not his to take. . . . In the final analysis, it's the actor's job to deliver and perform the lines as written. (Coons 1993b:5)

It is debatable how successful efforts have been to render soaps' multiple authors invisible to viewers by perpetuating the actor-as-author myth. Some viewers do in fact believe that actors create their characters, while others have a strong sense of the soap opera production process and are highly critical of the backstage activity of writers and producers (Seiter et al. 1989). Regardless of the degree to which they accept the myth, fans have a long history of making private moral claims about the authorship of daytime narratives. They have great reverence for soaps but contradictorily feel that they, rather than the production staff, possess or own the stories and characters: "Fans felt that [the British soap opera] 'Crossroads' was *their* show and its leading character, Meg, belonged to them rather than to the producers" (Fiske 1992:40, referring to the 1982 study by Dorothy Hobson). While these struggles have historically been located in private idiocultures, they are beginning to go public as a result of shifts within the production industry and the daytime press. These shifts have important consequences for fans' interpretations of daytime texts, as well as for the construction of their mattering maps (Grossberg 1992a).

## Fans' Struggles Go Public

Fans make moral claims to authorship not only in private conversations with each other but also in letters and phone calls to producers, writers, and actors suggesting ideas for character or plot development. Historically, these claims have been treated with bemused tolerance by those in the production industry. Fan letters are usually read, but specific suggestions are largely ignored, both to protect against plagiarism charges and because the suggestions lag behind the current story line. Explains Kay Alden, co-head writer of *The Young and the Restless*, "We will often get an influx of mail where people are livid or shocked by the point we are at in a story. As the writers, we know that this is only a point in the story. We are beyond that" (Weiss 1993:45).

While producers may not respond directly to fans' suggestions and complaints, they express little of the antagonism toward fans that is typical of other media (Bacon-Smith 1992; Jenkins 1992b). That virtually no publicized confrontations occur over copyright infringement or legal ownership is due in part to the unique kinds of activities engaged in by daytime fans. The long-term, ongoing nature of the soap text does not generate the range of fan activities that finite texts such as *Star Trek* and *Twin Peaks* do (Bacon-Smith 1992; Jenkins 1992b). Of the hundreds of daytime viewers we surveyed, only a handful ever write original narratives based on soap characters and only one does it on a regular basis, for personal rather than communal uses. Few create the type of song tapes and artwork common to other fan communities. Daytime writers and producers do not face legal threats of fan appropriation of textual material and thus are more tolerant of fans' moral claims to daytime stories.

But this genial relationship is undergoing a noticeable shift, which is creating new tension between fans, daytime critics, and industry participants, and which has important implications for fans' role in the interpretive process. Along with a coordinated attempt to present the *actor* as creator of daytime narratives, our data indicate, networks, producers, press agents, and fan magazines are increasingly encouraging fans to believe that *fans themselves* create daytime stories. They are inviting fans to help author daytime serials, in the "actual" rather than "moral" sense of the term.[7] For example, a recent fan magazine promotion invited readers to submit story-line suggestions for their favorite programs, and the winning entries were published in a subsequent issue (*Soap Opera Digest* 1993g). Another publication held a contest inviting *As the World Turns* viewers to submit fictional conclusions to the Carolyn Crawford murder mystery, which were later printed in the newsletter (Coons 1992). While fans love these promotions, their sincerity and appropriateness are questionable. Suspicion about their veracity — and debate about the role of the fan in story telling — has crept into every aspect of the daytime industry. A recent network promotion and the fan response to it tellingly illustrate the current conflict. NBC ran a contest in 1992 giving winners the chance to pick the name for Jack and Jennifer Devereaux's new baby (the two were wildly popular characters on *Days of Our Lives*). The producers had already picked the name, of course, which angry fans only belatedly realized. This gaffe made *TV Guide*'s list of "1992: The Worst in Soaps": "Legions of fans spent money to vote on a name for the Devereaux baby in a 1–900 contest. Maybe we're just sticklers, but shouldn't NBC have held the contest *before* taping the episode that revealed the kid's name?" (Logan 1993:30).

Fan magazines increasingly invite fans to tell daytime stories and be publicly validated as soap "authors." They offer more and more space and voice to fans in terms of opinion columns, letters to the editor, descriptions of interactions with celebrities, and promotional contests like the one noted above. In short, fans' private moral convictions that daytime stories are theirs to tell are beginning to go public. Those convictions extend to *dis*owning a story (or a show) when it goes awry. Below, a fan rejects *Guiding Light*'s efforts to convince viewers to accept narratives they have already abandoned: "Even burning down the lighthouse failed to spark the viewers' interest, or for that matter, light a spark under couples [whom] Executive Producer Jill Phelps and Headwriter Nancy Curlee keep telling the viewers we are going to love" (*Soap Opera Now!* 1994:6). Viewer demands have spawned a vocal turf battle over authorship, to the consternation of all involved in daytime production. Actress Deidre Hall, who plays Marlena on *Days of Our Lives,* complained in a daytime magazine about fans' claims to authorship:

> The audience has changed, and I'm not sure I like the change a lot. [The audience] has become much more actively involved in storytelling and much more demanding, and they know a lot more about contracts, about renewals and about personalities, which I think destroys the story for anyone who just wants to be taken away and entertained. (*Soap Opera Digest* 1993c:94)

Meanwhile, critics have joined in the debate. Soap columnist Michael Logan observes that the industry is merely catching up with what is already common practice in prime time and feature film. The following editorial by Mimi Torchin of *Soap Opera Weekly* defends the practice of giving fans a public voice:

> There are a few people in the industry who have criticized our practice of allowing readers/viewers to critique a show in print. The consensus in some quarters is that criticism should be left to professional critics. . . . I strongly disagree with that opinion. Many readers have an enormous amount of time and emotion invested in the soaps. . . . Whose opinions matter most? Those of a handful of professional jour-

nalists, or those of the millions of viewers who love the soaps? . . .
Many of the viewing public, when given a chance to make their views
known, have just as much right to be heard. (Torchin 1992:4)

But as Logan observes, when daytime executives and soap producers take
into consideration suggestions coming from too narrow (and unrepresen-
tative) a segment of the audience, the results can be disastrous. Describing
the firing of actress Ellen Parker from *Guiding Light* at the suggestion of a
viewer focus group, Logan says:

> The response [to the character by focus group members] was one of
> general disinterest, so GL confidently killed off the beloved character in
> a car crash — a decision that triggered an avalanche of calls and let-
> ters. . . . To this day, the firing of Parker . . . still has a negative impact
> on the show — and probably will continue to do so for years to come.
> (1993a:31)

The invitation to fans to author texts is not unique to the daytime
community. For example, in 1988 Warner Communications, Inc., which
holds copyright on the Batman narrative, let consumers decide via a 900
telephone number whether the character of Robin should be killed off or
retained as part of the story (readers voted to kill him; see Meehan 1991).
More recently, Fox's *Martin* invited viewers to call in their preference for
an ending to a two-part episode. But these are exceptions; only in the soap
opera community do we see widespread efforts to incorporate viewers
into the story-telling process.

Again, an accurate understanding of the fan-as-actual-author trend depends in part on whether or not the invitations and promotions are sincere. Evidence suggests they are not. The name-the-baby contest on *Days
of Our Lives* was clearly fabricated and makes us question the veracity
behind other promotional contests as well. Most space given to fan voices
in publications seems reserved for fans' squabbles with one another over
narrative and character interpretation. (There are notable exceptions,
however; the fan letters published in *Soap Opera Now!* receive in-depth
responses from critics.) Further, writers and actors are quick to say that
having knowledge of narrative or character history doesn't mean that

viewers are capable of actually authoring soap operas. One writer told us that viewers are "completely unknowledgeable" of the writing process. Most telling, perhaps, are producers' and head writers' acknowledgments that it doesn't really matter what viewers think of particular story lines as long as they keep watching. Says Linda Gottleib, former executive producer of *One Life to Live*: "In general, the fans write when they don't like something. Negative fan mail means the fans are watching. They are upset, but they are watching!" (Weiss 1993:46). And according to Ken Corday, executive producer of *Days of Our Lives*: "When [fans] say 'I hate what you're doing with X, Y and Z,' you know parenthetically they're saying, 'I'll watch to see what they're up to.' If you let them dictate the show, you can get into trouble" (McGarry 1993:12).

This "let them wait" attitude is criticized by both fans and industry insiders, especially in the case of *Days of Our Lives*, widely believed to be the soap least considerate of fan interests. Says daytime critic Alison J. Waldman in a published response to a fan inquiry: "[*Days of Our Lives*] prefers to keep up the air of omnipotence and omniscience. . . . I believe DOOL has reached a point of arrogance when it comes to their loyal, vocal followers. I don't think DOOL respects the fans. It believes, no matter what, DOOL fans always stay tuned" (*Soap Opera Now!* 1993d:5). Most soap producers seem to prefer that daytime viewers remain at arm's distance (at least) from the story-telling process. According to columnist and critic Michael Logan, that disinterest is shortsighted:

> This is a medium that is very much affected by what the audience thinks. If the audience doesn't like your romance, in not enough numbers, you'll be on the unemployment line by Tuesday. Or, if they liked you, who cares if they killed you, you'll be back. So they must realize listening to these folks, that is what it is about, because it [the soap medium] is not like any other end of the business. . . . Here, those fans out there will alter the course of where the show is going. So why are they not being respected, why are they not being treated like intelligent, sophisticated folks, when in fact they control these shows?

In this light, the fan as actual author seems nothing more than a marketing strategy to retain soap opera's gradually dwindling audience.

But fans' increasing acceptance of the notion of themselves as authors does have real consequences. One is a change in the function and power of daytime critics. As literary theory points out, critics need a text to be singly authored (however illusory that image is), so that they can then place themselves as the expert decoder of textual meanings (Heath 1972). In soaps, the history of presenting the actor as author was reflected in the daytime press in two ways. Initially, magazines devoted most of the interview and pictorial space to actors, thus legitimating and celebrating their status as interpreters of the narrative. More recently, magazines placed the right to express critical opinions in the hands of on-staff expert critics, who relied in part on public taste to validate their judgments (Becker 1982). As secondary texts increasingly validate the reader/viewer as expert/author, they not only invite viewers to participate in the story-telling process but validate their unique interpretations of textual meanings. The fan-as-author shift thus implies public acceptability of the fan as expert decoder. The fan/author legitimates the fan/critic.

In fact, the role of the fan/critic is increasingly validated within the daytime industry itself, as evidenced by a recent invitation to readers that appeared in *Soap Opera Digest* in a column titled "Now It's Your Turn": "In our series critiquing the soaps—and their hottest stories—we have our say. Now, we want to hear what *you* think about your shows: What would you change? Selections from letters will be printed in an upcoming issue. Please send us your opinions" (1994b:5).

A second consequence is a shift from the myth of soap operas as singly authored by the actor to public recognition of multiple authorship, a shift that has already occurred within the comics industry (Uricchio and Pearson 1991). But there is an important distinction between the two industries. Comics are characterized by numerous authors creating multiple, simultaneous, and often competing narratives. For example, four or five versions of the Superman story may coexist at any given time. In contrast, the nature of soap production (along with characterizations of the soap fan community) would more likely lead simply to the public acknowledgment of the preexisting collaborative process, with the fan recognized as a key player in shaping the primary narrative.

Despite the intriguing possibilities of the fan-as-actual-author trend, most evidence suggests that invitations to fans are not genuine efforts to validate viewers' moral claims. There is, however, another realm of the soap fan world in which moral claims are routinely made, and in which new possibilities for producer-fan relationships exist. This is the quasi-public world of electronic bulletin boards (BBSs), a forum that makes visible fans' status as legitimate interpreters of daytime texts.

## The Cyberworld of Fan Discourse

"This is much better than yelling at the television!" writes one soap fan to other users of a BBS, an emerging means of fan communication. Commercial on-line services currently have approximately five million subscribers and by some accounts are growing at a rate of 30 percent a year (Roberts and Sandberg 1994). Through either a monthly subscription fee or on-line charges, members can correspond with all other subscribers of the service day and night, seven days a week. They have access to each other through a variety of file topics under which they may post public messages and replies. While messages are typically posted under one's name, in most cases the individuals are not, at least initially, personal acquaintances. As a result, they are not relying upon social similarity or location in common social networks as a basis for deciding with whom to communicate (or whether to communicate at all).

BBS dialogue is sequential and can be immediate, but it differs from typical conversational interaction in that it does not typically reveal age, social class, ethnicity, or gender, characteristics known to impact conversational dynamics (see Boden and Bielby 1983; Stone 1990; Zimmerman and West 1975). One of our respondents describes the world of BBSs as an "intermediate realm" existing somewhere between isolated viewership and contact with the formal world of fan clubs, mall events, and celebrity luncheons. BBSs provide a space where diverse groups of fans can share ideas, hunches, insights, history, insider information, and backstage rumors. As we noted earlier, fans who participate on BBSs are less likely to join fan clubs or to seek out formally organized fan events.

What do BBSs provide that other forms of fan expression cannot? First, BBSs allow fans to engage in fan activity at a safe or removed distance.

BBS communication does not require fans to reveal their identities, although many eventually choose to do so. This allows fans to engage other fans on an equal footing: "For the first time individuals engage in telecommunications with other individuals, often on an enduring basis, without considerations that derive from the presence to the partner of their body, their voice, their sex, many of the markings of personal history" (Poster 1990:117). BBSs thus create a space where only the fan identity is relevant; fans' mattering maps converge in a space that both celebrates and validates their knowledge. This is enormously gratifying for fans who would not otherwise have access to a large, articulate, readily available, and informed community of like-minded viewers:

> I disagree, as you predicted. That's what is fun about the [bulletin board], different viewpoints.

> The only people I could chat with before [joining the bulletin board] were my sister and stepmother and they both live across the country. I have gotten my principal and one of the teachers I work with to tune [in to soap operas].

> Before I discovered this [bulletin board], the only person I had to talk . . . to was my roommate. Now everyone here gives me the scoop. . . . [Bulletin board members] are more fun than she is anyway!

BBSs create a forum for a unique kind of moral claims-making that differs in important ways from more conventional outlets for fans' claims. In terms of private claims-making, the activity that occurs on BBSs might seem the same as what occurs in group viewing of soap operas, since both contexts may include large numbers of people with diverse points of view (see Lemish 1985). There is, however, an important difference. In studies of group viewing, claims-making occurs in the process of viewing and is thus interruptable by the broadcast itself or by other viewers. In contrast, not only do most BBS users have the freedom to make uninterruptable claims but most come together to share insights *after* having viewed the daily episode. They have time to reflect on what they have seen, and their commentary is often more detailed, complex, analytical, and nuanced than that occurring in immediate face-to-face interaction, even though the gossip may look similar and functions in similar ways (Bielby and Harrington 1994).

BBS claims-making also differs significantly from public claims made visible by the daytime press. For one thing, BBS messages are not subjected to the same degree of selection, censoring, or editing that published fan letters are, so they allow for a freer exchange of information.[8] More important, fan letters are only belatedly interactive. Because of the time lag in the publication of fan magazines, while fans might be able to respond to each other across issues, the forum does not adequately allow for truly interactive communication. With BBSs, however, discussion is interactive; it can be immediate if not simultaneous, and it allows for the evolution of fan discussion. In these ways, this intermediate realm validates fans' claims outside the private and intimate world of family and friends and circumvents the limitations of public claims-making, while at the same time connecting fans to a large, like-minded community. In short, it mimics the immediacy of private claims-making while providing the relative anonymity and diversity of public claims-making.

BBSs also allow the public emergence of fans *as* fans. While in all forms of information sharing status emerges on the basis of who holds the most valued information (Barber 1983; Rosnow and Fine 1976), most of those status hierarchies are not only informal but essentially invisible.[9] While private groups of fans might validate each other's expert knowledge, the status so granted does not transcend the confines of the small, intimate group; outside the confines of the group, traditional status markers prevail. BBSs, however, dismantle the power relations that govern the traditional forms of information sharing. "Factors such as institutional status, personal charisma, rhetorical skills, gender, and race—all of which may deeply influence the way an utterance is received—have little effect. . . . Equality of participation is thereby encouraged" (Poster 1990:122–123).

While all BBS members are free to participate and contribute to the shared body of knowledge, some members gain status in the group over time on the basis of their wit, knowledge, and reliable insights. Status is thus earned within the community rather than granted ascriptively. One researcher found that "some of the people who enjoy extremely high status . . . tend to be secretaries, who are low status at work. But their exhaustive knowledge of soaps gives them status" (quoted in Grimes 1992:C14). Fans grant status to other fans who have the most knowledge about a celebrity or serial or executive producer, or who have reliable access to such knowledge, and they orient to them as expert information providers (Harrington and Bielby 1995). A veteran member of a group of *The Bold and the Beautiful* fans who chat regularly on a BBS is anointed "Mother" and teased about owning a crystal ball for her ability to antici- pate plot outcomes. Another fan says her college viewing clique conferred the title "soap queen" on the member with the longest history of watching *As the World Turns*. Knowledge of a serial's history is a valued resource for viewers who rely on others to update them on the intricacies of past story lines or missed episodes, or to dish inside scoops on a favorite celeb- rity. The intermediate realm of BBSs thus publicly grants status on the basis of talents and skills not legitimated outside the community. This is a reciprocal process: knowledge grants status, and the status in turn further legitimates the value of the knowledge.

This fact of reciprocity affects the authorship question in a unique way. Because this system of claims-making is self-generating and self-fulfilling, it is almost beside the point that the claims do not directly engage the soap opera production industry. For these viewers, the legitimation and value of their claims within the community is sufficient reward; their seeming invisibility for what they call the "powers that be" is not of foremost concern. Although BBS participants also write letters to producers or call networks to voice concerns or make complaints, choosing to make claims in public arenas as well as in quasi-public ones, such public claims do not replace or subsume private or quasi-public ones. They emerge in different contexts and serve different purposes.

While the quasi-public nature of the medium could render BBS dia- logues invisible to the daytime industry, it leaves open the possibility that insiders *do* pay attention to them, which raises interesting questions in terms of authorship. BBS users know that their conversations might be overheard by industry insiders; they use the term *lurkers* to refer to these possible eavesdroppers:

> I've wondered myself whether [the powers that be] read this. It seems too much of a coincidence awhile back when [BBS members] started

threatening to bring the Fashion Police notes back [Fashion Police refers to members' criticisms of characters' wardrobes] . . . lo and behold
[one character] made [a] fashion police comment to [another charac-
ter]. It sure sounded like the dialogue writers were way ahead of the
wardrobe people.

Other fans directly invite industry insiders to listen in:

Dear production team: we love you, we really do, and we admire and
respect your work. But speak to our minds, as well as our hearts, and
we'll all be happy!

There is so much more the writers could do with these characters. Why
do they insist on rehashing old material. If they are out of ideas, they
should read this [bulletin board]. Some of the people on here can really
come up with great ideas.

Still other fans feel convinced that industry insiders are paying attention to
their dialogues:

If . . . TPTB [the powers that be] would put [a character] back like she
used to be — funky and spunky then what a team she and [her father]
would be. . . . I hope the lurker is picking up on this!!!

I figure the writers think we won't [notice the stupidity of a plot point].
I hope the lurker is watching.

Some evidence suggests that industry insiders tune in to BBS conversations, at least casually (Grimes 1992). Patrick Mulcahey, former co–head
writer of *Guiding Light,* has chatted with fans on CompuServe. Some
actors are highly aware of the medium and participate both directly and
indirectly through friends and relatives (see *Soap Opera Digest* 1994a:
77). As one fan reported on a BBS: "[An actor at a personal appearance]
asked if anyone in the audience [belonged to the service]. He said . . . that
his [relatives] had it. He wanted to know if anyone who had it knew
anything about a rumor that he'd been told was posted [on the boards]."
An actor's mother participated for a short time on a BBS, providing fans
with insider information about her son's unexpected firing from his show.
Another actor who recently returned to daytime offered a preview to BBS

members through his sister, who was also a subscriber, about his character's reintroduction to the narrative.

*Soap Opera Magazine*'s Mary Ann Cooper, *Soap Opera Now!*'s Michael Kape, and *Soap Opera Digest* contributing editors Donna Hoke Kahwaty and Stephanie Sloane have interacted with viewers on at least one electronic bulletin board, offering hints about plot direction and opinion about industry developments. For example, Michael Kape, monitoring one BBS, chose to intervene in an exchange regarding the departure of a soap's headwriters: "Ya'll got it all wrong (including M. Logan, by the way) about why Mr./Mrs. Demorest were fired as headwriters. . . . To learn more, as always, read the 1/31/94 issue of Soap Opera Now! — which carried the WHOLE story." While Cooper's and Kape's interaction has been intermittent, both Kahwaty and Sloane had ongoing contact with board members, answering questions and previewing news and information about to appear in print; it is uncertain whether they carry viewer opinion back to industry insiders.

We have little indication that anyone directly connected with the serials or the networks systematically monitors bulletin board dialogues; if they do, it is unclear what becomes of this information. To be sure, the explosion in BBS membership has caught the attention of network executives, among them Alan Cohen, senior vice-president of marketing for NBC: "There is a lot of buzz about this whole industry right now. . . . We were waiting for the industry to get to a place where there is enough of a reach to make it worth our while. This is the superhighway that's here today" (quoted in Cerone 1994:82). Each of the networks now provides bulletin board services on at least one of the major commercial computerized information systems, and some include regularly scheduled chats with celebrities. For example, *Days of Our Lives* stars Robert Kelker-Kelly (Bo) and Kristian Alfonso (Gina) conversed in spring 1994 with their fans via America-Online, with excerpts reprinted in *Soap Opera Update* (Weiss 1994: 56). While this might be an effective mechanism for generating viewer interest in a soap, it is probably not used as a means for channeling viewer feedback to "the powers that be."

Daytime industry insiders' participation and lurking on BBSs raises interesting questions in terms of authorship. Recall that in the fan-as-actual-author trend, controversy focuses on how much attention should be given to fan voices. Critics, actors, producers, and fans themselves are embroiled in a heated battle over fans' rights to author daytime narratives. Industry insiders are paying attention to these claims, as evidenced at the most obvious level by their publication in the form of fan letters. In this way, insiders are forced, at some level, to be accountable to fans' public expressions of their interests. But in the BBS community, insiders cannot be held accountable for their actions unless they choose to participate on BBSs. If producers, actors, or writers choose merely to lurk, they gain access to fans' claims without actually having to deal with or respond to fans. They thus could receive all of the benefits of fans' insights with none of the negative repercussions, if being accountable to fans is indeed perceived negatively. Both the trends — one in the daytime press, the other on BBSs — most likely disempower fans. In the first, fans appear to have some impact, but their control is illusory. In the second, if fans do have impact, they are not fully aware of it because their contributions are never made public. Fans' relationships with the daytime industry create unique problems in their struggles over textual interpretation as well as in their struggles to create and sustain their mattering maps. Fans must continually negotiate ways to sustain the pleasure they find in soap opera, which means that constructing their mattering maps is an ongoing, dynamic, and agentic process.

The inclusion of fans' voices in the world of daytime television has important consequences for the fan subculture. While all media fans can express their fanship, soap fans have a unique opportunity to publicly engage the daytime industry from a private setting via the professional daytime press. This seems to legitimate soap fans' voices in a way not possible in other fan communities, where fans must construct alternative publications and alternative sites (such as formal conventions) for their voices to be heard. Having a professional and easily accessible outlet for their opinions makes soap fans' struggles with authorship seem easier than similar battles in other fan communities. The nasty skirmishes that *Star Trek* fans routinely engage in are legendary, and the Trekker community is forced to relate to the production industry as Us versus Them. Such a division contributes to the marginalized status of most media fans, whose identities and activities necessarily exist in direct opposition to that of which they are fans.

From the outside, the relationship of soap fandom to the daytime industry does not look like Us or Them, but a more harmonious We. Soap fans are not forced to adopt a marginalized status to participate in public fandom, which leads to the amorphous and loose organization and structure of the daytime fan world. But if the daytime fan-producer relationship resembles a We, the trends we have discussed suggest that this We is partly illusory. Fans might be temporarily pacified by having their claims appear in the daytime press, but little evidence suggests that the industry actually listens to individual fan voices. While Michael Logan asserts that "the shows absolutely read the magazines," and that, indeed, letters published in them may be fans' most direct route to decision makers, producers seem to listen to fans only at the grossest level. They care about Nielsen ratings and the volume of fan letters, but they pay little attention to the nuances of fan interests and desires.[10] In spite of considerable differentiation among soap viewers and fans in terms of their specific interests, levels of sophistication, ages, socioeconomic backgrounds, and so on, the common stereotype remains unchanged, and the daytime production industry persists in treating viewers as an undifferentiated mass.

This raises the issue of who is most qualified to speak for the daytime fan. Those who write letters to the daytime press? Those who bypass the press and write directly to executive producers at the studio? Those who phone the studio? Those who attend annual fan club gatherings? Those who organize letter-writing campaigns to the studio? Participants in producers' latest novelty, the focus group? In a recent critique in *TV Guide*, columnist Michael Logan describes the potentially negative consequences of relying upon focus groups: "What if these groups — which usually consist of only 12 to 24 people — don't speak for the audience as whole? Worse, what if their conclusions are just plain wrong?" (1993a:31). Critics worry that fans might be wrong; fans complain that producers, writers, and directors *are* wrong; and, despite fairly dramatic changes in fans' position within the daytime industry, debates over authorship continue to rage. In the end, only fans can speak for fans, but how their voices are accommodated within the daytime industry has yet to be resolved.

# Chapter Six

## Fandom in Everyday Life

There is a comfort in these shows. People talk about "the addiction," but I think the addiction is far more a comfort with these programs. There is that ease and comfort of wanting to come back and be with your pals. There is something about going home and snuggling up with your TV, knowing you can count on it. In an interesting and in a sad way it's replacing the human connections that people so desperately need. I don't know if that's good or bad, I just know that's a level in which people are responding to these things. I think this is more what America is about . . . more than the screaming yelling "It's Bo! I want your autograph" kind of thing. [It's the] emotional attachment that you develop, and so when you screw with it, it's not the same as doing something to a character on *L.A. Law* or *Coach* or something like that. There is a much deeper bond that has developed, and you mess with that and you are asking for trouble. You absolutely are. How we have become so much more sophisticated and what that emotional bond is, to me, the key to what this is all about. That's why you're coming back; [it's] because there is a deep need; it's not the need for entertainment; it's what your emotional investment is for escape into those worlds.

— *TV Guide* columnist Michael Logan

Speaking from the dual vantage point of columnist/critic and dedicated viewer, Michael Logan offers several explanations for why the soap medium is so profoundly enmeshed in viewers' everyday lives. In his view, soap watching generates social and personal bonds that are organized through a perception of comfort with the fictional world of the soap narrative. He reinforces what our respondents say is essential to their personal experiences as soap fans and anticipates our final observations about fans, their fanship, and fandom.

We emphasize that being a fan is not just a social but a personal phenomenon; by exploring both dimensions we have been able to consider
fanship as a normal, everyday phenomenon. In taking that stance, we
targeted the characteristics of dedicated soap viewers and their identities,
pleasures, and struggles as fans. The experience of affect in the pursuit of
pleasure is the central organizing feature of soap subculture, in contrast to
other media fan subcultures, which emphasize the production of cultural
artifacts. Soap fanship is distinctive in that fans and industry participants
reciprocally construct the subculture, doing so across a range of sites
and through myriad social processes. That cooperation differentiates soap
fandom from those that must struggle to overcome industry efforts to
suppress them. This cooperation has significant consequences for the daytime fan community. First, soap fandom does not exist as an outlet for
participants' expressions of opposition to dominant culture, as is more
commonly the case with other fandoms. Second, because of industry en-
dorsement, soap fans have neither to define themselves as marginalized to
participate nor to develop an alternate identity to be fans. These distinctions raise considerations about how fans and fandoms vary in degree of
embeddedness within mainstream society. Such variation allows fan communities to exist as outlets for socially legitimate emotion and pleasure in
some cases but not in others.

The hundreds of dedicated viewers who thoughtfully replied to our
lengthy questionnaire gave us an overview of the scope and diversity of
soap fan subculture. In-depth interviews provided us with a more complete understanding of the motivation for and significance of fans' attachment to the genre. Insights we gained from the questionnaires and interviews were validated by the countless other fans we interacted with or
observed at organized events, through soap magazines, and in the cyber-
world of electronic bulletin boards. As participants ourselves, we supplemented these insights with our own experiences as fans and our interactions with fan friends and colleagues. Participants in the soap industry,
including actors, journalists, editors, producers, writers, and casting directors, helped to contextualize these insights by opening their workplaces
to us and candidly discussing their relationships with fans. Their observations about the medium reinforced our understanding that the everyday

experience of fanship is a normal outcome of interaction between dedicated viewers and the soap industry.

## Fandom in Everyday Life: Pleasure, Power, and Agency

Soap fans are viewers first, and the content and form of the genre is essential to understanding the way soaps are integrated into their lives. Daytime stories are not just the stories that air on television. They are also the industry stories (secondary texts) and the oral stories (tertiary texts) that fans create through verbal discourse with one another (Fiske 1987). But fans also create their own unique story. They construct their own narratives by blending their viewing histories, memorable moments in the story lines, personal friendships, celebrity encounters, inside information (the "fourth text" described in Chapter Two), and other peak experiences with significant events in their real lives. What do we make of fans' creation of highly personalized stories, and what does it suggest about the importance of fanship as both an identity and as a normal leisure activity?

Most soap fans do not speak directly about their fan identities, nor do they consciously talk about the meanings they derive from being a fan. However, their statements reveal their awareness of the personal significance of their interests and activities. We learned how they incorporate their fan identity into their lives and manage its public manifestations. For example, soap fan identity varies in salience and is disclosed to varying degrees, just as other aspects of the self are integrated, engaged, and revealed to others. Fans manage the considerable stigma associated with identifying as a fan in many ways. Their awareness of the dangers of excessive fanship is reflected in their regulation of their own behavior. This richness and diversity of the fan experience is overlooked by scholars who view fanship simply as an ideological reaction against dominant or oppressive social institutions. Fanship is not always a reactive response by marginalized groups. Quite the contrary. Viewers participate in soap subculture to defend, advocate, and display their commitments to a medium that reflects and comments on what is socially significant to them in their personal lives.

Soap fans' pleasures (and displeasures) are the result of their conscious participation in finely coordinated play with the boundary between fiction and reality. Their pleasures are individual, private, and personal. The emotional involvement that pleasures create — affiliation, attachment, catharsis — is readily understood by other fans, and the sharing of pleasures further underpins the collective experience of affect that binds the subculture. Consequently, while soap fans' pleasures are personal and specific, they are not socially isolating. The social bonds fans establish — the intense bond between themselves and the genre, and their equally intense claims of ownership over narratives — account for some otherwise inexplicable behavior. This behavior is rooted in play in the transitional realm, routinely engaged in by normal adults but hidden from outsiders. Scholars need to address this aspect of fan behavior in order to reconceptualize the ways people engage with cultural forms, taking into account normal ranges of seemingly underdistanced behavior that might otherwise be labeled deviant.

The viewing practices fostered by soap fans' pleasures invite us to rethink domestic viewing practices and the power relations that shape them. Current scholarship argues that the domestic context impacts television viewing but often simply concludes that television viewing typically occurs within groups (which precludes privacy) and that males dominate program choices (e.g., Lull 1988; Morley 1986). These presumptions overlook the range of viewing arrangements practiced by our informants, as well as the emotions, pleasures, and subjectivities that are the basis for their engagement. Soap fans not only lay claim to the television, to the VCR, and to viewing time, they also create private and personal space to watch alone and to their own satisfaction in their own homes. Their viewing arrangements often more closely resemble those of filmgoers who select times to view and do so with anticipated pleasure that is based upon knowing what the experience will deliver. Future research should reconsider how viewers' subjective involvements shape the intersection of television viewing and domestic power.

Our suggestions may seem remarkably similar to Radway's conclusions concerning readers of romance novels, but they differ in an important way: we do not find soap fans' control over space to be fundamentally organized by ideological concerns, as Radway interprets romance readers' to be. Instead, soap fans' practices are guided by a sense of agency — an awareness of their ability as socially embedded individuals to initiate and control behavior (Shibutani 1991). Soap fans' viewing choices and practices emerge for a myriad of reasons, including pleasure and the experience of emotion. The concept of agency more adequately captures the general process of intentionality that is obscured by a focus on hegemonic resistance. Recent work parallels ours and extends the concept of agency beyond the viewing process itself. Lembo (1994), for example, conceptualizes the "mindfulness" of viewers as they construct a self as viewer within a context of programming choices, readings, and other activities, including nonviewing ones. Central to Lembo's thinking is the viewer's control over the continuity between the self when viewing and the self when not viewing. The complementary concepts of mindfulness and agency suggest a purposiveness to viewers' actions and readings. Applied to soap fans, these concepts suggest that what fans are or what they do are extensions of their integration and participation in viewing and in everyday life.

More than other fanships, soap fanship has a strong link to the social organization of the medium's industry. This industry not only invites particular fan interests and pleasures, it also endorses specific activities. But while the industry prefers to treat viewers as passive, soap fan idioculture is neither passive nor uncritical. As Michael Logan observes, the soap audience can be best characterized as taking the position that "even though we get it [programming] for free, we are still consumers." The struggles over narrative ownership testify to that stance, as do the extremely critical judgments fans level at story lines, production values, acting, casting, or any other aspect of the medium that stretches credibility beyond the customary give-and-take at the boundaries of the genre.

While writing this book, one of us taught a women's studies course on soap operas and romance novels and required students to watch *All My Children* as one of the class texts. Midway through the semester, a class session was devoted to students' questions and commentary about the narrative, story line, and actors. For a solid seventy-five minutes students argued over current plot lines, debated characters' shifting personalities, shared backstage rumors, and revived long-forgotten story elements to help new viewers understand the show. In other words, they gossiped. At the end of the class the students were asked, "We've just spent over an hour talking about *All My Children*. Is our ability to do this valuable? Is this a valuable skill?" The students responded with stunned silence, followed by raucous laughter and a resounding no. Why did they automatically discount and devalue their own behavior, even behavior they enjoyed? Can we think of the cultural competency of soap viewers as socially valuable?

This is a difficult question to answer, in large part because it implies that soap viewing either provides a source of meaning that does not exist elsewhere in people's lives or is a substitute for and displaces meaningful interaction. The knowledge and skills the students demonstrated in that hour-plus of gossiping — reading emotion, motivation, and intention; exercising relational memory and historical memory skills; juggling fifteen balls (characters) in the air and knowing how dropping any one would impact the other fourteen — might lie outside their conscious ability to name *precisely because* they are so closely integrated into the students' everyday world of experience. Viewers enjoy the fictional world of soaps not because they lack fulfilling lives themselves — the real and the fictional are not so clearly separable. Instead, soap operas offer viewers the chance to stand on the boundaries between multiple worlds and see real life as connected to, and informed by, a variety of perspectives. They cannot name the value of their soap-watching skills any more readily than they could the value of skills used to do the laundry or write a term paper or chat at a party. This is not particularly unique in terms of how people understand their own leisure choices. What is unique is soap viewers' ready awareness that their meanings and pleasures are not socially acceptable. Students saw nothing valuable not because they themselves find no value and pleasure in what they watch, but because they know that the culture values nothing about soaps and soap watchers. Daytime fans' interpretation of their individually experienced and collectively shared pleasure always occurs within a context of social disdain and ridicule.

## Rethinking Soap Subculture, Marginality, and Stigma

Soap subculture is loosely bounded and constituted, drawing from individual interests and localized idiocultures. It is organized through the shared experience of emotion and the celebration of a medium that offers opportunities for that experience, rather than through either the production of artifacts scavenged from dominant texts or the enactment of alternative life-styles. A heterogeneous collection of individuals from all gender, racial, age, and socioeconomic groups, the members of the subculture do not identify themselves as belonging to a marginalized group. It is less an expression of deviance or difference as a consequence of blocked social or economic opportunities than a means through which affect associated with human social interaction can be recognized and celebrated. What do these features suggest about rethinking the concept of subculture as a feature in everyday life?

The cultural studies tradition ties the existence of subculture to notions of marginality, difference, resistance, or opposition. Henry Jenkins's poachers, Constance Penley's slashers, and Camille Bacon-Smith's fanziners, for example, are groups that ostensibly organize as alternatives to marginalized social status. These studies, which concentrate on fans' activities and interests that resist dominant society, sidestep issues central to the sociological concept of subculture that would explain how they are embedded in society. How does self-identification as a marginalized member of society affect acceptance by the group? Under what conditions do members of a group struggle to neutralize the stigma associated with their interests? Through what personal or institutional means does the group seek legitimacy?

Sociologists outside the cultural studies tradition have examined the social construction of subculture, but they tend to adopt a cumbersome set of assumptions about its basis. For example, Howard Becker's (1963) seminal study of marijuana users explicitly ties the concept of subculture to deviance. To sociologists, deviant behavior is that for "which there is a probability of negative sanctions subsequent to its detection" (Black and Reiss 1970:63). In this perspective, outsiders label the activities of the subculture as deviant, and members are aware of being labeled as such. Conventional deviance scholarship defines a subculture as a group whose "members interact with one another more frequently and more intimately than they do with members of other social categories; its members' way of life, and their beliefs, are somewhat different from members of other social categories; and its members think of themselves as belonging to a specific group, and they are so-defined by those who do not share this trait" (Goode 1994:258).

To be sure, fanship has negative connotations, especially for fans of a genre that is among the lowest on cultural taste hierarchies and is targeted at a female audience. Well aware of their stigmatization by nonviewers, soap fans become skilled at managing and neutralizing it. But the disapproval of soap fans' interests and activities rarely takes the form of significant social sanctions. Moreover, the members of soap subculture do not consciously define themselves as participants in an exclusive group; most do not speak directly about their identities as fans, nor do they consciously express the meanings they derive from participation with soap fandom. Although they are conscious of being stereotyped, are attentive to crossing the line and losing control, and manage observers' assumptions about their interest in soaps, being a soap fan is only one of several identities (and activities) in their lives, and it is incorporated as one among others. In short, soap fanship constitutes a subculture, but one whose members can successfully maintain reputability.

Soap fans' pleasures are sanctioned by the industry, and their struggles with producers are legitimated by the daytime press and endorsed by the expanding role of critics. Thus, organizational elements of soap fandom itself help viewers maintain reputability by legitimating their claims to identity, pleasure, activity, interests, and meaning, and by sanctioning their activities as leisure, not deviance. These institutional resources take several forms, one of which is the patronage that extends from the soaps to their fans. We have used the metaphor of the family reunion to describe the atmosphere at fan club luncheons. All of the industry participants in the soap opera world — the actors, directors, writers, producers, critics, press members, and others — see the fans as part of the family, as participants in daytime story telling, and as integral to the production and success of soap opera. The daytime industry does not stigmatize its own fans. With some other forms of fandom, the object of fans' admiration rejects and abnormalizes fan behavior: think of William Shatner's "Get a life!" condemnation of *Star Trek* fans (Jenkins 1992b). Most media fans find industry doors slammed in their faces and their desires and suggestions routinely dismissed; they are the overeager, uninvited strangers at the reunion to whom family members nod hello and smile politely and wonder who invited them. In contrast, soap fans are expected guests at the party; the daytime industry does not abnormalize their behavior and interests but rather cultivates and legitimates them. Not that this relationship works perfectly; fans' advice is not always taken, their demands aren't always met, and they are occasionally misled, but they are insiders of sorts. A greater degree of communication and a more formalized set of expectations exists between soap fans and the daytime industry than between any other form of fandom and its media counterpart. Because of their common ghettoization, soap fans and industry participants rely on one another to an extent unparalleled within the entertainment world.

Another important institutional resource is the secondary text. While the soap press exists largely as a publicity arm for the industry, the allocation of increased space in national fan magazines to fans' voices, opinions, and interactions not only authorizes fans as players in control over the narrative but validates and legitimates them in their own eyes. *Pure Soap,* which ran on E! Entertainment Television from early fall 1993 to the end of 1994, offered daily opportunities on live national television for fans to interact with the host and each other over plot updates and news, and with soap celebrity guests, providing immediate access to this resource. The increased role of fan magazine critics who patrol the borders of the genre through commentary about its representation to outsiders and through in-house criticism offers further validation. These developments are occurring in a medium that has always been more responsive to its audience than other mediums. But faced with a dwindling audience, whether the soap industry can continue to politely ignore fan claims to ownership of the narrative to the degree that it has in the past remains a question.

Another institutional resource is the collective organization of the fan community itself, a development still in its formative stages, at least at a national level. Unlike other media-based fandoms, soap fanship was not organized out of resistance to preferred readings of the narrative; its fandom did not originate through national conventions to celebrate perceived differences. Instead, the fandom emerged through localized idiocultures, and subsequently through annual fan club gatherings sponsored by the soaps themselves. Electronic bulletin boards have greatly facilitated more broadly based fan idiocultures and may introduce novel opportunities for fans to recognize similarities among themselves, identify differences with the industry, produce alternative texts, and engage industry participants. Regardless of the evolutionary status of their community, fans have always been a considerable resource to each other in their ability to validate, rationalize, and advance their interests. What has changed is that soap fans now have easier routes to more extensive networks of others. What kinds of issues they will mobilize around and what goals they might pursue as a national (or international) fan community remain to be seen: whether they adopt a stance of difference toward outsiders who devalue their interests, whether they modify individual strategies of neutralization, or whether their participation in the industry modifies the industry itself.

The consequences of a subculture's having institutional resources at its disposal are several. First, access enlarges the repertoire of cultural, social, and personal resources members can draw upon for legitimating their interests at a collective as well as at a personal level. Second, while a subculture may emerge through networks of like-minded acquaintances, its idiocultures are also sustained by contributions originating beyond localized interactions. Third, institutional resources can be used to undermine as well as to enhance the existence of a subculture; for example, soap fanship would undoubtedly be transformed should the soap industry modify the boundaries or the content of the medium, abandoning the interests and emotional investments of its current fans. In short, a subculture's reputability can vary both at the hands of its members and as the result of institutional-level dynamics. This suggests that fan subcultures more generally can vary in the extent to which they are shaped by individual and collective activities of their members on the one hand, and by commercial, organizational, and other institutional forces on the other. Moreover, the maintenance or undermining of reputability is likely to vary across subcultures depending on the relative interests and influence of individual, collective, and institutional participants (cf. Lachmann 1988).

## Rethinking Soap Subculture in Everyday Life

We need to broaden the concept of subculture to incorporate groups organized around shared interests, not just those considered wholly separate, marginal, or oppositional. This agenda calls for greater attention to " 'invisible' networks of small groups submerged in everyday life" that are embedded within the ongoing structure of society (Keane and Mier 1989: 6). While we hardly think television viewing qualifies as a social movement, it does offer a collective outlet for exploring the expression of emotion and pleasure. As Orrin Klapp (1969) has observed, a "poverty of cultural ritual" prevails in contemporary society, in the sense that the connection between strong emotion and dramatic cultural ritual has been severed. Television viewing, guided in particular by the conventions of specific genres, may become one of the few meaningful rituals for the expression of collective (and individual) emotion. Within the soap genre, the ritual is enacted through the social bonds that viewers form with characters, pro ducers, and other viewers (see Bielby and Harrington 1992). How those bonds are shaped by social structural sensibilities, including social history and political contexts, merits further consideration (see Cruz and Lewis 1994).

Our study considers the multiple levels through which the subculture of soap fans is socially constructed and explores the intersection of individual agency, social bonds, and social organization. At one level, the structure of an industry—which includes serials, networks, production companies, daytime press, actors, fan clubs, and ancillary sites like BBSs—shapes the ways social bonds are formed, sustained, and managed individually and collectively. For example, some actors launch their careers by creating and managing perceived intimacy with viewers, while executive producers promote the popularity of their shows by capitalizing upon actors who have attracted fervent and dedicated fans. At another level, fans form friendships and then mobilize to analyze and critique the course of the narrative, the performances of their favorite actors, and the popularity of a given serial. Mediating between fans and the soaps are the industry press, fan clubs, computer bulletin boards, and other means through which members of the subculture communicate. These segments of the industry profit from the functions they offer the subculture, while simultaneously providing a site for fans' creation of meaning.

But our study does more than delineate the social organization in which the creation of meaning takes place. It also reveals why the meanings and pleasures that fans derive from that social organization take a distinctive form. Identity, pleasure, and control over ownership of the narrative are issues central to the private realm in which both the narrative and the viewer reside, and the particular forms those issues take among soap fans — stigma, limerence, and moral claims — are fundamental to the moral arena of the individual viewer. The experience and emotion of a viewer's subjective engagement with the narrative is the business of collective sharing at the sites through which fans communicate. That those sites are embedded within a commercially organized industry structure makes the soap subculture a particularly intriguing case for reconsidering assumptions about individual and collective action and the cocreating of meaning in social research on subcultures and popular culture.

# Appendix

Our project was designed to study the diverse population of soap opera fans, not a representative sample of viewers. Studies of television audiences consider a viewer to be anyone who is present in a room with a television turned on, regardless of level of participation in spectatorship (Ang 1991). We designed our study to reach dedicated viewers, not casual spectators. Besides the fans themselves, our informants include the individuals involved in the production of soap operas, daytime journalists, fan club officers, and others who contribute to the industry. We also analyzed the objects produced by the subculture and the industry, including the soaps themselves, daytime magazines, and fan-generated materials. In addition, we were participants or observers in settings where soaps are produced, where fans gather, and where the business of the industry is conducted.

## The Survey

In January 1991 we designed a questionnaire to be administered to viewers of soap operas. Containing both closed- and open-ended items, the questionnaire assessed daytime serial viewing habits and related fan activities. For example, respondents were asked which daytime serials they regularly view; their reasons for viewing; their involvement in fan clubs; whether they have written to actors, writers, or producers; if they purchase or subscribe to fan magazines; and so forth.

Participants for the study were obtained through advertisements and referrals. In February 1991 we advertised our study, inviting interested readers to write us for a copy of our survey. Our ad was placed in the newsletters of the National *Days of Our Lives* Fan Club and the Fans of *General Hospital, Soap Opera Weekly,* and on one electronic bulletin board (BBS). The ad ran once in each of the fan club newsletters and the fan magazine, and for several weeks on the BBS. Participants were also obtained through an item in our questionnaire that invited respondents to recommend others for our study. Through mid-July 1991, we mailed surveys to each of those recommended along with a cover letter describing our study and an invitation to participate.

A total of 931 surveys were sent out, 871 to individuals who either responded to the advertisements or were referred by a respondent and 60 to the president of the *General Hospital* fan club, to be passed on to longtime fan club members. Completed surveys were collected through late September 1991; we received 706 usable questionnaires. However, a precise response rate cannot be calculated because we do not know how many fans actually received a questionnaire, for several reasons. First, several participants requested multiple copies of the questionnaire, which they may or may not have distributed. Second, it became apparent that some participants were making copies of the questionnaire for friends or family to complete, rather than having them write to us directly. Third, it is unclear whether the president of the *General Hospital* fan club actually distributed all 60 questionnaires to fan club members.

## The Sample

Like most soap opera viewers, our sample was predominantly female and white, although not exclusively so. Six percent were male, and 7 percent were nonwhite. Nearly half (48 percent) were currently married, and another 12 percent were widowed, divorced, or separated. The remaining 40 percent were single. Our respondents ranged from fourteen to seventy-eight years of age, and the median age was thirty-five years. Most of our sample consisted of individuals in their twenties (28 percent), thirties (29 percent), and forties (19 percent), with 10 percent in their fifties, slightly over 4 percent over sixty, and 7 percent under twenty.

All fifty states and the District of Columbia were represented in our sample, with the largest number of responses coming from the populous states of California (12 percent of our sample) and New York (9 percent). Florida, Illinois, Ohio, New Jersey, Pennsylvania, and Texas each contributed at least 4 percent to our sample. Thirteen percent of our respondents resided in rural areas, over 56 percent in small to midsized communities, and nearly 29 percent in large metropolitan areas.

Our sample was diverse in its socioeconomic profile. Nearly half (47 percent) were employed in some capacity. A plurality (43 percent) of our respondents worked in white collar occupations, with nearly 27 percent of them in professional or managerial capacities, 16 percent in sales and clerical positions, and 4 percent in service or craft occupations. Twenty-nine percent were not in the labor force because they are either retired (7 percent), unemployed (6 percent), or students (16 percent). Another 23 percent reported "Other" for occupational status, and most of them identified themselves as homemakers. The median educational level for our sample was thirteen years of schooling. At least 29 percent had attained a college education (including several with advanced degrees), 40 percent had a high school education, and 8 percent had an eighth-grade education or less.

Our sample was reasonably affluent, as measured by total household income. Fifty-one percent report combined household earnings between $15,000 and $49,000, with slightly over 35 percent of that group reporting earnings between $25,000 and $49,000. Twenty-six percent reported income of at least $50,000; 23 percent reported a total household income of less than $15,000.

Our sample includes viewers of all eleven soap operas airing at the time of data collection. However, *Days of Our Lives, General Hospital,* and *All My Children* are the shows most favored by our respondents. Because some of our respondents were contacted through national fan clubs representing those serials, it is not surprising that they were more prevalent in our sample.

## The Interviews

To supplement the surveys, we interviewed fans who had diverse backgrounds, experiences, and involvements with the daytime medium. To select interviewees, we categorized survey respondents based on the breadth and depth of their involvements. We defined breadth in terms of factors such as whether the fan followed several soaps, dropped in and out of different serials, purchased numerous fan magazines, wrote letters, and so forth. Our intent was to include those engaged in a broad way with the soap genre as a whole, not with a single show, actor, character, or activity. The depth classification identified those who followed only one or two serials (or actors or characters) and were very emotionally invested in them, regardless of whether they engaged in activities related to their viewership. Such fans tended to be less involved with the medium as a whole but identified strongly with one aspect of it.

Three tiers emerged from our classification. Nearly 90 percent of the completed surveys comprised tier 3, a group with a fairly typical level of involvement in terms of both depth and breadth. These fans typically watch several shows regularly, occasionally read fan magazines, and may have attended fan club events. Another 8 percent comprised tier 2. These fans had a greater level of involvement than those in tier 3 in terms of either breadth or depth. They tended to watch two or three serials regularly or invest heavily in a single show, subscribe to a number of fan magazines, belong to several fan clubs, and regularly attend fan activities. Finally, twelve respondents comprised tier 1. These fans exhibited an extraordinary investment in soap viewing and fan events. They were extremely invested in a particular serial or closely watched a number of different serials, carefully followed industry news, and frequently corresponded with writers, actors, or producers. These fans were both introspective and articulate about their involvement with serials.

In August 1991 we began the second phase of our data collection, interviewing survey respondents. We interviewed fans from all three tiers. Almost all of our respondents, including those in tier 3, were serious and committed soap viewers. Those from tier 3 provided us with invaluable information on typical viewing habits and fan activity, while those from tiers 1 and 2 gave us insights into unusually rich investments in daytime serials. We interviewed by telephone all twelve tier 1 respondents, and four respondents each from tiers 2 and 3. One additional interview was conducted with a woman who had not completed a survey but was referred to us by a tier 1 respondent. We decided to interview her because of her unusually intense emotional involvement with daytime serials.

Interviews consisted of open-ended questions about daytime serial viewing and involvement in fan activities. They ranged in length from thirty minutes to two and a half hours. Respondents were encouraged to elaborate on the information they had provided in the survey, as well as to address broader issues associated with their soap viewing, including their initiation into daytime viewing, their self-identification as fans, their perceptions about the production of daytime serials, and so forth.

## Participation/Observation

We employed participation, observation, and textual analyses to capture the ways in which viewers individually and collectively contribute to the production and interpretation of textual meanings, and to illustrate how viewers interact as consumers of and contributors to the soap industry. In late August 1991, we began interviewing writers, producers, actors, journalists, and others active in the soap industry. In all, we interviewed seven actors and observed or interacted with countless others at work and at industry and charity events. The six writers we interviewed held responsibilities ranging from head writer to dialog writer. They worked on a variety of serials, including some that are now defunct. We also interviewed an executive producer and a casting director and spoke with two network executives. Extensive interviews were conducted with members of the daytime press, including six journalists representing five publications, and four free-lance photographers. We interviewed six fan club staff members and spoke to numerous others at fan club events. Formal interviews were conducted by telephone or in person and lasted from forty minutes to several hours.

In our fieldwork we participated in fan activities and fan club gatherings; attended celebrity personal appearances and charity events; visited the studio of a soap and viewed the videotaping of an episode; sat in on the production of *Pure Soap,* the now defunct daily soap program; and observed the taping of two nationally televised soap industry events. At the many fan gatherings we attended or saw by way of video recordings, we observed social interaction among fans and celebrities and the organized rituals in which they participate. Our studio visit provided the opportunity to observe the art world of actors, directors, makeup artists, wardrobe and set designers, lighting and sound technicians, camera operators, and others who carry out on a daily basis the vision created by writers and producers. Our observations gave us insight into the technical origins of the narratives and images upon which soap fanship is based. At *Pure Soap* we obtained a firsthand look at an important segment of the industry that mediates the relationship between fans and serials. Finally, attending nationally televised soap industry events gave us a behind-the-scenes look at how industry participants construct an image of themselves for the medium's fans.

We carefully monitored the soap press for its coverage of the production of serials; critiques of the shows, actors, writing, directing, and other aspects of production; fan feedback and interaction; interviews with actors, directors, and other industry participants; and soap publicity and gossip. Since 1980, we have read a variety of publications that focus exclusively upon the soap medium or devote a portion of their coverage to it, and during this project, we regularly followed all of them: *Soap Opera Digest, Soap Opera Magazine, Soap Opera Now! Soap Opera Weekly, Soap Opera Update, Daytime TV, People, Star, TV Guide,* and the now defunct *Viewers' Voice, Soap Opera Illustrated,* and *Episodes.* In addition, we noted coverage of the industry in the *Los Angeles Times, New York Times, Wall Street Journal,* and the two major entertainment industry trade papers, *Daily Variety* and *The Hollywood Reporter.*

Fan-generated texts were an important source of data for our analysis. These texts are produced primarily in two contexts. One is letters to fan magazines, where fans analyze, criticize, and comment upon soap story lines, characters, performances, production values, and the views that have been expressed by other fans, journalists, producers, and others in the industry. Second, electronic bulletin boards on services such as Prodigy, CompuServe, GEnie, and America-Online serve a similar function for the exchange of views.

Finally, we drew upon our own experiences as soap fans to inform our study. One of us began viewing soaps on and off in 1963 and regularly in 1980, while the other has been watching steadily since 1978. While we have both skipped around in the serials we follow, between the two of us we have watched at some point every serial currently airing as well as several that are no longer in production. Like many fans, each of us has a private video collection of past episodes of serials and edited story lines, televised promotionals, prime-time specials, industry awards shows, and guest appearances by actors and other industry participants on talk shows, at charity and mall events, and in other mediums. In addition to our personal viewing histories, we have attended numerous fan club luncheons as fans, and between us we have participated as members in six fan clubs, including clubs for actors as well as those for serials. Fans who have become personal friends have shared materials from their private collections, including videos, photographs, letters, scrapbooks, and other memorabilia. Some participants in our survey shared similar materials with us.

Both of us continue to be embedded in networks of viewers and fans via face-to-face relationships and by long-distance connections maintained through letters e-mail, electronic bulletin boards, and telephone. Like most soap viewers, we have engaged in countless discussions with other fans about memorable episodes, story lines and scenes, favorite actors and characters, and the industry in general. Inevitably, our discussions delve into criticism of the serials themselves, actors' performances, "the powers that be" who oversee the production of serials, and the daytime press's coverage of the industry. In sum, our own engagement in the social networks that comprise the subculture of soap fanship permits us invaluable insights and further understanding of what drives viewers and fans to invest so intensely in soap opera narratives.

# Notes

## Introduction

1. For exceptions, see the recent investigations of prime-time and movie fan communities that focus on fans of *Star Trek* (Bacon-Smith 1992; Jenkins 1992b; Penley 1991, 1992).

2. However, fans of fictionalized sports are also subjected to marginalization. Professional wrestling enthusiasts are denigrated because the outcomes of matches and championships are scripted in advance (Jenkins forthcoming).

3. For discussion of the fan-celebrity-industry link, see Jenkins 1988, 1992a, b.

4. We do not mean to imply that the difference between viewer and fan is clear-cut; indeed, we explicitly argue against such an interpretation throughout the book. For our purposes here, however, we acknowledge that the category "fan" implies a participation in public activities that the category "viewer" does not.

## Chapter One

1. As we discuss later, few daytime fans create derivative products; only a few write fictional pieces that extend daytime narratives or create the type of artwork or song tapes for which other media fans are known. The only types of derivative texts routinely produced by soap opera fans are specially edited videotapes of favored characters or story lines, scrapbooks, and yearbooks chronicling the activities of fans who attend soap events together.

2. A shift under way within the daytime industry is creating new tension between producers and viewers; see Chapter Five.

3. In late 1994, *Soap Opera Digest* reported a total paid circulation of 1,607,500 and *Soap Opera Weekly* reported 523,579 copies sold.

4. As Trinajstick states: "Fan clubs are non-profit, UNLESS they sell a lot of merchandise or are run from the celebrity's office by a paid employee. In the latter case, this is NOT a 'fan club,' but then becomes a promotional organization for the celebrity, and would be classified as a business" (1991:45). Also see Dawn Mazzurco's 1991 article "Everything You Need to Know about Fan Clubs."

5. The first science fiction fanzines date to the 1920s. They began to be ex-

changed by fans in earnest in the early 1930s, and their success is linked to the emergence of science fiction fan clubs during the same era (Bainbridge 1986).

## Chapter Two

1. Some research examines gratifications that come through viewing daytime serials as a member of a group—in college dormitories, sororities and fraternities, the workplace, and other public locations (e.g., Lemish 1985). Viewing in prisons, the military, and professional sports teams has received little attention.

2. While some scholars assume specific social structural factors must be present for the emergence of a subculture (see, for example, Cloward and Ohlin 1960; Hebdige 1979; Yinger 1960), we make no such assumptions (following Fine and Kleinman 1979). We rely upon work by Clark et al. (1981) for our conceptualization of culture and subculture. Culture refers to "that level at which social groups develop distinctive patterns of life, and give *expressive form* to their social and material life-experience. Culture is the way, the forms, in which groups 'handle' the raw material of their social and material existence; . . . it is the practice which realises or *objectivates* group-life in meaningful shape and form. . . . The 'culture' of a group or class is the peculiar and distinctive 'way of life' of the group or class, the meanings, values and ideas embodied in institutions, in social relations, in systems of beliefs, in *mores* and customs, in the uses of objects and material life. Culture is the distinctive shapes in which this material and social organisation of life expresses itself. A culture includes the 'maps of meaning' which make things intelligible to its members. These 'maps of meaning' are not simply carried around in the head: they are objectivated in the patterns of social organisation and re-lationships through which the individual becomes a 'social individual.' Culture is the way the social relations of a group are structured and shaped: but it is also the way those shapes are experienced, understood, and interpreted" (53). Subculture "takes shape around the distinctive activities and 'focal concerns' of groups. They can be loosely or tightly bounded. Some subcultures are merely loosely-defined strands or 'milieux' within the parent culture: they possess no distinctive 'world' of their own. Others develop a clear, coherent identity and structure" (56). We will be describing a subculture that is loosely bounded.

Our conception of the subculture of serial fanship also differs from the concept of taste publics as developed by Herbert Gans (1974). According to Gans, members of taste publics organize primarily on the basis of shared values and the cultural forms that express those values. But serial fans do not necessarily engage the medium on the basis of a shared set of aesthetic values, and thus they do not precisely conform to the definition of a taste public. Daytime fans do share an interest in a particular content, namely, narratives that address concerns about the private realm. However, their aesthetic values about that content are quite diverse, ranging from enjoying watching attractive female characters who are dressed seductively (as some male fans readily admit) to interest in viewing intergenerational interaction over a family crisis (as is the case for some of the other male and female fans we know). Accordingly, they do not comprise a homogeneous taste public in Gans's sense. As Gans himself notes, cultural values cannot be inferred from cultural content, at least without knowing how people choose content. Individuals may choose the same content based on different aesthetic values (1974:11).

3. But there is a difference of opinion as to whether subjectivity as conceptualized by film theorists applies to television viewing (see Press 1991:17–19). Subjectivity in film viewing assumes spectatorship is done individually and voyeuristically. As Andrea Press notes, television viewing usually occurs in domestic, group settings that preclude highly individualized viewing. See also Fiske 1987:57.

4. Evidence of fan gossip comes primarily from ethnographic studies of soap viewers as spectators, which establish how the gossip originates mainly through fans' collaborative interpretations of the soap and to a lesser extent from individual, isolated interpretations (Seiter et al. 1989:233).

5. The term *charismatic* is often used to describe the performance of a very popular actor. Charisma is defined as "a certain quality of an individual's personality by virtue of which he is set apart from ordinary men and treated as endowed with supernatural, superhuman, or at least superficially exceptional qualities" (Weber, *Max Weber on Charisma and Institution Building*, 1968:329). Richard Dyer (1979:35) notes that there are problems in transferring the notion of charisma as it is found in the political order (as Weber was concerned with) to the realm of entertainment. He elaborates: "As Alberoni has pointed out, the star's status depends upon her/his not having any institutional political power. Yet there is clearly some correspondence between political and star charisma, in particular the question of how or why a given person comes to have 'charisma' attributed to her or him. E. A. Shils in *Charisma, Order, and Status* suggests: 'The charismatic quality of an individual as perceived by others, or himself lies in what is thought to be his connection with (including possession by or embedment in) some very central feature of man's existence and the cosmos in which he lives. The centrality, coupled with intensity, makes it extraordinary.'" Leo Braudy (1986:71) argues that the structured arrangement between performers and audiences "force[s] the

performer to project an invisible audience to play to, and *star* quality . . . mean[s] the ability to play to an audience of anonymous others and make them think you meant each one of them alone [emphasis added]."

6. According to Dyer (1991), markers of authenticity are lack of control, such as when gestures and facial expressions are redundant with words; lack of premeditation, when gestures seem spontaneous; and privacy, when intimacy or essentialness are connoted by nonpublic actions.

7. One casting director says that for the most part her colleagues are unable to predict what qualities will capture the audience's interests.

8. While fan interest would seem to presume talent as a prerequisite for an actor's popularity (see Gamson 1994), one fan club president noted that "there are countless instances in serial history where the popularity of a character far exceeds the presence of the actor playing the part."

9. Every industry participant we interviewed — actors, journalists, producers, and fan club officials — had a story about fans who go too far in their pursuit of information (see Chapter Three).

10. Elsewhere we have studied the impact of sharing exclusively obtained information with others who are, at least initially, nonintimates. The negotiation of trust, authenticity, and truth are central to the intimacy that develops between fans (see Harrington and Bielby 1995).

11. The contribution of celebrity to soap fanship contrasts with its role in other media-based fanships. In other television-based fanships, actors are largely untouched by the textual poaching activity of fans (e.g., Bacon-Smith 1992; Jenkins 1992b). For fanships organized around charismatic live performers, such as musicians (Weinstein 1991), celebrity is based upon an artist's persona, not scripted fictional characters under the exclusive control of professional writers. Film celebrity may be more relevant to our examination of soap actors, but its analysis rarely goes beyond discussion of the fan's psychological identification with the actor's screen image (Dyer 1979; Stacey 1991).

12. In contrast to other genres where fan clubs and conventions are fundamental to the organization of fan subculture because they provide "space where interpretations are negotiated between readers" (Jenkins 1992b:88), daytime serial fan clubs are less relevant to fans' ability to construct tertiary texts around viewing.

13. *Episodes,* launched in 1990, violated the traditional boundaries among the textual layers that differentiate producers from consumers. It was produced by a producer of the primary text in contrast to other publications constituting the secondary text. Considered successful with more than a million subscribers, sustaining it became too costly (*Wall Street Journal* 1993).

14. Even insiders lament its status. As one former daytime actor told us, "Soaps are rinky dink, not because they don't try, but because they don't have the time to do things right."

15. In "Day for Night: NBC Wins with Emmy Awards" the industry trade paper the *Hollywood Reporter* (1992:3–5) noted that the prime-time broadcast of the 1992 daytime Emmy awards won its time period with a twenty-six share.

## Chapter Three

1. According to Becker (1963:14), what is defined as "rule-breaking" behavior depends in part on the nature of the activity (that is, whether or not it violates norms of social organization) and in part on what others do about it.

2. The work by Mills (1940) and others about vocabularies of motive is relevant here. According to Mills, individuals whose behavior is labeled as violating social norms devise responses that justify and explain the behavior, usually in terms that neutralize how it is perceived.

3. We follow Kay Deaux's understanding of identity. First, there is an emphasis on social identity, meaning that when we identify ourselves in a certain way, we speak not only of personal characteristics but of characteristics shared with others (e.g. a specific subculture). Second, we have multiple identities. Finally, identities are socially constructed through experience (1991:78). Deaux's perspective integrates established psychological and sociological approaches to identity that are usually studied separately (see, for example, Burke and Reitzes 1991; Mead 1934; Stryker 1968; Tajfel 1981).

4. Fan identities illustrate ideas of the postmodern self. As postmodern theorists suggest, the relationship between the individual and social institutions is being redefined, offering increased freedom from societal restrictions. Whereas the self in the modern era was defined largely through commitments to institutional structures (e.g., work, family, religion, and marriage), the postmodern self is located in "impulse" (Turner 1976:991). The "impulsive" individual experiences the true self by breaking free from social and institutional constraints; what is important is emotion, affect, and nonlinear/nonrational modes of thought. Some have suggested that a rise in various forms of fanship is occurring in postmodern culture "partly because there seems to be no other space available" that is equally receptive to emotion and pleasure (Grossberg 1992a:63).

5. This research supports earlier work that characterized celebrity-fan relationships as parasocial, based on fans' misperceptions that the interactions they have with performers are real. The fan might indeed experience the relationship as real,

but it is actually "one-sided, nondialectical, controlled by the performer, and not susceptible of mutual development" (Horton and Wohl 1956:215).

6. The line between fantasy and reality became even fuzzier following the bizarre 1992 murder of a popular Brazilian soap actress by her on-screen lover, distraught at the writers' decision to end the characters' romance. One commentator concluded: "Brazilians discovered virtual reality years ago. . . . They never know when they are entering the screen and when they are leaving it" (Guillermoprieto 1993:44; see also Gliatto 1993).

7. A recent article in *Soap Opera Weekly,* "Close Encounters of a Fan Kind," explored the issues of what actors owe their fans and what they expect in return (Martin 1993).

8. Indeed, while we do not feel these women engaged in erotomaniac behavior, their cases illustrate the degree to which fans can become engaged with soap operas, to the point of feeling that their fanship is damaging to themselves and their families. It is important to note that neither woman presented a physical danger to Evans or Nichols, although the rumors generated by the Patch/Kayla support group might have been personally painful to the actors. The repercussions of their "addiction" were thus experienced privately, not publicly. This supports a study conducted by criminologist Park Dietz and his colleagues (1991) that found little association between fans' verbal threats and harassment of celebrities and "approach behavior." In our view, these fans' actions might be more easily understood in terms of research on sports fans, who are known to "identify so strongly with their team that they respond to team outcomes as if they directly affect the self" (Hirt et al. 1992:725). Clearly, Sandra's and Phyllis's emotional and physiological reactions to the Patch/Kayla story line indicate extreme identification with the characters.

9. The Super Couple trend is declining, due primarily to the difficulty writers have in continuing the story lines for characters who have been portrayed as perfect lovers (Reep 1992).

10. For a brief time in 1991, NBC aired a commercial featuring *Days of Our Lives* viewers as screaming, frantic, desperate people. While the commercial accurately reflected *Days* fans' poor reputation within the industry, the commercial was pulled from the air quickly. Insiders suspect the withdrawal was due to viewer complaints.

## Chapter Four

1. Valerie Walkerdine notes that "psychoanalytically oriented film theory [from which these insights about fantasy are drawn], despite its many strengths, still

elides certain problems about subjectivity when it implies that subject-positions are produced *within* the discourses of filmic representations. . . . Readers will read films not in terms of a pre-existing set of relations of signification or through a pathology of scopophilia [the pleasure of looking], but by what those relations *mean to them*" (1986:189–190).

2. We suggested in Chapter One that one reason fans of daytime television (in contrast to female fans of male-centered texts) rarely participate in textual poaching is that they *are* able to identify more easily with the primary narrative, particularly with female characters and female-oriented story lines. Because the text is more accessible to them, there is little motivation to create alternative texts. As a second comparison consider the fantasy-gaming subculture, only 5–10 percent female. Fine (1983:62) suggests that because women who choose to play fantasy-oriented games such as Dungeons and Dragons must portray male characters, it is more difficult for women than for men to identify with and find pleasure in the game. These contrasts suggest that the genderedness of any cultural object is crucial to the development of the subculture that emerges around it.

3. Katz and Liebes (1984:195) have examined how fans identify with characters — specifically, the processes through which they engage them: "certain groups use [a] program 'referentially': that is, they relate the narrative to real life. Others speak much more analytically, or 'poetically,' relating to the dramatic construction of the story rather than to its reality." These differences were found to be related to ethnic identity and not necessarily to gender.

4. Research on the viewer's role in the interpretive process is indebted to Stuart Hall's (1980) work on encoding/decoding. Hall theorized that despite dominant meanings encoded in cultural texts, the different positions that viewers might take in the decoding process (dominant-hegemonic, negotiated, or oppositional) allow for viewer agency in interpretation.

5. The pleasures of speculation are not limited to soap viewers. In *Claims to Fame: Celebrity in Contemporary America*, Joshua Gamson suggests that many celebrity watchers derive great pleasure simply from circulating and discussing information about stars and care little about the resolutions of stars' private troubles. "What's important here is a process rather than an endpoint, a game rather than an outcome" (Gamson 1994:268). What differentiates soap fans from many celebrity watchers is their investment in the outcome of such information, insofar as it impacts story line or character developments.

6. Henry Jenkins (forthcoming) suggests that professional wrestling fans provide a fascinating contrast to soap fans, in that while the latter find intense pleasure in looking for the real behind the fictional (as this chapter elaborates), the former are constantly looking for proof that the purportedly real sporting events are, in

fact, staged. One respondent, a sports fan and the son of a former leading daytime actor, observed that the huge salaries paid to sports figures raise expectations for "performances" by them at sporting events.

7. Identification (and fantasy) is constrained by the psychological and social position of the viewer, the social context of viewing, and the medium itself (see Brown 1990; Mulvey 1975; Press 1991).

8. Regarding actors' ad-libs, we offer two examples from fans, both involving Jack Wagner and Kristina Malandro, who played the popular Frisco and Felicia on *General Hospital*. One respondent declares, "I loved the 'solid' scene. So it wasn't an adlib then? When he said 'Solid like I am,' I thought that maybe that part wasn't scripted." And another says: "Remember when they went to Ohio and Frisco got on her train? Well, Felicia is supposed to be mad at him, but Kris is smirking throughout most of the scene. He is grabbing her by the belt and pulling her into the seat and she is thinking it's funny and is not nearly as mad as Felicia is supposed to be."

9. Scheff (1990) does not directly discuss people's affective bonds with fictional others. His theory implies, however, that the celebrity-fan relationship is a form of an insecure bond.

10. In 1992, the largest commercial computer service was Prodigy with 1.75 million users, followed by CompuServe with 1.69 million and GEnie with 350,000 (Grimes 1992:C13). By late 1993, America-Online had 500,000 subscribers (Mossberg 1994:B1). In addition, millions access bulletin boards on the Internet via both commercial and noncommercial services.

11. Levine (1988), for example, shows how Shakespeare's popularity transformed over time, shifting from the participatory (and underdistanced) pleasure of mass audiences to the appreciative (but overdistanced) pleasure of most audiences today.

## Chapter Five

1. Regarding literary theory, see, for example, Roland Barthes's classic article "The Death of the Author," which argues that historically the author was thought the sole creator of a text, including the full range of its meanings; "[to] give a text an Author is to impose a limit on that text" (1977:147) and the possible meanings it might engender. The growing impact of reception theory on literary criticism led to a shift in focus from the author to the text and its readers (Crawford and Chaffin 1986; Holland 1975; Holub 1984; Iser 1978). Reconceptualized as the result of an interaction between text and reader, meaning is constituted (and reconstituted) by

the reader in each successive reading. In this view, neither the text nor the reader completely determines meaning; rather the reader activates a text's meanings. Television studies, also impacted by reception theory of the 1970s, awarded the consumer precedence over the text in terms of meaning making as a result of three transformations (Brunsdon 1989): audience studies, which focused on *how* people watch television; feminist theory and criticism, which addressed women's repetitive consumption of female-centered narratives and shifted attention from the "bad" text to the "good" audience; and scholarship that recognized the difficulty of separating a primary text from other texts that surround it (Morley 1989:23) and thus shifted to consumers as a focus of analysis (Bennett and Woollacott 1987; Brunsdon 1989; Morley 1989).

2. For a discussion of the legal history of ownership and copyright of cultural texts, see Jane M. Gaines's *Contested Culture: The Image, the Voice, and the Law* (1991). As Gaines points out, we have a long history of confusing the legal owner of a text with its author.

3. This familiar view of cultural stratification might be changing. Richard A. Peterson argues that the elite-to-mass (or "snob to slob") theory is being replaced by an "omnivore to univore" distinction, wherein high status groups participate in a wide range of leisure activities (both elite and nonelite) while low-status groups focus on a single activity or genre for leisure investment (1992:252–254).

4. The relationship between a novelist and a reader is mediated by any number of industry figures, including literary agents, publishers, critics, editors, reviewers, and booksellers. In the process of getting published, "novelists' works can take on lives that were never authorially intended" (Rogers 1991:163).

5. In some cases, a head writer's influence transcends even death. Fan newsletter editor Michael Kape applauded the writing staff of *As the World Turns* for remaining faithful to the story projections of the legendary Douglas Marland, who died in early 1993 (*Soap Opera Now!* 1993c:2).

6. This relative powerlessness seems true for all forms of acting. For example, cinema studies scholar Barry King argues that technological advances in film production have so altered actors' performances that they have little or no control over their characters. The actor "is anything but the sole author of the discourse he or she has produced" (in Gaines 1991:35).

7. Mikhail Bakhtin (1981) and Michel de Certeau (1984), among others, suggest that fans author original creations when they create their own meanings out of texts. In that sense, all viewers, readers, and fans are authors. We are suggesting that soap opera fans are being invited to actually author the primary text.

8. Some bulletin board services do censor public messages for appropriateness

of topic or suitable language because they consider themselves "family" boards. Users are aware of this and often comment on ways to comply with the censors or gleefully share the tricks they discover to bypass the censors and keep the content and form of their message intact. For example, curse words are modified with asterisks to avoid censorship: sh*t, g*ddamn, etc.

9. Even though soap fandom is a loosely organized subculture, elements of a status hierarchy exist just as in more tightly bounded subcultures that serve as life-style alternatives (see Fox 1987; Hebdige 1979).

10. This is true of virtually all entertainment industries. According to Joshua Gamson in *Claims to Fame: Celebrity in Contemporary America,* those who work in media production have little idea of viewers' and fans' interests or opinions of cultural texts. "The idea that one can understand audiences is itself a joke, pun-ished with ridicule. . . . The central link between the celebrity industry and the consuming publics operates with very tenuous knowledge about those publics" (1994:179–180; see also Gitlin 1983).

# References

A. C. Nielsen Company. 1981. "Individual Network Program Audiences (Total Duration): Monday-Friday Daytime." (February and May).

Alasuutari, Pertti. 1992. " 'I'm Ashamed to Admit It but I Have Watched Dallas': The Moral Hierarchy of Television Programmes." *Media, Culture and Society* 14:561–582.

Alberoni, Francesco. 1972. "The Powerless Elite: Theory and Sociological Research on the Phenomenon of the Stars." In *Sociology of Mass Communications,* edited and translated by Denis McQuail, 75–98. London: Penguin.

Allen, Robert C. 1983. "On Reading Soaps: A Semiotic Primer." In *Regarding Television,* edited by E. Ann Kaplan, 97–108. Frederick, Md.: University Publications of America.

———. 1985. *Speaking of Soap Operas.* Chapel Hill: University of North Carolina Press.

Ang, Ien. 1985. *Watching Dallas: Soap Opera and the Melodramatic Imagination.* New York: Methuen.

———. 1988. "Feminist Desire and Female Pleasure: On Janice Radway's 'Reading the Romance: Women, Patriarchy and Popular Literature' (Chapel Hill and London: University of North Carolina Press, 1984)." *Camera Obscura* 16:179–190.

———. 1990. "Melodramatic Identifications: Television Fiction and Women's Fantasy." In *Television and Women's Culture,* edited by Mary Ellen Brown, 75–88. Newbury Park, Calif.: Sage.

———. 1991. *Desperately Seeking the Audience.* New York: Routledge.

Archer, Jane. 1992. "The Fate of the Subject in the Narrative without End." In *Staying Tuned: Contemporary Soap Opera Criticism,* edited by Suzanne Frentz, 89–102. Bowling Green, Ohio: Bowling Green State University Popular Press.

Arrigo, Mary. 1990. "Rebel with a Cause." *Soap Opera Digest* 15 (December 11):30–32, 142.

Babad, Elisha. 1987. "Wishful Thinking and Objectivity among Sports Fans." *Social Behavior* 2:231–240.

Bacon-Smith, Camille. 1992. *Enterprising Women.* Philadelphia: University of Pennsylvania Press.

Bainbridge, William Sims. 1986. *Dimensions of Science Fiction.* Cambridge: Harvard University Press.

Bakhtin, Mikhail. 1981. *The Dialogic Imagination.* Austin: University of Texas Press.

Barber, Bernard. 1983. *The Logic and Limits of Trust.* New Brunswick, N.J.: Rutgers University Press.

Barthes, Roland. 1975. *The Pleasure of the Text.* New York: Hill and Wang.

———. 1977. "The Death of the Author." In *Image/Music/Text,* edited by Stephen Heath, 142–148. London: Fontana.

Becker, Howard S. 1963. *Outsiders: Studies in the Sociology of Deviance.* New York: Free Press.

———. 1982. *Art Worlds.* Berkeley and Los Angeles: University of California Press.

Bennett, Tony, and Jane Woollacott. 1987. *Bond and Beyond: The Political Career of a Popular Hero.* London: Macmillan.

Bernard, Jessie Shirley. 1981. *The Female World.* New York: Free Press.

Bialkowski, Carol. 1992. "Fan Fare." *Soap Opera Digest* 17 (July 7):100–102.

Bielby, Denise D., and C. Lee Harrington. 1992. "Public Meanings, Private Screenings: The Formation of Social Bonds through the Televisual Experience." In *Perspectives on Social Problems,* edited by Gale Miller and John Holstein, 3:155–178. Greenwich, Conn.: Jai.

———. 1994. "Reach Out and Touch Someone: Viewers, Agency, and Audiences in the Televisual Experience." In *Viewing, Reading, Listening: Audiences and Cultural Reception,* edited by Jon Cruz and Justin Lewis, 81–100. Boulder, Colo.: Westview.

Bielby, William T., and Denise D. Bielby. 1994. "'All Hits Are Flukes': Institutionalized Decision-Making and the Rhetoric of Network Prime-Time Program Development." *American Journal of Sociology* 99:1287–1313.

Black, Donald J., and Albert J. Reiss Jr. 1970. "Police Control of Juveniles." *American Sociological Review* 35:63–77.

Boden, Deirdre, and Denise D. Bielby. 1983. "The Past as Resource: A Conversational Analysis of Elderly Talk." *Human Development* 26:309–319.

Bourdieu, Pierre. 1984. *Distinction: A Social Critique of the Judgment of Taste.* Cambridge: Harvard University Press.

Brake, Mike. 1974. "The Skinheads: An English Working Class Subculture." *Youth and Society* 6:179–199.

Braudy, Leo. 1986. *The Frenzy of Renown.* New York: Oxford University Press.

Brower, Sue. 1992. "Fans as Tastemakers: Viewers for Quality Television." In *The Adoring Audience,* edited by Lisa A. Lewis, 163–184. New York: Routledge.

REFERENCES / 207

Brown, Mary Ellen. 1987. "The Politics of Soaps: Pleasure and Feminine Empowerment." *Australian Journal of Cultural Studies* 4:1–25.

———. 1989. "Soap Opera and Women's Culture: Politics and the Popular." In *Doing Research on Women's Communication: Perspectives on Theory and Method,* edited by Kathryn Carter and Carole Spitzack, 161–190. Norwood, N.J.: Ablex.

———. 1990. *Television and Women's Culture.* Newbury Park, Calif.: Sage.

Brunsdon, Charlotte. 1981. "Crossroads: Notes on Soap Opera." *Screen* 22:32–37.

———. 1989. "Text and Audience." In *Remote Control,* edited by E. Seiter, H. Borchers, G. Kreutzner, and E. Warth, 116–129. London: Routledge.

Burke, Peter, and D. Reitzes. 1991. "An Identity Theory Approach to Commitment." *Social Psychology Quarterly* 54:39–51.

Byars, Jackie. 1988. "Gazes, Voices, Power: Expanding Psychoanalysis for Feminist Film and Television Theory." In *Female Spectators,* edited by Deidre Pribam, 110–131. Verso: London.

Cancian, Francesca. 1987. *Love in America.* Cambridge: Cambridge University Press.

Cantor, Muriel, and Suzanne Pingree. 1983. *The Soap Opera.* Beverly Hills, Calif.: Sage.

Caughie, John. 1981. Introduction to part two of *Theories of Authorship,* edited by John Caughie, 123–130. London: Routledge and Kegan Paul.

Cavell, Stanley. 1982. "The Fact of Television." *Daedalus* 111:75–96.

Cawelti, John G. 1976. *Adventure, Mystery, and Romance.* Chicago: University of Chicago Press.

Cerone, Daniel. 1994. "Hollywood On-Line." *Los Angeles Calendar,* April 17, 7–8, 82–83.

Chodorow, Nancy. 1978. *The Reproduction of Mothering: Psychoanalysis and the Sociology of Gender.* Berkeley and Los Angeles: University of California Press.

Ciotti, Paul. 1992. "Fan-Mail Firm Gets Peek at Private Lives." *Los Angeles Times,* May 8, F25A, D.

Clark, John, Stuart Hall, Tony Jefferson, and Brian Roberts. 1981. "Subcultures, Cultures, and Class." In *Culture, Ideology, and Social Process,* edited by Tony Bennett, et al., 53–79. London: Batsford Academic and Educational in association with Open University Press.

Cloward, Richard, and Lloyd Ohlin. 1960. *Delinquency and Opportunity.* New York: Free Press.

Compesi, Ronald. 1980. "Gratifications of Daytime TV Serial Viewers." *Journalism Quarterly* 57:155–158.

Comstock, George. 1989. *The Evolution of American Television*. Newbury Park, Calif.: Sage.

Coons, Joanna. 1992. "An Inside Look." *Soap Opera Now!* 10 (April 27):4.

———. 1993a. "An Inside Look." *Soap Opera Now!* 11 (August 23–30):5–6.

———. 1993b. "Should Actors Have Unlimited Input in Their Storylines?" *Soap Opera Now!* 11 (January 4):5.

Cox, Dan. 1994. "WGA, 3 Nets OK Contract." *Daily Variety* 246 (December 16):1, 30.

Crane, Diana. 1992. *The Production of Culture*. Newbury Park, Calif.: Sage.

Crawford, Mary, and Roger Chaffin. 1986. "The Reader's Construction of Meaning." In *Gender and Reading*, edited by Elizabeth A. Flynn and Patrocinio P. Schweikart, 3–30. Baltimore: Johns Hopkins University Press.

Cruz, Jon, and Justin Lewis. 1994. Introduction to *Viewing, Reading, Listening: Audiences and Cultural Reception*, edited by Jon Cruz and Justin Lewis, 1–18. Boulder, Colo.: Westview.

Csikszentmihalyi, Mihaly. 1975. *Beyond Boredom and Anxiety*. San Francisco: Jossey-Bass.

Davidson, Sara. 1973. "Feeding on Dreams in a Bubble Gum Culture." *Atlantic Monthly* 232 (October):62–72.

*Daytime TV.* 1993a. "Pillow Talk." Vol. 24 (September):43–53.

———. 1993b. "We Get Letters." Vol. 23 (February):42.

Deaux, Kay. 1991. "Social Identities: Thoughts on Structure and Change." In *The Relational Self: Theoretical Convergences in Psychoanalysis and Social Psychology*, edited by Rebecca C. Curtis, 77–94. New York: Guilford.

de Certeau, Michel. 1984. "Reading as Poaching." In *The Practice of Everyday Life*, 165–176. Berkeley and Los Angeles: University of California Press.

De Lacroix, Marlena. 1992. "Critical Condition: Attack of the Killer Tomatoes." *Soap Opera Weekly* 3 (July 14):38.

Deri, Susan. 1978. "Transitional Phenomena: Vicissitudes of Symbolization and Creativity." In *Between Reality and Fantasy*, edited by Simon Grolnick, L. Barkin, and W. Muensterberger, 45–60. Northvale, N.J.: Jason Aronson.

Derry, Charles. 1985. "Television Soap Opera: 'Incest, Bigamy, and Fatal Disease.'" In *American Television Genres*, edited by Stuart Kaminsky with Jeffrey H. Mahan, 85–110. Chicago: Nelson-Hall.

DeVault, Marjorie. 1991. "Novel Readings: The Social Organization of Interpretation." *American Journal of Sociology* 95:887–921.

*Diagnostic and Statistical Manual of Mental Disorders-III-Revised.* 1987. 3d edition (DSM-III-R). Washington, D.C.: American Psychiatric Association.

Dietz, Park Elliott, D. B. Matthews, C. Van Duyne, D. A. Martell, C.D.H. Parry, T. Stewart, J. Warren, and J. D. Crowder. 1991. "Threatening and Otherwise Inappropriate Letters to Hollywood Celebrities." *Journal of Forensic Sciences* 36:185–209.

DiLauro, Janet. 1994. "Memorial Days Delight." *Soap Opera Weekly* 5 (June 21):34–36.

Dolan, Carrie. 1992. "Labor of Love: Watching the Soaps Is a Calling for Some." *Wall Street Journal,* December 17, A1–5.

Douglas, Mary. 1963. *Natural Symbols.* New York: Pantheon.

Dunlop, Joyce L. 1988. "Does Erotomania Exist between Women?" *British Journal of Psychiatry* 153:830–833.

Dyer, Richard. 1979. *Stars.* London: BFI.

———. 1991. "*A Star Is Born* and the Construction of Authenticity." In *Stardom: Industry of Desire,* edited by Christine Gledhill, 132–140. London: Routledge.

Eco, Umberto. 1985. "Innovation and Repetition: Between Modern and Postmodern Aesthetics." *Daedalus* 114:161–184.

*Fans of "General Hospital" Newsletter.* 1991. August 26.

Farberman, Harvey. 1981. "Fantasy in Everyday Life: Some Aspects of the Intersection between Social Psychology and Political Economy." *Symbolic Interaction* 3:3–21.

Fine, Gary Alan. 1979. "Small Groups and Culture Creation: The Idioculture of Little League Baseball Teams." *American Sociological Review* 44:733–745.

———. 1983. *Shared Fantasy: Role-Playing Games as Social Worlds.* Chicago: University of Chicago Press.

Fine, Gary Alan, and Sheryl Kleinman. 1979. "Rethinking Subculture: An Interactionist Analysis." *American Journal of Sociology* 85:1–20.

Finn, Seth. 1992. "Television 'Addiction'? An Evaluation of Four Competing Media-Use Models." *Journalism Quarterly* 69:422–435.

Fiske, John. 1987. *Television Culture.* New York: Methuen.

———. 1992. "The Cultural Economy of Fandom." In *The Adoring Audience,* edited by Lisa A. Lewis, 30–49. New York: Routledge.

Flynn, Elizabeth A. 1986. "Gender and Reading." In *Gender and Reading,* edited by Elizabeth A. Flynn and Patrocinio P. Schweikart, 267–288. Baltimore: Johns Hopkins University Press.

Fowles, Jib. 1992. *Why Viewers Watch.* Newbury Park, Calif.: Sage.

Fox, Joan. 1987. "Real Punks and Pretenders: The Social Organization of a Counterculture." *Journal of Contemporary Ethnography* 16:344–370.

Freedman, L. Z. 1981. "Desperate to Fill an Emotional Void, Some Fans Become Dangerous to Their Idols." *People Weekly* 15 (April 20):38–39.

Gaines, Jane M. 1991. *Contested Culture: The Image, the Voice, and the Law.* Chapel Hill: University of North Carolina Press.

Gamson, Joshua. 1992. "The Assembly Line of Greatness: Celebrity in Twentieth-Century America." *Critical Studies in Mass Communication* 9:1–24.

———. 1994. *Claims to Fame: Celebrity in Contemporary America.* Berkeley and Los Angeles: University of California Press.

Gans, Herbert J. 1974. *Popular Culture and High Culture.* New York: Basic.

Geraghty, Christine. 1991. *Women and Soap Opera.* Cambridge: Polity.

Gilligan, Carol. 1982. *In a Different Voice.* Cambridge: Harvard University Press.

Gitlin, Todd. 1983. *Inside Prime Time.* New York: Pantheon.

Gledhill, Christine. 1987. *Home Is Where the Heart Is: Studies in Melodrama and the Woman's Film.* London: BFI.

Gliatto, Tom, with Karla Bruner and Steve Yolen. 1993. "Kiss of Death." *People Weekly* 39 (January 18):96, 98.

Goode, Eric. 1994. *Deviant Behavior.* 4th edition. Englewood Cliffs, N.J.: Prentice-Hall.

Greenberg, Jay R., and Stephen A. Mitchell. 1983. *Object Relations in Psychoanalytic Theory.* Cambridge: Harvard University Press.

Greene, A. L., and Carolyn Adams-Price. 1990. "Adolescents' Secondary Attachments to Celebrity Figures." *Sex Roles* 23:335–347.

Griggs, Robyn. 1991. "Peaks Freaks Seek to Keep Weak Show." *Mediaweek,* April 29, 2.

Grimes, William. 1992. "Computer as a Cultural Tool: Chatter Mounts on Every Topic." *New York Times,* December 1, C13–14.

Griswold, Wendy. 1987. "The Fabrication of Meaning: Literary Interpretation in the United States, Great Britain, and the West Indies." *American Journal of Sociology* 92:1077–1117.

Grossberg, Lawrence. 1987. "The Indifference of Television." *Screen* 28:29–45.

———. 1992a. "Is There a Fan in the House? The Affective Sensibility of Fandom." In *The Adoring Audience,* edited by Lisa A. Lewis, 50–65. New York: Routledge.

———. 1992b. *We Gotta Get Out of This Place.* New York: Routledge.

Guillermoprieto, Alma. 1993. "Obsessed in Rio." *New Yorker* 69 (August 16):44–55.

Hall, Stuart. 1980. "Encoding/Decoding." In *Culture, Media, Language,* edited by S. Hall, A. Lowe, and P. Willis, 128–139. London: Hutchinson.

Handel, Leo. 1950. *Hollywood Looks at Its Audience: A Report of Film Audience Research.* New York: Arno.

Hansen, Miriam. 1991. "Pleasure, Ambivalence, Identification: Valentino and Female Spectatorship." In *Stardom: Industry of Desire,* edited by Christine Gledhill, 259–282. London: Routledge.

Harrington, C. L., and D. D. Bielby. 1995. "Where Did You Hear That? Technology and the Social Organization of Gossip." *Sociological Quarterly* 36.

Haskell, Molly. 1987. *From Reverence to Rape: The Treatment of Women in the Movies,* 2d edition. Chicago: University of Chicago Press.

Heath, Stephen. 1972. *The Nouveau Roman: A Study in the Practice of Writing.* London: Elek.

Hebdige, Dick. 1979. *Subculture: The Meaning of Style.* London: Metheun.

Hirt, Edward R., D. Zillmann, G. A. Erickson, and C. Kennedy. 1992. "Costs and Benefits of Allegiance: Changes in Fans' Self-Ascribed Competencies after Team Victory versus Defeat." *Journal of Personality and Social Psychology* 63:724–738.

Hobson, Dorothy. 1982. *Crossroads: The Drama of a Soap Opera.* London: Methuen.

Hochschild, Arlie. 1989. *The Second Shift: Working Parents and the Revolution at Home.* New York: Viking.

Holland, Norman N. 1975. *5 Readers Reading.* New Haven: Yale University Press.

*Hollywood Reporter, The.* 1992. "Day for Night: NBC Wins with Emmy Awards." Vol. 322 (June 25):3–5.

Holub, Robert C. 1984. *Reception Theory: A Critical Introduction.* London: Methuen.

Hornik, Susan. 1994. "Industry News." *Soap Opera Now!* 12 (July 4):4.

Horton, Donald, and R. Richard Wohl. 1956. "Mass Communication and Para-Social Interaction: Observations on Intimacy at a Distance." *Psychiatry* 19:215–229.

Iser, Wolfgang. 1978. *The Act of Reading: A Theory of Aesthetic Response.* London: Routledge & Kegan Paul.

*Jack's Fan Connection.* 1991. No. 7.2 (June).

Jenkins, Henry. 1988. "'Star Trek' Rerun, Reread, Rewritten: Fan Writing as Textual Poaching." *Critical Studies in Mass Communication* 5:85–107.

———. 1990. " 'If I Could Speak with Your Sound': Fan Music, Textual Proximity, and Liminal Identification." *Camera Obscura* 23:149–176.

———. 1992a. " 'Strangers No More, We Sing': Filking and the Social Construction of the Science Fiction Fan Community." In *The Adoring Audience,* edited by Lisa A. Lewis, 208–236. New York: Routledge.

———. 1992b. *Textual Poachers: Television Fans and Participatory Culture.* New York: Routledge.

———. 1993. "Ninja Turtles, the Macho King, and Madonna's Navel: Taking Popular Culture Seriously." Seminar in the Special Summer Program, Massachusetts Institute of Technology, Boston, June 7–11.

———. Forthcoming. "Never Trust a Snake: WWF Wrestling as Masculine Melodrama." In *Gender, Race and Sports,* edited by Adam Barker and Todd Boyd. Bloomington: Indiana University Press.

Jensen, Joli. 1992. "Fandom as Pathology: The Consequences of Characterization." In *The Adoring Audience,* edited by Lisa A. Lewis, 9–29. New York: Routledge.

Johnson, Richard. 1986/87. "What Is Cultural Studies Anyway?" *Social Text* 16:38–80.

Kahwaty, Donna Hoke. 1993. "Get Them to the Church on Time." *Soap Opera Digest* 18 (August 31):20–21.

Kaminsky, Stuart, with Jeffrey H. Mahan. 1985. *American Television Genres.* Chicago: Nelson-Hall.

Kape, Michael. 1993. *Soap Opera Now!* 11 (June 14):2.

Kaplan, Cora. 1986. "The Thorn Birds: Fiction, Fantasy, Femininity." In *Formations of Fantasy,* edited by Victor Burgin, James Donald, and Cora Kaplan, 142–166. New York: Methuen.

Kaplan, E. Ann. 1983. "The Realist Debate in the Feminist Film: A Historical Overview of Theories and Strategies in Realism and the Avant-Garde Theory of Film (1971–81)." In *Women and Film: Both Sides of the Camera,* 125–141. London: BFI/OU.

Katz, Elihu, and Tamar Liebes. 1984. "Mutual Aid in the Decoding of 'Dallas': Preliminary Notes from a Cross-Cultural Study." In *Television in Transition,* edited by Phillip Drummond and Richard Paterson, 187–198. London: BFI.

Keane, John, and Paul Mier. 1989. Preface to *Nomads of the Present,* by Alberto Melucci, 1–9. Philadelphia: Temple University Press.

Kelm, Rebecca Sturm. 1989. "The Lack of Access to Back Issues of the Weekly Tabloids: Does It Matter?" *Journal of Popular Culture* 23:45–50.

Kielwasser, Alfred P., and Michelle A. Wolf. 1989. "The Appeal of Soap Opera: An

Analysis of Process and Quality in Dramatic Serial Gratifications." *Journal of Popular Culture* 23:111–123.

King, Andrea. 1991. "Celebrity Stalkers Finding Hollywood's Guard Is Down." *Hollywood Reporter* 45 (January 22):6.

Klapp, Orrin. 1969. *The Collective Search for Identity.* New York: Holt, Rinehart and Winston.

Kubey, Robert. 1990. "Psychological Dependence on Television: Application of DSM-III-R Criteria and Experience Sampling Method Findings." Paper presented at the annual meeting of the American Psychological Association, Boston.

Kubey, Robert, and Mihaly Csikszentmihalyi. 1990. *Television and the Quality of Life: How Viewing Shapes Everyday Experiences.* Hillsdale, N.J.: Lawrence Erlbaum Associates.

Kuhn, Annette. 1984. "Women's Genres." *Screen* 25:18–28.

Lachmann, Richard. 1988. "Graffiti as Career and Ideology." *American Journal of Sociology* 94:229–250.

Lang, Kurt. 1958. "Mass, Class, and the Reviewer." *Social Problems* 6:11–21.

Lembo, Ronald. 1994. "Is There Culture after Cultural Studies?" In *Viewing, Reading, Listening: Audiences and Cultural Reception,* edited by Jon Cruz and Justin Lewis, 33–54. Boulder, Colo.: Westview.

Lembo, Ronald, and Kenneth H. Tucker Jr. 1990. "Culture, Television, and Opposition: Rethinking Cultural Studies." *Critical Studies in Mass Communications* 7:97–116.

Lemish, Dafna. 1985. "Soap Opera Viewing in College: A Naturalistic Inquiry." *Journal of Broadcasting and Electronic Media* 29:275–293.

Levin, Jack. 1993. "Confessions of a Soap Opera Addict." In *Sociological Snapshots,* 34–37. Thousand Oaks, Calif.: Pine Forge.

Levine, Lawrence W. 1988. *Highbrow/Lowbrow: The Emergence of Cultural Hierarchy in America.* Cambridge: Harvard University Press.

Lewis, Lisa A. 1992. Introduction to *The Adoring Audience,* edited by Lisa A. Lewis, 1–6. New York: Routledge.

Livingstone, Sonia. 1990. *Making Sense of Television: The Psychology of Audience Interpretations.* Oxford, England: Pergamon.

Logan, Michael. 1993. "1992: The Worst in Soaps." *TV Guide* 41 (January 2):30.
———. 1993a. "Focus Groups Blur Creativity." *TV Guide* 41 (November 6):31.

London, Mary. 1991. "The Other Wagner." *Soap Opera Update* 39 (October):38–39.

Lull, James. 1982. "How Families Select Television Programs: A Mass-Observational Study." *Journal of Broadcasting* 26:801–811.

———. 1988. "The Family and Television in World Cultures." In *World Families Watch Television,* edited by James Lull, 9–21. Newbury Park, Calif.: Sage.

Martin, Deirdre. 1993. "Close Encounters of a Fan Kind: What, If Anything, Do Actors Owe Their Admirers?" *Soap Opera Weekly* 4 (April 20):37–38.

Mayne, Judith. 1988. *Private Novels, Public Films.* Athens: University of Georgia Press.

Mazzurco, Dawn. 1991. "Everything You Need to Know about Fan Clubs." *Soap Opera Update* 39 (October):36–37.

McGarry, Mark. 1993. "Breaking Up Is Hard to Do." *Soap Opera Weekly* 4 (August 31):12–14.

McIlwraith, R., E. Smith Jacobvitz, R. Kubey, and A. Alexander. 1991. "Television Addiction." *American Behavioral Scientist* 35:104–121.

Mead, George H. 1934. *Mind, Self, and Society: From the Standpoint of a Social Behaviorist.* Edited by C. W. Morris, Chicago: University of Chicago Press, 1962.

Meehan, Eileen R. 1991. " 'Holy Commodity Fetish, Batman': The Political Economy of a Commercial Intertext." In *The Many Faces of Batman: Critical Approaches to a Superhero and His Media,* edited by Roberta E. Pearson and William Uricchio, 47–65. New York: Routledge.

Mellencamp, Patricia. 1990. "TV Time and Catastrophe, or Beyond the Pleasure Principle of Television." In *Logics of Television: Essays in Cultural Criticism,* edited by Patricia Mellencamp, 240–266. Bloomington: Indiana University Press.

Meloy, J. Reid. 1989. "Unrequited Love and the Wish to Kill." *Bulletin of the Menninger Clinic* 53:477–492.

———. 1992. *Violent Attachments.* Northvale, N.J.: Jason Aronson.

Meyrowitz, Joshua. 1985. *No Sense of Place: The Impact of Electronic Media on Social Behavior.* New York: Oxford University Press.

Mills, C. Wright. 1940. "Situated Actions and Vocabularies of Motive." *American Sociological Review* 5:904–913.

Modleski, Tania. 1982. *Loving with a Vengeance: Mass-Produced Fantasies for Women.* New York: Methuen.

———. 1983. "The Rhythms of Reception: Daytime Television and Women's Work." In *Regarding Television,* edited by E. Ann Kaplan, 67–75. Los Angeles: American Film Institute Monograph Series/University Publications of America.

Morley, David. 1986. *Family Television: Cultural Power and Domestic Leisure.* London: Comedia.

——. 1989. "Changing Paradigms in Audience Studies." In *Remote Control,* edited by E. Seiter, H. Borchers, G. Kreutzner, and R. Warth, 16–45. New York: Routledge.

Mossberg, Walter S. 1994. "Personal Technology." *Wall Street Journal,* January 6, B1.

Mulvey, Laura. 1975. "Visual Pleasure and the Narrative Cinema." *Screen* 16(3): 6–18.

Nell, Victor. 1988. *Lost in a Book.* New Haven: Yale University Press.

Oakley, Ann. 1974. *The Sociology of Housework.* New York: Pantheon.

Ostling, Richard N. 1989. "A Fatal Obsession with the Stars." *Time Magazine* 134 (July 31):43–44.

Penley, Constance. 1991. "Brownian Motion: Women, Tactics, and Technology." In *Technoculture,* edited by Constance Penley and Andrew Ross, 135–161. Minneapolis: University of Minnesota Press.

——. 1992. "Feminism, Psychoanalysis, and the Study of Popular Culture." In *Cultural Studies,* edited by L. Grossberg, C. Nelson, and P. Treichler, 479–494. New York: Routledge.

*People Weekly.* 1990. "When Fans Turn into Fanatics, Nervous Celebs Call for Help from Security Expert Gavin De Becker." Vol. 33 (February 12):103–106.

Peterson, Richard A. 1992. "Understanding Audience Segmentation: From Elite and Mass to Omnivore and Univore." *Poetics* 21:243–258.

Poster, Mark 1990. *The Mode of Communication. Poststructuralism and Social Context.* Chicago: University of Chicago Press.

Press, Andrea. 1991. *Women Watching Television: Gender, Class, and Generation in the American Television Experience.* Philadelphia: University of Pennsylvania Press.

Radway, Janice. 1984. *Reading the Romance: Women, Patriarchy, and Popular Literature.* Chapel Hill: University of North Carolina Press.

Rayner, Eric. 1991. *The Independent Mind in British Psychoanalysis.* Northvale, N.J.: Jason Aronson.

Reep, Diana C. 1992. "The Siren Call of the Super Couple: Soap Operas' Destructive Slide toward Closure." In *Staying Tuned: Contemporary Soap Opera Criticism,* edited by Suzanne Frentz, 96–102. Bowling Green, Ohio: Bowling Green State University Popular Press.

Reeves, Jimmie L. 1990. "Rewriting Culture: A Dialogic View of Television Authorship." In *Making Television: Authorship and the Production Process,* edited by Robert J. Thompson and Gary Burns, 147–160. New York: Praeger.

Roberts, Johnnie L., and Jared Sandberg. 1994. "TCI Holds Talks with America-Online and Microsoft About On-Line Services." *Wall Street Journal,* September 13, A2, 10.

Rogers, Mary F. 1991. *Novels, Novelists, and Readers.* Albany: SUNY Press.

Rosen, Ruth. 1986. "Search for Yesterday." In *Watching Television,* edited by Todd Gitlin, 42–67. New York: Pantheon.

Rosnow, Ralph A., and Gary Alan Fine. 1976. *Rumor and Gossip: The Social Psychology of Hearsay.* New York: Elsevier Scientific.

Ross, Andrew. 1989. *No Respect: Intellectuals and Popular Culture.* New York: Routledge.

Rouverol, Jean. 1984. *Writing for the Soaps.* Cincinnati: Writer's Digest.

———. 1992. *Writing for Daytime Drama.* Boston: Focal.

Rubin, Lillian B. 1984. *Intimate Strangers.* New York: Harper and Row.

Sarris, Andrew. 1981. Extract from "Notes on the Auteur Theory in 1962." In *Theories of Authorship,* edited by John Caughie, 62–65. London: Routledge and Kegan Paul.

Scheff, Thomas J. 1979. *Catharsis in Healing, Ritual, and Drama.* Berkeley and Los Angeles: University of California Press.

———. 1990. *Microsociology.* Chicago: University of Chicago Press.

———. 1993. "Gender Wars: Emotions in Much Ado about Nothing." *Sociological Perspective* 36:149–166.

Schickel, Richard. 1985. *Intimate Strangers: The Culture of Celebrity.* Garden City, N.Y.: Doubleday.

Schindehette, Susan. 1990. "Vanna White and Teri Garr Ask the Courts to Protect Them from Fans Who Have Gone Too Far." *People Weekly* 14 (July 16):40.

Scott, James C. 1985. *Weapons of the Weak: Everyday Forms of Peasant Resistance.* New Haven: Yale University Press.

Seiter, Ellen, Hans Borchers, Gabriele Kreutzner, and Eva-Maria Warth. 1989. "Don't Treat Us Like We're So Stupid and Naive: Toward an Ethnography of Soap Opera Viewers." In *Remote Control,* edited by E. Seiter, H. Borchers, G. Kreutzner, and E. Warth, 223–247. New York: Routledge.

Shibutani, Tamotsu. 1991. "Human Agency from the Standpoint of Pragmatism." In *Verstehen and Pragmatism: Essays in Interpretive Sociology,* edited by Horst Helle, 183–194. Frankfurt, Germany: Peter Lang.

Shils, Edward A. 1965. "Charisma, Order, and Status." *American Sociological Review* 30:100–213.

Sloane, Stephanie. 1993. "Full Speed Ahead." *Soap Opera Digest.* 18 (June 8):70–73.

*Soap Opera Digest.* 1990. "Real Life Couples." Vol. 15 (December 25):24–32.

———. 1993a. "Editor's Note." Vol. 18 (February 16):112.

———. 1993b. "Isn't It Romantic?" Vol. 18 (February 16):28–30.

———. 1993c. "Look Who's Watching: Forget the Stereotypes, Soap Watchers Are a New Breed." Vol. 18 (April 13):62–66.

———. 1993d. "NBC Gossip." Vol. 18 (April 13):95.

———. 1993e. "NBC Gossip." Vol. 18 (August 3):94.

———. 1993f. "Paparazzi." Vol. 18 (May 25):33.

———. 1993g. "You Write the Stories." Vol. 18 (August 17):58–61.

———. 1994a. "Eavesdropping." Vol. 19 (April 12):77.

———. 1994b. "Now, It's Your Turn." Vol. 19 (January 4):5.

*Soap Opera Illustrated.* 1993. "The Hayes Heyday." Vol. 2 (Spring):18.

*Soap Opera Magazine.* 1994. "A Father's Day Photo Album." Vol. 4 (June 21):30–31.

*Soap Opera Now!* 1992. "Letters to the Editor." Vol. 10 (November 30):2.

———. 1993a. "Letters to the Editor." Vol. 11 (June 28):2.

———. 1993b. "Letters to the Editor." Vol. 11 (August 9):5.

———. 1993c. "Managing Editor's Corner." Vol. 11 (July 26):2.

———. 1993d. "Should Actors Use Their Fans to Help Get Their Storylines Changed?" Vol. 11 (April 26):5.

———. 1994. "Letters to the Editor." Vol. 12 (January 24):6.

*Soap Opera Update.* 1990a. "A Stephen Nichols Fan Bids Him a Fond Farewell." Vol. 3 (October 8):10.

———. 1990b. "Jack Wagner and Kristina Malandro Talk about Their Greatest Gift." Vol. 3 (December 24):25–29.

———. 1993a. "The 9 Most Provocative Women on Daytime." Vol. 6 (September 21):59, 61.

———. 1993b. "What's On Your Mind? ("Heartbroken over Harley and Mallet"). Vol. 6 (September 21):14.

———. 1993c. "What's On Your Mind? Vol. 6 (February 23):15.

*Soap Opera Weekly.* 1993. "Public Opinion." Vol. 4 (April 20):42–43.

*Soap World.* 1994. "Classified." No. 7:32.

Spacks, Patricia Meyer. 1986. *Gossip.* New York: Knopf.

Spencer, Richard. 1992. "They're Too Much Alike . . ." *Soap Opera Update* 5 (October 20):60–63.

*Springfield Journal.* 1992. Vol. 11 (August/September/October/November):12.

———. 1993. Vol. 12 (February/March):7–8.

Stacey, Jackie. 1991. "Feminine Fascinations: Forms of Identification in Star-

Audience Relations." In *Stardom: Industry of Desire,* edited by Christine Gledhill, 141–163. London: Routledge.

Stone, A. 1990. "Cyberspace and the Limits of Social and Cultural Reality." *Newsletter of the Sociology of Culture* 5.

Stryker, Sheldon. 1968. "Identity Salience and Role Performance." *Journal of Marriage and the Family* 30:558–564.

Swan, M. 1987. "Soap Star Computes." *Personal Computing* 11 (September):282.

Tajfel, H. 1981. *Human Groups and Social Categories.* Cambridge: Cambridge University Press.

Tannen, Deborah. 1990. *You Just Don't Understand: Men and Women in Conversation.* New York: Ballantine.

Tanner, Julian. 1978. "New Directions for Subcultural Theory: An Analysis of British Working-Class Youth Culture." *Youth and Society* 9:343–371.

Tennov, Dorothy. 1979. *Love and Limerence.* Chelsea, Mich.: Scarborough House.

Thorp, Margaret Farrand. 1939. *America at the Movies.* New Haven: Yale University Press.

Thurber, James. 1948. "Soapland." In *The Beast in Me and Other Animals,* edited by James Thurber, 189–260. New York: Harcourt.

Timberg, Bernard. 1981. "The Rhetoric of the Camera in Television Soap Opera." In *Television: The Critical View,* edited by Horace Newcomb, 132–147. New York: Oxford University Press.

Torchin, Mimi. 1992. "Speaking My Mind." *Soap Opera Weekly* 3 (March 17):4.

———. 1993a. "Speaking My Mind." *Soap Opera Weekly* 4 (April 6):4.

———. 1993b. "Speaking My Mind." *Soap Opera Weekly* 4 (August 24):4.

———. 1994a. "Speaking My Mind." *Soap Opera Weekly* 5 (January 25):4.

———. 1994b. "Speaking My Mind." *Soap Opera Weekly* 5 (June 14):4.

Trinajstick, Blanche. 1989. *The Fan Club Guide.* Pueblo, Colo.: National Association of Fan Clubs.

———. 1991. *The Fan Club Directory.* Issue 16 (November): Pueblo, Colo.: National Association of Fan Clubs.

Tulloch, John. 1990. *Television Drama: Agency, Audience, and Myth.* New York: Routledge.

Turner, Ralph. 1976. "The Real Self: From Institution to Impulse." *American Journal of Sociology* 81:989–1016.

Uricchio, William, and Roberta E. Pearson. 1991. "I'm Not Fooled by That Cheap Disguise." In *The Many Faces of Batman: Critical Approaches to a Superhero and His Media,* edited by Roberta E. Pearson and William Uricchio, 182–213. New York: Routledge.

Vine, Dorothy. 1993. "Marital Bliss." *Soap Opera Weekly* 4 (October 5):5.

Walkerdine, Valerie. 1986. "Video Replay: Families, Films, and Fantasy." In *Formations of Fantasy,* edited by Victor Burgin, Donald James, and Cora Kaplan, 167–199. London: Methuen.

*Wall Street Journal.* 1993. "Capital Cities/ABC Closing Its Magazine for Soap-Opera Fans." May 13, A7.

Warner, Lloyd W., and William E. Henry. 1948. "The Radio Day Time Serial: A Symbolic Analysis." *Genetic Psychology Monographs* 37:1–71.

Weber, Max. 1968. *Max Weber on Charisma and Institution Building.* Chicago: University of Chicago Press.

Weinstein, Deena. 1991. *Heavy Metal: A Cultural Sociology.* New York: Lexington.

Weiss, Hildee. 1993. "Can You Change a Storyline?" *Soap Opera Update* 6 (November 2):44–47.

———. 1994. "Computerized Soaps — Part 2." *Soap Opera Update* 7 (September 20):56.

Welkos, Robert W. 1991. "The Best Days of Their Lives." *Los Angeles Times,* May 30, F1, 10.

Wertham, Fredric. 1973. *The World of Fanzines.* Carbondale: Southern Illinois University Press.

Westen, Drew. 1991. "Cultural, Emotional, and Unconscious Aspects of Self." In *The Relational Self: Theoretical Convergences in Psychoanalysis and Social Psychology,* edited by Rebecca C. Curtis, 181–210. New York: Guilford.

Whetmore, Edward Jay. 1992. *American Electric.* New York: McGraw Hill.

———. 1993. *Mediamerica, Mediaworld: Form, Content, and Consequence of Mass Communication.* 5th edition. Belmont, Calif.: Wadsworth.

Whetmore, Edward Jay, and Alfred P. Kielwasser. 1983. "The Soap Opera Audience Speaks: A Preliminary Report." *Journal of American Culture* 6:110–116.

Williams, Carol. 1992. "It's Time for My Story: Oral Culture in the Technological Era — Towards a Methodology for Soap Opera Audience Study." In *Staying Tuned: Contemporary Soap Opera Criticism,* edited by Suzanne Frentz, 69–88. Bowling Green, Ohio: Bowling Green State University Popular Press.

Williams, L. 1985. "A Jury of Their Peers: Questions of Silence, Speech, and Judgment in Films by Women." Paper presented at the Society for Cinema Studies Annual Conference, New York City.

Winnicott, D. W. 1971. *Playing and Reality*. London: Tavistock.

Wuthnow, Robert. 1987. *Meaning and Moral Order: Explorations in Cultural Analysis*. Berkeley and Los Angeles: University of California Press.

Yinger, Milton. 1960. "Contraculture and Subculture." *American Sociological Review* 25:625–635.

Zimmerman, Don H., and Candace West. 1975. "Sex Roles, Interruptions, and Silences in Conversations." In *Language and Sex: Difference and Dominance*, edited by B. Thorne and N. Henley, 105–129. Rowley, Mass.: Newbury.

# Name Index

*Text pages in parentheses follow indexed note pages to identify the context in which note references occur.*

# Subject Index

*Text pages in parentheses follow indexed note pages to identify the context in which note references occur.*